A SHORT HISTORY OF CHINESE ART

LUDWIG BACHHOFER

A SHORT HISTORY OF CHINESE ART

PANTHEON

PRINTED BY L. F. WHITE COMPANY, INC. · NEW YORK
BOUND BY RUSSELL-RUTTER COMPANY, NEW YORK
DESIGNED BY JACQUES SCHIFFRIN
COPYRIGHT 1946 BY PANTHEON BOOKS INC.
41 WASHINGTON SQUARE, NEW YORK

PREFACE

Huizinga, the Dutch philosopher, once remarked that sooner or later every scholar reaches a point where he wearies of the drudgery of investigating special problems and wants to draw a coherent picture of his ideas. Having dealt with many topics of Chinese art in various papers during the last thirteen years, I came to that point some time ago. The results I arrived at often differed considerably from current notions. New material that turned up tended to confirm rather than to upset the ideas I had formed about the development of Chinese art. These ideas I have tried to present in this book.

No explanation should be necessary for the great emphasis laid upon problems of form. Form is the only means of expression an artist has at his disposal, whatever considerations may have determined his subject matter. It is form alone that makes a vessel, a statue, or a painting a work of art. But form never remains the same. It changes continually, and I saw my main task in describing these changes. They revealed themselves as so many phases of a logical, orderly, and organic evolution.

I am profoundly indebted to Miss Rosalie Green who in her quiet, efficient, and intelligent way prepared the manuscript for printing; and to my wife who prepared the index. I also want to extend my sincerest thanks to those who generously provided me with photographs. They are Professor B. Karlgren of the Museum of Far Eastern Antiquities, Stockholm; Mr. R. Grousset, Musée Cernuschi, Paris; Bishop W. C. White of the Royal Ontario Museum of Archæology, Toronto; Mr. G. Del Drago, New York; Mr. R. H. Bidwell, Springfield, Mass.; Mr. C. T. Loo, New York; Mr. Alfred H. Pillsbury, Minneapolis; Mr. L. Wannieck, Paris; the Tonying Company, New York.

Chicago, Summer 1944   LUDWIG BACHHOFER

ACKNOWLEDGMENT

By courtesy of Museum of Fine Arts, Boston, fig. 21, 63, 71, 84, 97, 101, 102, 105, 106, 108, 113, 118, 129; Gardner Museum, Boston, fig. 55; Fogg Museum, Cambridge, fig. 37, 92; Art Institute, Chicago, fig. 13, 16, 26, 27, 29, 32, 38, 39, 40, 45, 67, 75, 80, 123; W. R. Nelson Gallery, Kansas City, fig. 11, 17, 23, 54, 64, 68, 88; Metropolitan Museum, New York, fig. 15, 59, 70, 73, 77, 78, 82; University Museum, Philadelphia, fig. 36, 56, 58, 61, 62, 66; Museum of Art, Toledo, fig. 99; Freer Gallery, Washington, fig. 6, 14, 30, 47, 57, 65, 83, 98, 109, 112, 119, 121, 122; Royal Ontario Museum of Archæology, Toronto, fig. 52, 60, 76; British Museum, London, fig. 87; Victoria and Albert Museum, London, fig. 18, 20; Louvre, Paris, fig. 9, 28, 46, 49; Staatliche Museen, Berlin, fig. 8, 93, 104; Museum für Völkerkunde, Munich, fig. 1, 127; Museum of Far Eastern Antiquities, Stockholm, fig. 3, 4, 5, 7.

CONTENTS

LIST OF ILLUSTRATIONS	11
CHINESE DYNASTIES	15
THE NEOLITHIC AGE	
POLYCHROME POTTERY IN CHINA	17
KANSU	19
HONAN	22
LUNG SHAN OR BLACK POTTERY	24
THE BRONZES	
SHANG	
White Pottery: A link with the Neolithic	26
Bronzes with graphic décor	28
Bronzes with plastic décor	33
WESTERN CHOU	36
THE HSIN CH'ÊNG STYLE	41
THE LI YÜ STYLE	42
THE HUAI STYLE	45
THE CHIN TS'UN STYLE	46
MIRRORS	50
CONCLUSION	53
SCULPTURE	
SHANG TO HAN	55
TOMB FIGURES FROM HAN TO WEI	60
BUDDHIST SCULPTURE	63
Fifth Century	64
Sixth Century	66
Seventh to Ninth Century	73
Ninth to Eleventh Century	77
Twelfth to Seventeenth Century	80
PAINTING	
SHANG TO FORMER HAN	86
FIRST TO FIFTH CENTURY	90
FIFTH TO SEVENTH CENTURY	95
SEVENTH TO NINTH CENTURY	98

Tenth Century	107
Eleventh Century	110
Twelfth Century	113
Thirteenth Century	116
Fourteenth Century	117
Fifteenth Century	121
Sixteenth to Eighteenth Century	125
NOTES	129
INDEX	133

LIST OF ILLUSTRATIONS

Frontispiece: Lu Chao-yang: Peacocks and Peonies. Silk. Dated A.D. 1552. Height 1.78 m. Del Drago Collection, New York

1. Amphora from Pan Shan. Diam. 29 cm. Museum für Völkerkunde, Munich
2. Amphora from Pan Shan. Height 34 cm. L. Wannieck, Paris
3. Amphora from Ma Ch'ang. Height 34 cm. Museum of Far Eastern Antiquities, Stockholm
4. Pot from Ma Ch'ang. Height 20.5 cm. Museum of Far Eastern Antiquities, Stockholm
5. Pot from Ma Ch'ang. Height 19.2 cm. Museum of Far Eastern Antiquities, Stockholm
6. White Pottery Amphora. Height 33 cm. Freer Gallery, Washington
7. *Ting*. Museum of Far Eastern Antiquities, Stockholm
8. *P'ou*. Height 19.3 cm. Staatliche Museen, Berlin
9. *P'ou*. Louvre, Paris
10. *Tsun*. Height 22.7 cm. C. T. Loo, New York
11. *Ting*. Height 13.2 cm. W. R. Nelson Gallery, Kansas City
12. *Chia*. Height 26.6 cm. C. T. Loo, New York
13. *Kuei*. Height 17 cm. Art Institute, Chicago
14. *Yu*. Height 36.1 cm. Freer Gallery, Washington
15. *Yu* from Pao Chi. Height with Socle 47 cm. Metropolitan Museum, New York
16. *I*. Height 32.5 cm. Art Institute, Chicago
17. Four-legged *Ting*. Height to Rim 17.8 cm. W. R. Nelson Gallery, Kansas City
18. *Yu*. Height 36.5 cm. Victoria and Albert Museum, London
19. *Yu*. Height 22 cm. Mrs. Otto H. Kahn, New York
20. *Yu*. Height 20 cm. Victoria and Albert Museum, London
21. Chalice-shaped *Kuei*. Height 17.6 cm. Museum of Fine Arts, Boston
22. *Kuei*. Height 30.3 cm. C. T. Loo, New York
23. *Kuei*. 825 B.C. Height 30.3 cm. W. R. Nelson Gallery, Kansas City
24. *Kuei*. Height 33.5 cm. C. T. Loo, New York
25. *Hu* from Hsin Ch'êng. Height ca. 100 cm. Honan Provincial Museum
26. *Fu*. Height 18.5 cm. Art Institute, Chicago
27. *Ting*. Height 33.6 cm. Art Institute, Chicago
28. *Ting* from Li Yü. Louvre, Paris
29. Basin. Diam. 59.7 cm. Art Institute, Chicago
30. Basin. Diam. 51.8 cm. Freer Gallery, Washington
31. Bell *Chung*. Height 58.7 cm. C. T. Loo, New York
32. Pilgrim's Bottle. Height 36 cm. Art Institute, Chicago
33. *Hu*. Height 45.6 cm. C. T. Loo, New York
34. *Hu*. Ohta Collection
35. Vase with Inlay in Gold and Silver. Height 23.5 cm. C. T. Loo, New York
36. Vase *Fang*. Inlay of Malachite. Height 37.3 cm. University Museum, Philadephia

37. Finial. Length 19 cm. Art Institute, Chicago
38. Finial. Length 20 cm. Fogg Museum, Cambridge
39. Small *Hu*. Inlay in Gold and Silver. Height 12.2 cm. Art Institute, Chicago
40. *Hu*. Height 45 cm. Art Institute, Chicago
41. Mirror. Diam. 12.3 cm. C. T. Loo, New York
42. Mirror. Diam. 18.6 cm. C. T. Loo, New York
43. Mirror with Inlay. Marquis Hosokawa, Tōkyō
44. Mirror. Diam. 16 cm. C. T. Loo, New York
45. "*TLV* Mirror." Made in the Shang-fang Atelier. First century A.D. Diam. 21 cm. Art Institute, Chicago
46. The Camondo Elephant. Bronze. Length 96.5 cm. Louvre, Paris
47. Tiger. Bronze. Length 75.7 cm. Freer Gallery, Washington
48. Buffalo. Bronze. Length 20 cm. Alfred H. Pillsbury, Minneapolis
49. Lid of Four-legged *Ting* from Li Yü. Louvre, Paris
50. Dragon. Bronze. Length 65 cm. A. Stoclet, Brussels
51. Kneeling Servant. Bronze. Height 24.7 cm. R. H. Bidwell, Springfield, Mass.
52. Kneeling Servant. Bronze. Height 26.1 cm. Royal Ontario Museum of Archæology, Toronto
53. Boy Dancing on a Toad. Bronze. Height 10 cm. C. T. Loo, New York
54. Horse. Bronze. Height 21 cm. W. R. Nelson Gallery, Kansas City
55. Two Bears. Gilt Bronze. Height 15.5 cm. Gardner Museum, Boston
56. Chimæra. Stone. Third to fourth century A.D. Length ca. 2.15 m. University Museum, Philadelphia
57. Buddha. Gilt Bronze. Dated 451 A.D. Height 12 cm. Freer Gallery, Washington
58. Maitreya. Gilt Bronze. Dated 536 A.D. Height 61 cm. University Museum, Philadelphia
59. Maitreya. Gilt Bronze. Dated 477 A.D. Height 1.40 m. Metropolitan Museum, New York
60. Buddha. White Marble. Height 1.27 m. Royal Ontario Museum of Archæology, Toronto
61. Monk. Grey Limestone. Height 1.65 m. University Museum, Philadelphia
62. Avalokiteśvara. Grey Limestone. Height 1.90 m. University Museum, Philadelphia
63. Avalokiteśvara. Grey Limestone. Height 2.48 m. Museum of Fine Arts, Boston
64. Bodhisattva. Stone. Height 1.32 m. W. R. Nelson Gallery, Kansas City
65. "Paradise of the West." Grey Limestone. Length 3.27 m. Freer Gallery, Washington
66. (a) Avalokiteśvara and (b) Mahāsthāmaprapta. Grey Limestone. Height 1.36 m. and 1.31 m. University Museum, Philadelphia
67. Bodhisattva. Grey Limestone. Height 1.72 m. Art Institute, Chicago
68. Bodhisattva from T'ien-lung Shan. Height 97.8 cm. W. R. Nelson Gallery, Kansas City
69. Horse. Glazed Clay. Height 85 cm. Formerly L. Bernheimer, Munich
70. Stela with Mahāsthāmaprapta and Avalokiteśvara. Grey Limestone. Height 1.64 m. Metropolitan Museum, New York
71. Bodhisattva from T'ien-lung Shan. Sandstone. Height 1.31 m. Museum of Fine Arts, Boston
72. Bodhisattva. White Marble. Height ca. 1.50 m. L. Wannieck, Paris
73. Avalokiteśvara. Marble. Height 2.23 m. Metropolitan Museum, New York
74. Kuan-yin. Wood. Dated 1168 A.D. Height 1.63 m. Tonying Co., New York
75. Kuan-yin. Wood. Height 1.58 m. Art Institute, Chicago

76. (a) Avalokiteśvara and (b) Mahāsthāmaprapta. Wood. Dated 1195 A.D. Height 1.90 m. and 1.89 m. Royal Ontario Museum of Archæology, Toronto
77. Avalokiteśvara. Wood. Dated 1282 A.D. Height 99.5 cm. Metropolitan Museum, New York
78. Fēng Hsiao-chung: Avalokiteśvara. Wood. Dated 1385 A.D. Height 77 cm. Anonymous Loan. Metropolitan Museum, New York
79. Avalokiteśvara. Wood. Height 1.92 m. Royal Ontario Museum of Archæology, Toronto
80. Head of Pi-hsia Yüan-chün. Grey Limestone. Height 50.5 cm. Art Institute, Chicago.
81. Avalokiteśvara. Cast Iron. Dated 1511 A.D. Height 70 cm. Formerly L. Bernheimer, Munich
82. Avalokiteśvara. Lacquered Wood. Dated 1624 A.D. Height 21 cm. Metropolitan Museum, New York
83. Basin. Bronze with Inlay. Diam. 61.4 cm. Freer Gallery, Washington
84. Scene from a Painted Tomb Slab. Height 19.5 cm. Museum of Fine Arts, Boston
85. The Attempted Recovery of a Chou *Ting*. Rubbing. Hsiao T'ang Shan
86. Paragons of Filial Piety. Detail of the "Painted Basket." Lacquer Painting. Height with Border 8.5 cm. Museum of Keijō
87. Emperor Ch'ēng and Lady Pan. From the Copy of a Scroll by Ku K'ai-chi. Silk. Height 24.5 cm. British Museum, London
88. Engravings on Tomb Slab. Length 2.23 m. W. R. Nelson Gallery, Kansas City
89. Fresco in Cave 118/A of Tun-huang
90. Amitābha in His Western Paradise. Fresco in Cave 146 of Tun-huang
91. Amitābha in His Western Paradise. Fresco in Cave 139/A of Tun-huang
92. Head of Kāśyapa, a Bodhisattva and two Lokapālas. Fragment of Fresco from Cave 139/A in Tun-huang. Height 68.6 cm. Fogg Museum, Cambridge
93. Mourners. Detail of Fresco from the Kinnarī Cave, Kumtura. Staatliche Museen, Berlin
94. Mountain Landscape. Paper. Palace Museum, Peking
95. Landscape on a Sixfold Screen. Silk. Tōji, Kyōto
96. Winter Landscape. Silk. Height 1.25 m. Palace Museum, Peking.
97. Winter Landscape. Silk. Height 1.82 m. Museum of Fine Arts, Boston
98. Winter Landscape. Silk. Height 1.87 m. Freer Gallery, Washington
99. Kuo Hsi: Winter Landscape. Section of a Scroll. Silk. 4.80 m. by 0.50 m. Museum of Art, Toledo, Ohio
100. Chao-Ta-nien: House by the Lake. Silk. Height 29 cm. Akaboshi Collection, Tōkyō
101. Trees and Rocks. Silk. Diam. 24 cm. Museum of Fine Arts, Boston
102. Ma Yüan: Lady Ling-chao Standing in the Snow. Silk. Height 26 cm. Museum of Fine Arts, Boston
103. Summer. Silk. Konchiin, Kyōto
104. Li Kung-nien: Waterfall. Silk. Diam. 23 cm. Staatliche Museen, Berlin
105. Liu Sung-nien: Landscape. Silk. Diam. 25 cm. Museum of Fine Arts, Boston
106. Hsia Kuei: Landscape. Silk. Diam. 25 cm. Museum of Fine Arts, Boston
107. Hsia Kuei: Landscape. Silk. Height 25.3 cm. G. Del Drago, New York
108. Ma Yüan: Landscape. Silk. Diam. 24 cm. Museum of Fine Arts, Boston
109. Hsia Kuei: Mountain Brook. Silk. Height 1.37 m. Freer Gallery, Washington
110. Landscape. Paper. Height 37 cm. Viscount Akimoto, Tōkyō

111. Landscape. Silk. Height 28.5 cm. G. Del Drago, New York
112. Mountains. Silk. Height 1.49 cm. Freer Gallery, Washington
113. Wu Chēn: Bamboo. Paper. Height 75 cm. Museum of Fine Arts, Boston
114. Huang Kung-wang: Landscape. Dated 1353 A.D. Paper. Yamamoto Collection, Tōkyō
115. Ni Tsan: Landscape. Silk. Height 25.2 cm. G. Del Drago, New York
116. Detail of "Departure of Wēn-chi"
117. Chao Mēng-fu: Departure of Wēn-chi. Silk. Dated 1301 A.D. Height 1.29 m. G. Del Drago, New York
118. Two Horsemen in Landscape. Silk. Height 1.08 m. Museum of Fine Arts, Boston
119. Landscape. Silk. Height 1.90 m. Freer Gallery, Washington
120. Scholar Watching Birds. Silk. Height 24.5 cm. G. Del Drago, New York
121. Landscape. Silk. Height 1.71 m. Freer Gallery, Washington
122. T'ang Yin: A Scholar and a Priest Drinking Tea. Section of a Scroll. Paper. 1.16 m. by 23 cm. Dated 1509 A.D. Art Institute, Chicago
123. Tai Chin: Storm along the River. Section of a Scroll. Paper. 11.13 m. by 0.30 m. Freer Gallery, Washington
124. Chang Lu: Scholar Wandering along a Mountain Stream. Paper. Height 1.65 m. G. Del Drago, New York
125. Landscape. Paper. Height 1.40 m. Formerly Yamanaka
126. Detail of the "Portrait of an Old Lady." Silk. G. Del Drago, New York
127. Landscape. Paper. Height 23.5 cm. Museum für Völkerkunde, Munich
128. Ch'iu Ying: Scholar in Mountain Landscape. Silk. Height 1.15 m. W. H. Wells, Munich
129. Lēng Mei: Girl Listening to Flute Player. Silk. Height 1.15 m. Museum of Fine Arts, Boston

CHINESE DYNASTIES

SHANG	ca. 1523 - 1027 B.C.
CHOU	1027 - 221 B.C.
WESTERN CHOU	1027 - 771 B.C.
EASTERN CHOU	
Period of "Spring and Autumn Annals"	ca. 722 - ca. 481
Period of the "Warring States"	ca. 481 - 221
CH'IN	221 - 207
FORMER HAN	202 - 9 A.D.
LATER HAN	25 - 220
THE SIX DYNASTIES	220 - 589
SUI	581 - 618
T'ANG	618 - 906
THE FIVE DYNASTIES	907 - 960
LIAO	907 - 1123
NORTHERN SUNG	960 - 1126
CHIN	1114 - 1234
SOUTHERN SUNG	1127 - 1279
YÜAN	1271 - 1368
MING	1368 - 1644
CH'ING	1644 - 1912

THE NEOLITHIC AGE

POLYCHROME POTTERY IN CHINA

IN China and her borderlands, as everywhere else, the spade of the archæologist was the key that unlocked the doors of the past. Though little has been done in the way of scientifically conducted excavations, this little enormously increased knowledge about the beginnings of Chinese civilization. The material dug up clarified vague notions and corrected false ones about the early historical epochs; and it revealed the existence of a neolithic age in China.

The first late stone age settlement was discovered in 1921 by Professor J. G. Andersson, a Swedish geologist in the service of the Chinese government. It was in the neighbourhood of Yang Shao Ts'un, a village in western Honan. The site was surprisingly large; it covered an area of 480 m. by 600 m. No houses were found, only circular pits, ca. 1.90 m. to 2.80 m. in diameter, and 50 cm. to 1.90 m. deep. Some of them had rather large bottoms and very narrow necks. Later on, a house was excavated at Ch'ing Tai, another site of this culture. This house had been built of pounded earth, but was subsequently converted into one solid brick by the deliberate or accidental application of fire.

The village near Yang Shao Ts'un was inhabited by peasants who cultivated millet and rice, possibly wheat, and raised pigs and cattle. The dog was tamed, but not the horse. Since whorls were found, spinning must have been practised. Sewing was done with needles of bone and horn that were sometimes kept in little bone tubes. Awls were made of bone, knives of stone. The latter were rectangular or semilunar in shape, with one sharpened edge and one or two holes to fasten the piece of hide that served as handle. Also of stone were short broad hoes, celts of varying forms, and weapons, namely arrow-heads with a slight midrib and a short tang, and some large pieces that could be called spears. No trace of any metal was discovered.

The pottery of these people fell into two distinct classes. One was very coarse in texture because of an ample admixture of sand. It was grey in colour, and fired at a very low temperature. The vessels of this ware were made by hand, with their necks and mouths often finished on a turntable. This last, a board pivoted on a pole, was a forerunner of the potter's wheel. The outside of such vessels was roughened, either by the pressure of mats or by a comb-like instrument. The only things that could be called ornamentation without abuse of the word were one or more horizontal ridges with impressions of finger tips.

THE NEOLITHIC AGE

The shapes varied widely. Most characteristic were pots and flasks with pointed bottoms, and two kinds of tripods. The one consisted of a deep bowl with three slender and solid legs; the other of three hollow, bulging legs. It was seen at once that these correspond to the tripods called *ting* and *li* by students of Chinese bronzes. Here was definite evidence that the Chinese culture of historical times had sprung from that of the neolithic age.

With this coarse grey pottery was inextricably mixed a very different kind of ceramics. Its clay was very carefully washed; it was fired at a temperature of about 1100° C. and it resounded on percussion. The vessels were built by the coiling method, i.e. from a long roll. The finished ware was grey to red, and usually painted in white, black and red. Very few intact vessels were found, though thousands of sherds. The bowls were painted on the outside only, seldom down to the bottom, usually within the upper half. The most important motive was the spiral.

So utterly different was the painted ware from the coarse one that Andersson thought of it as an intruder. Painted pottery was known from many sites in the west, ranging from northern India and Russian Turkistan to eastern Europe. If painted ware had come to central China from any of these places, it must have entered the country through Kansu, its westernmost province.

To Kansu, then, went Andersson in 1923. In the valley of the T'ao-ho he recovered material in such abundance as to surpass the boldest dreams. Settlements of a neolithic people were found on the loess terraces along the river, and their graves were discovered high up on the mountain ridges. The tombs yielded hundreds of intact vessels. They were made by the coiling method, fired at a high temperature, and painted with many patterns in black and red. The most striking décor consisted of several double spirals so linked as to form an endless ornament (fig. 1). It recurred in many variations.

A somewhat coarser ware accompanied the fine polychrome pottery. It also was made by the coiling method, and decorated with files of small plastic dots, sometimes in patterns that occur on the painted vessels. And everywhere was found the rough ware known from Honan with its leading types, the vessel with pointed bottom and the *li* tripod. The painted ceramics of many sites, especially in southern Kansu, are so closely related to those of Honan that Andersson called both of them Yang Shao.

The discovery of polychrome pottery in Kansu confirmed the opinion that the practice of painting vessels in indestructible colours had come to China from outside. It did not answer the question about its origin.

Of all the painted ceramics that were made at different times and different places farther west, only that of eastern Europe corresponds in ware and decorative system to that of China. It was made of extraordinarily fine clay, was fired at a high temperature, and rang when touched sharply; its colour scheme was white, black and red; its décor, which covered only the upper part of the vessel, was based on the double spiral. Another characteristic feature of this polychrome pottery is the way in which the décor was produced: the clay or white slip was covered with black in such a way as to let the intended pattern stand out on a black background. In other words, it was the background that was painted, and not the pattern. This procedure has been called "negative ornament," a term that would be better applied to the result. At any rate, this peculiar technique was not used anywhere else, except in the early sites of Kansu, in Honan, and Jehol, Manchuria.

It was the last phase of the painted pottery in eastern and southeastern Europe that provided the patterns for the painted pottery of China. And since it is not vessels that wander, but men, there must have been a powerful stimulus which drove the Vase Painters, as they have been called, from their homes in Europe across the steppes of Asia to China.

Archæological evidence shows that practically all the settlements of the Vase Painters came to a sudden and violent end. They were destroyed by an invader, the "Corded Ware" or "Battle-Axe" folk, so called after their characteristic ware and weapon. This was a warlike people which subdued most of Europe from the Vosges to the Ural mountains. They can be traced by their graves where their dead lie sprinkled with red ochre, accompanied by stone battle-axes and vessels with real or mock impressions of cord.

The conquest of southeastern Europe by these neolithic warriors took place in the nineteenth century B.C. This must have been the time when a few Vase Painters set out on the eastbound trek that brought them to Honan and Kansu.

KANSU

At the beginning, the painted wares of Kansu and Honan were practically identical. Their décor consisted of "negative ornaments." Some designs resemble flowers with large waving petals; some are combinations of elliptical and leaf-like shapes; others may be described as more or less complete, and still others as dissolved volutes. All these motives and their unique presentation are closely related to those of the last phase of the painted pottery in southeastern Europe. But whereas this peculiar art degenerated in Honan, it blossomed forth in Kansu. In some early sites, e.g., in Lo Han T'ang and Ma Chia Yao, the "negative ornaments" were either produced or accompanied by bundles of thin, parallel lines. This element became more and more important; and hand in hand with its increasing use went a shift from the negative to a positive rendering. In many cases, it is impossible to tell what counts, the black lines or the intervals between them that were left blank. In the end, however, the positive representation prevailed, and a new style was born. It is neither feasible nor necessary to enumerate all the designs rendered in the new manner; the most conspicuous ones are bands of straight and wavy lines, segments of concentric circles, long spirals, and combinations of them. Though most of these ornaments were painted in black, they were sometimes done in red, too.

THE NEOLITHIC AGE

The bundled lines, the most characteristic feature of this new style, were well-known and employed in the polychrome wares of southeastern Europe; so was another distinctive element that goes with them, red or black dots that mark the junctions of different linear themes. But these old means were used by the Kansu potters to new and better ends. Their painted vessels surpass anything ever created in the West; especially their bowls, with a neatly set off rim, decorated on the outside with flowing lines and in the interior with combinations of concentric circles and curves, are delightfully elegant in shape and ornamentation. The latter, with its effect of brisk and endless movement, shows a vigour and forcefulness that distinguish it very advantageously from the sluggish decoration of the European pots. It is as if a shoot of a weak and sickly plant had been transferred into new fertile soil and a healthier climate. It may well be that the admixture of some alien strain had brought about this good result.

During this second phase the double spiral was by no means neglected. The basic form remained unaltered, though the connecting stem usually was rendered with bundled lines; and, as in the West, the double spiral was one ascending to the right.

The next stage saw a reversal of this direction: the spirals ascend now to the left. The most common décor of this group, called Pan Shan after its main site, is a combination of four such spirals on the shoulder of a vessel. The spirals are red, and the nuclei they form when they merge, very small; the long and sweeping stems are accompanied by lines alternately black and red; the black ones usually are serrated.

It has been said that every ornament is a problem of mental discipline; from this point of view, the spiral décor of the Pan Shan group certainly ranks very high. It is an enormously active décor: the curves seek and flee the nuclei which appear at regular intervals. They are the points of articulation where the movement of the lines slows down almost to a halt; but only to start off again in a lively tempo. This décor of interlocked spirals that was confined to a frieze upon the shoulder of a vessel was also quite common in southeastern Europe; the best known vases of this type were

I. Vase from Schipenitz, Galicia   II. Amphora from Pan Shan

THE NEOLITHIC AGE

discovered in Petreny, in Bessarabia. These western pieces possess all the characteristics of their kind, the negative rendering, the right turn of the volutes, and a certain limpness of form; yet all these differences mean very little against the evident kinship of the polychrome wares of Kansu and eastern Europe. This family resemblance is especially striking if the décor is somewhat unusual.

The main problem is in reality not the relationship between the two areas in the West and the East, but the fact that the Vase Painters of Kansu successively took up certain types of ornamentation that were more or less simultaneous in Europe, according to our present knowledge. An answer to that may be found in the increasing tendency toward order and discipline, so obvious in the evolution of the decorative systems in Kansu. It was but natural that the potters chose and developed those designs that lent themselves to their intentions, neglecting and abolishing those that were unfit.

The leading types of vessels in the Pan Shan group are a short amphora with a low neck and broad mouth, and a tall amphora with a high neck and narrow mouth. These two types are not only similar to, but identical with the leading types of the corded ware. The fact, however, that such amphoræ, with and without handles, were made already in Kansu during the two stages preceding Pan Shan, and that the Pan Shan vessels plainly are their descendants, is not favourable to the idea of a corded ware influence.

Within a comparatively short time, it seems, the spiral décor of the Pan Shan stage underwent considerable changes. The nuclei grew in size; and finally the status of stem and nucleus was reversed: large disks, or ovals, occupy the whole surface between the borders, while the stems and accompanying lines have shrunk to mere fillings.

Along with this change went a trend toward rectilinear patterns. In some cases, the disks were turned into lozenges, and rows of lozenges became a frequent motive (fig. 2). The attitude toward form had radically altered: formerly it was impossible

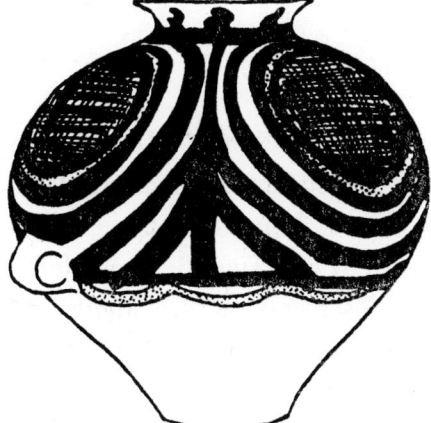

III. Amphora from Pan Shan   IV. Amphora from Pan Shan

21

THE NEOLITHIC AGE

to cut up a décor without immolating it, now its elements can be separated without serious harm; as a result, the continuous movement of the original designs was supplanted by rigid immobility.

The insertion of straight lines between two disks gave rise to a zig-zag pattern that is characteristic of the next phase, Ma Ch'ang (fig. 3).

The volute, which had never quite disappeared, was finally subjected to these new ideals, and turned into a meander (fig. 4). In other cases, the ground was so filled with thin parallel lines as to let a tilted, angularly broken S appear (fig. 5). This is a late, and rather unexpected, rebirth of the "negative ornament."

A fifth group of painted ware is called Hsin Tien, after its main site. Its sherd is much coarser than that of the four preceding stages; its amphoræ usually have thick swollen necks; they are often carinated, and have their lower halves covered with fine mat impressions. The heavy necks are often adorned with rows of meanders, the shoulders with a combination of two short volutes, in the shape of a buffalo's horns. Scattered between these designs are sometimes small figures of animals, such as dogs and what looks like a horse, and of men. The latter are represented in the typical primitive manner that breaks up the human form into a series of triangles and is best known from the geometric phase of Greek vase painting. It may be added that the sequence Pan Shan — Ma Ch'ang — Hsin Tien is well established, by internal and external evidence. Internally, because the vessels and designs of Hsin Tien can be traced back to Pan Shan via Ma Ch'ang; externally, by the stratification of an excavated site, near Hsin Tien.

Hsin Tien graves contained a very few objects in copper and bronze. It was at this stage that the art of painting vessels deteriorated in Kansu. A sixth group, Ch'i Chia, has only a pattern of boxed triangles hanging from the necks of its ungainly pots, and this but very rarely. Ch'i Chia ware must have been roughly contemporary with Hsin Tien, as it was found together with late Ma Ch'ang, Hsin Tien, and other bronze age sherds in the site of Chu Chia Chai.

HONAN

The polychrome ware of Honan is but an extension of the first stage of painted pottery in Kansu. Such charming designs as those on some bowls from Ching Ts'un recur on vessels from Kansu.

As pointed out, such designs were derived from the old spiriform décor; others display a closer and more evident relation to it, and to the parent stock of southeastern Europe. A sherd from Ch'in Wang Chai shows a spiral ascending to the right, its curve rendered by parallel lines in white and red; black was only used to insert the background, and to produce a "negative ornament." The same forms and technique had been used in the West.

THE NEOLITHIC AGE

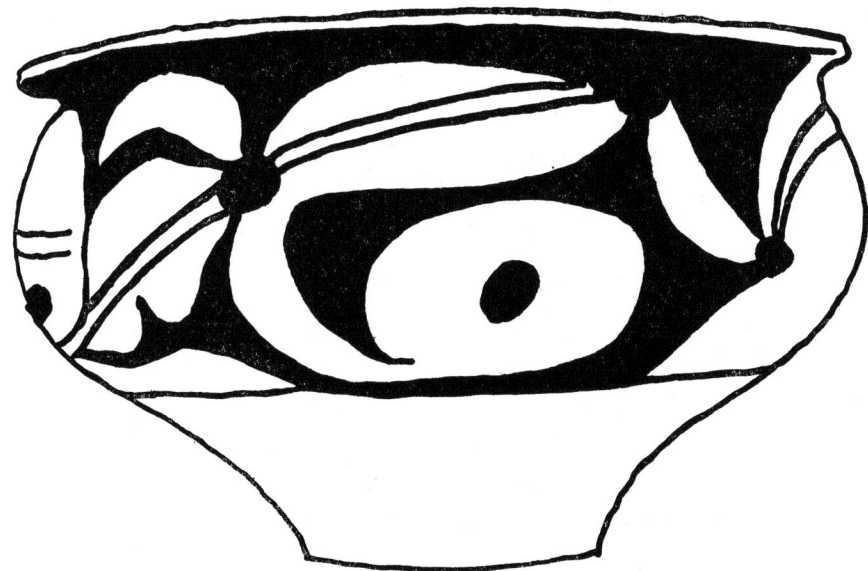

V. Bowl from Ching Ts'un

The painted ware of central China was not subjected to the strong discipline as that of Kansu; nor was there anything like the vigour, spiritedness and inventiveness that caused the lively evolution of polychrome ceramics in China's western province. On the contrary, a progressive disintegration of composition, a retrenchment of motives, and a reduction of the décor as a whole to a very modest level can be observed. At the end, there was nothing left but cross-hatching, the swathe, and a tripartite zigzag band with lopped off points. After a short time, the motives were not even painted, but incised. Finally, they vanished altogether. The Vase Painters had been absorbed by the native population.

VI. Sherd from Ch'in Wang Chai

VII. Vase from Cucuteni, Rumania

THE NEOLITHIC AGE

LUNG SHAN OR BLACK POTTERY

THE Yang Shao culture was superseded by another, called the Black Pottery culture, after its characteristic ware. This ware is also named Lung Shan pottery, after the town in Shantung in the vicinity of which it was first found. The chronological position of this culture is well established: at Hou Kang, in Honan, a Lung Shan stratum lay above a Yang Shao stratum, and nearby a Lung Shan stratum was overlaid by a Shang stratum. The contents of the two Lung Shan layers were identical. The same sequence was discovered in Hou Chia-chuang and in Ta Lai Tien.

Lung Shan pottery is thrown on the wheel. It must be divided in two classes. One is made of extraordinarily fine clay, is glossy of surface, coal black in colour, and sometimes incredibly thin. The other class consists of a coarser ware that is black to dark grey. This black pottery is accompanied by white, pink, red, and brown wares. The artisans of this culture used tools made of stone, bone, and, in the neighbourhood of the sea, of shell; these tools were practically identical with those of the Yang Shao culture. The vessel types *li* and *ting* are well known. From these two facts it can be inferred that the Lung Shan culture was the direct continuation of the Yang Shao culture.

This is corroborated by the form of all Lung Shan vessels, which are remarkable for the stress laid upon structure, an effect which is achieved by means of horizontal ridges and lines sharply separating the various parts. Such ridges had been used by the native potters of the Yang Shao period.

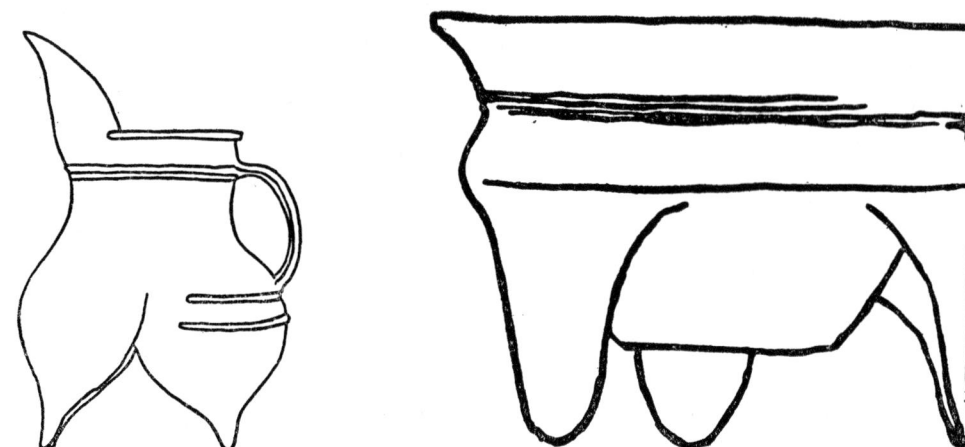

VIII. BLACK POTTERY "LI" FROM CH'ĒNG-TZŬ YAI   IX. BLACK POTTERY "TING" FROM CH'ĒNG-TZŬ YAI

Though Lung Shan pottery usually relies for effect upon a clear tectonic form and a polished smooth surface, some vessels carry small friezes with an incised trellis pattern, cross-hatchings, tripartite zigzag bands whose points are lopped off, the swathe, or a row of tiny circles.

24

THE NEOLITHIC AGE

The black ware does not indicate a new culture or a new people. It is the ceramics of the natives who had learned certain technical improvements. In a number of Yang Shao villages where intruders and natives had lived together, typical black pottery vessels were found along with red ware. The red ware was fired under oxidizing, the black under reducing conditions. This means a deliberate control of the fire in the kiln. It is something the natives could have learned only from the immigrants.

THE BRONZES

SHANG

WHITE POTTERY: A LINK WITH THE NEOLITHIC

SINCE late Chou times, the Chinese have spoken of the Hsia as their first dynasty. If there were anything like it, the Hsia kings were probably no more than the headmen of some neolithic towns and villages.

The Hsia were succeeded by the Shang. Their rise was an event whose importance cannot be exaggerated. It marked the transition from the stone to the bronze age; from prehistory to history; and from a state of illiteracy to one where writing was known. The Shang set the course of Chinese art for a millennium and a half.

A material link between the Lung Shan culture and that of the Shang is the white ware that had accompanied the black pottery. The creamy white colour of that ware is due to a large admixture of kaolin. Unlike the plain white Lung Shan ware, that of the Shang is covered with ornaments.

It has often been asserted that these ornaments are identical with those found on Shang bronzes. This is but partially true. At least four groups of ornaments can be discerned on the white sherds; and their relationship is such that they must be interpreted as the main phases of a changing decorative system.

The basic pattern of all four groups is the angular volute, or meander. At first, a vessel was evenly covered with small, choppy elements, all of them definitely rectangular. The effect is rather restless, because the whole lacks coherence. In the next stage, the meanders are no longer small and independent, but are combined in large continuous patterns; they are folded into one another in a very complicated way. At this stage a pattern was invented which was to have a great future: the T with the ends of the crossbar bent at right angles. The décor is still evenly spread; but instead of standing upright, the meander and the other motives are set slantwise.

The third group abandons the ideal of an evenly spread décor. A few main designs are worked out. They are of a purely geometric character, appearing as comparatively broad flat bands upon a background of small meanders and triangular volutes. In other words, a clear distinction is made between design and background. Such designs are two or more parallel zigzags, sometimes combined with large rectangular hooks, and the angular S, the "compound lozenges" and the "interlocked T." In all these cases the meander is relegated to a subservient rôle.

A few large fragments and the only intact vessel, an amphora in the Freer Gallery (fig. 6), show that at this time the friezes around the neck, shoulder, and foot of a

THE BRONZES

vessel were filled with a décor of a radically different, namely a theriomorphous character. It usually consists of a single eye or of a pair of them. Some are surrounded by meanders and T's; from others sprout lines or flat ribbons in either direction. Their ends are bent inward, at sharp angles, but with rounded off corners. Small hooks pointing toward the centre often spring from these bands. The whole design is set upon a background of small meandroid elements. Along with these vaguely zoömorphic motives appear representations of animals that can be recognized, for example the cicada. Little animal heads in the round were placed upon the vessels.

The fourth group comprises but a few sherds. They are decorated with broad smooth bands ending in pointed hooks. They can scarcely belong to anything except such theriomorphous forms as have gathered around one or two eyes. Such motives were formerly restricted to a few narrow friezes; now they have descended from the neck and shoulder to the walls of a vessel. They are rendered by very fine and shallow incisions, as is the background. Along with this change goes another, this one in the rendering of form. It affects the main designs as well as the small elements. All of these look as if they had been pressed toward one side. There is a definite tendency to avoid a pure right angle. Upright lines slant a little; and the corners are alternately rounded and pointed. For the first time line was subject to a rhythm that is specifically Chinese.

The decorated white Shang pottery sets a few problems of great interest and importance. As to the ware, it is directly descended from the white pottery of the Lung Shan culture. As to the décor, with its fundamental motive of the meander, no such relation can be discovered. The meander has no resemblance to any pattern found in Honan, Shansi or Shantung. It was, however, a prominent element in the late Ma Ch'ang, and the Hsin Tien group in Kansu. It is true that the meander was used by the Shang potters to build up an entirely different décor; but this has nothing to do with the question of where that design came from. The large zigzag bands and the compound lozenges were also known only in Kansu.

It is hard to believe that all these motives were invented anew by the craftsmen who worked for the Shang in central China. There are other facts that make such an assumption highly improbable, and a knowledge by the Shang of the late neolithic culture of Kansu rather certain. The Shang had weapons and implements in bronze that are almost identical with those found in the Ordos region; their knives can be traced via Ordos to Minussinsk in Siberia; their socketed celt came from central Europe, South Russia and Siberia; they sprinkled their dead with red ochre, a practice totally foreign to the neolithic cultures of central and eastern China; they used large flat rings of jade, as did the Vase Painters of Kansu. All this is evidence of the close affinity of Shang culture with that of the west and northwest. Whoever brought these

THE BRONZES

objects, customs, and ideas to central China must have done so by way of the T'ao-ho valley where the main sites of the Vase Painters lay.

By virtue of material and motive, the white pottery of the Shang is a link with the neolithic culture, though with two sections that were widely separated in space. By virtue of the animal décor that appears in the third group, it is a bridge to the bronzes. This, however, does not explain the origin of the animal décor and its peculiar style.

As nothing of this kind was known before, it is only plausible to assume that it was due to the Shang. A few of their bronze objects, such as knives and rein-holders, end in the heads of horses. They are done in the most summary fashion. It was a simple art. These heads have nothing in common with the plastic heads found everywhere on bronze, or on late white pottery vessels. Only the latter are identical in style and conception with the incised theriomorphous décor. They both have severely geometrized forms. Close inspection will show that these animal motives were built of the same elements used in the abstract décor: the meander, the triangle, the T, and the hook. It is possible that the craftsmen were of different origin and culture from the Shang for whom they were forced to work; and that after the consolidation of their rule, the Shang found the leisure to impose their will on them. They forced them to introduce animal motives, undoubtedly for their apotropæic quality, and to cast vessels in bronze for their rites.

BRONZES WITH GRAPHIC DECOR

Ritual bronzes are the sole monuments of ancient China that have survived the ravages of time and man. Of the temples, palaces and houses under the Shang and Chou, nothing is left. Religious beliefs did not call for representation of a deity in the shape of man or animal, certainly not in plastic isolation. What there was in the nature of sculpture during the Shang epoch was kept in the strict and inexorable bondage of architecture. And painting was to be long in coming into its own right.

The Shang worshipped the spirits of their ancestors, of the elements, of rivers and mountains, and this required vessels for offerings of food and liquids. Though practically all the bronze vessels in our collections came from tombs, most of them were probably kept in ancestral temples before they were put in a grave.

A great many of the bronzes are inscribed; and owing to the long, laborious and ingenious work of Chinese scholars, they can be deciphered. Till the end of the Shang dynasty, such inscriptions were usually very short. One or two characters may give the name of the family that had the vessel made. Vessels so inscribed may well have been used in everyday life. Other inscriptions, such as "For Father Ting," suggest a sacrificial function; and this is beyond question in the case of vessels whose inscriptions express the wish that sons and grandsons may use and treasure them for ten thousand years.

Some of these inscriptions, especially those of later times, are quite lengthy. They report on events in which the donor has played a rôle. Their primary function was to tell the ancestors about their descendant and the gifts with which he was rewarded. Such inscriptions are often very accurately dated, to the year, month, and day. Unfortunately, the only specification of such a date is "of the king." The clan, or family, knew of course what member was meant, and what king; we have to look for circumstantial evidence, which is often lacking or insufficient.

In a few cases, however, it is possible to identify the ruler or the person mentioned in the inscription. These are then the *pièces de repère* which permit reconstruction of the history of Chinese bronzes.

Very probably all ancient Chinese bronzes were cast by the *cire perdue*, or lost wax, process. A model of the vessel was formed in wax, over a core of clay, and the decoration applied. The model was then covered with a coating of clay. This mould was fired, and the wax flowed out through prepared vents. Liquid bronze was then poured in, taking the place of the wax. In some cases moulds in sections were used. These sections had tenons and mortices; they were covered with wax and then put together. More wax was added till the required thickness was reached. The mould was then removed and the wax model treated in the way described. This method permitted the casting of several identical vessels. The discovery of many broken moulds with tenons and mortices in Hsiao-t'un, near An-yang, gave rise to the hypothesis that direct casting was also practised.[1] Though the moulds themselves are not conclusive proof, the seams that are found on many early bronzes strongly support this view.

From the tenth century B.C. onward, many vessels were called by their current names in the inscriptions. The designs, however, are never mentioned. The large fantastic ogre of the Shang bronzes was called as early as in the third century B.C. *t'ao-t'ieh,* i.e., Glutton. This is certainly a misnomer, but by now it has been used for more than two thousand years.

A *ting* in Stockholm demonstrates very nicely the close connection between the two last groups of white pottery and the early bronzes (fig. 7). Under the rim is a frieze filled with that peculiar arrangement of lines and hooks on either side of a single eye which appeared in identical form on the amphora in the Freer Gallery (fig. 6). It is also found on many sherds in Toronto and Stockholm. The same holds for the compound lozenge pattern covering the *ting's* body. Other *ting* display large parallel zigzags such as occur on the white amphora, or interlocked T's. All these patterns are found in the third group of white pottery, but not earlier. The upright handles of the bronze *ting* are new; they were only practicable in metal.

Though an early work, the Stockholm *ting* is by no means one of the oldest existing bronzes. These are frequently found among the *p'ou,* round containers with sagging bodies, sloping shoulders, and narrow mouths. They are commonly decorated with the motives just mentioned; and in addition to them may carry on their shoulders a file of fish, or of little plastic frogs (fig. 8). These motives are not met with in later times. The ungainly shape and the rather slack casting suggest forcibly that the *p'ou* range among the first attempts at making bronze vessels.

The specimen in Berlin is a good representative of this group. Under the rim are two horizontal plastic lines, so-called bowstrings; then follows a frieze with a file of *monoculi,* a variation of the pattern described. The eye is differently rendered: it is a small knob, and inserted in curved, pointed lids. The bands extending on either side are of varying lengths. They are covered with little T's, and tiny hooks protrude from them. Then comes, between two flat strips, a row of fish, all of them looking in one direction. The main décor of interlocked T's is bordered by files of tiny circles. A small band of little meanders covers the lower half of the foot, which is in the shape of a truncated cone.

A *p'ou* in the Louvre tells about the aspirations of a younger generation (fig. 9). The body is lifted, its outline is tense and more vigorous. The structure is accentuated by a clear and sharp division of the parts. The body is divided into three vertical sections ornamented with the same design. It is definitely zoömorphic in character, and may be described as follows. On either side of a low vertical ridge are placed two eyes in pointed lids; from these emerge to the left and right horizontal bands ending in an upturned meander: they stand for body and tail. Similar elements, pointing toward the centre, are immediately above the eyes: they stand for the horns. The intervals between horns and tails are filled with a pattern faintly reminiscent of feathers. These are also found under the tails, and amid them, rather unexpectedly, is a very small eye without any recognizable attachment. Rectangular lines ending in curly hooks represent legs.

The low and smooth vertical ridge that separates the two identical halves of the animal reaches from the upper edge of the frieze about three quarters of the way down. It ends in two small meanders. Under it runs a rather long horizontal band. This is the mouth, which is the only element that connects the left with the right half.

The smaller, single-eyed animals on the shoulder are composed of exactly the same parts as the large animal on the body, but they are put together in a different way. Body and tail are placed on the "wrong" side of an eye. A row of quills, or feathers, fills the rest of the surface. The result is vaguely theriomorphous, but it has no resemblance whatsoever to anything that may occur in nature, and was never intended to have one. The query: "What animal had the ancient Chinese in mind when they decorated their bronzes?" is asked time and again. The question is wrongly put. A bronze caster would have turned away with the same silent contempt as would a Greek vase painter when asked what plants he wanted to depict by his combinations of volutes, palmettes, and tulip-like forms. The analogy of the floral décor of Greek vases with the animal décor of Chinese bronzes is rather illuminating. The former will help in understanding the latter. Both are floral and animal in a vague sense only. With a very few exceptions, neither purports to represent reality: they are abstract, as the term goes. What happened in both cases was that the artist interpreted his visual experience of plant or animal in customary terms. Thus a Shang artist would represent a body and a tail by a tapering meander, and use the same form for a horn. In fact, so little do these new forms differ from the old ones as to make their new meaning difficult to understand; were it not for the eyes, they would pass for purely geometric patterns. Another phenomenon must be pointed out: just as formerly the artist had grouped his elements, large and small meanders, triangles and hooks, in ever new combinations, so he did now with what appears to a modern spectator the parts of an animal. He created endless varieties of fantastic fauna. This explains how a body may get a head on either end. There is no need to attach a special magic meaning to such creatures. They are the products of a form fantasy that worked everywhere and at all times in much the same way.

A source of constant wonder is the fact that the big monsters of the main décor, the so-called *t'ao-t'ieh*, are rendered with one head and two bodies, one on either side of the head in the centre. To explain this phenomenon, it has been suggested that a *t'ao-t'ieh* was at first two animals confronting each other. There is no doubt that such combinations occur. But there is also no doubt that the oldest representations of the *t'ao-t'ieh* do not bear out that theory: they have always one big mouth shared by both halves. The head was the main and most important motive, and as such it occupies the centre. And with a marked centre the law of symmetry came into play at once. Once discovered, it was inexorably applied. Thus the maker of the amphora in the Freer Gallery (fig. 6) put bands to the left and the right of the eye.

But the Westerner should not be surprised at the splitting of the body. In our own Middle Ages, animals decorating the capitals of columns were treated in the same way. The Sumerians had done it at the beginning of the third millennium B.C. In all of these cases, the head of the animal marks the centre; and for the sake of symmetry, the body that under any other circumstances would have extended to one side only, was repeated on the other side. On a few occasions, tigers and serpents are represented on Chinese bronzes; they were depicted in a summary, but recognizable manner. The moment they occupy the centre of a frieze, they are given two bodies, like the *t'ao-t'ieh*.

A large vase of the type called *tsun* shows a further development (fig. 10). It is a vessel of the carinated variety, such as was known in the white pottery of Shang times. The parts are more strongly emphasized than before, by smooth horizontal bands. The three main fields of decoration, faintly indicated on the body of the *p'ou* (fig. 9) by slight vertical bands, are now sharply separated by small indented flanges. The friezes on the shoulder and the foot are similarly treated, their centres being marked by a little plastic head and a smooth vertical ridge, respectively. A smooth ridge also runs down the middle of the *t'ao-t'ieh*. The presence of ridges and flanges on one and the same vessel, each one on a definite place and in a definite function, disposes of the theories that the flanges sprang either from the ridges or from badly cast seams. They owe their existence to purely artistic considerations. They were used to accentuate a prominent part, and in this very rôle they had already been used by the indigenous potters of the neolithic age. A little later they were to replace the smooth ridges.

To make the flanges stop at the shoulder was a clever idea; thus foot, body, and shoulder were set off from neck and mouth. A file of serpents around the neck and above them a row of standing triangles admirably interpret the direction and decrease of force in these parts.

The décor as a whole gives the impression of wealth and variety. In fact, richness and variety were synonyms at this period. Yet it is very interesting to see with what little stock of forms that effect was achieved. The bodies of the snakes consist of a rectangular band, ending in a tapering meander. The same design served for the animals on the shoulder, for the *t'ao-t'ieh* and the dragons on the foot. The heads of the serpents are identical with the heads of cicadas as found on white pottery and bronze vessels. The very narrow frieze above the *t'ao-t'ieh* is adorned with two confronted dragons and two *monoculi*. One half of such a *monoculus* serves as the body of the adjacent dragon.

The workmanship is admirable. The designs are deeply incised, with sharp edges. It is very probable that the grooves were originally filled with a red or black pigment so as to make the décor distinct. When new, such bronzes shone like polished silver, and the contrast of the decorated with the undecorated parts must have been very striking.

The old pigments have often been preserved, as on a *ting* in Kansas City (fig. 11). Such vessels are not furrowed by deep lines, but have a smooth surface interrupted only by little plastic eyes, ridges, and sometimes flanges. The casting was not always good; there exist hundreds of bronzes with a shallow decoration and blurred lines. The range in quality and invention was very wide.

The *ting* in Kansas City shows the old *t'ao-t'ieh* with new horns. They turn outward and are broken at right angles. This type held the field for some time. It was also in this phase that the mouth was gradually changed. The ridge in the centre was drawn down to the lower edge; its lateral curls were increased in size, as were the hooks under the eyes. At the end, the horns changed again; they took the shape of a recumbent C. The final form can be seen on the magnificent four-legged *chia* (fig. 12).

The design is now presented with great lucidity. By reducing in size the meanders of the background, and by spacing widely those in the interior of the animals, the main themes stand out very clearly. This was not always so. For some time it was often dubious whether an element belonged to an animal, or was part of its surroundings. On early bronzes one or two eyes seem to float in a sea of hooks and meanders; and only a very close inspection reveals the faint contours of bodies, tails, and horns (cf. fig. 9).

At this time a great many types were in use. The *p'ou*, the *ting*, the *tsun*, and the *chia* have been mentioned. The *chia* usually had but three legs, and so had the *chüeh*, which looks like an inverted helmet. *Chia* and *chüeh* have a pair of short, capped columns standing on their rims, to facilitate their removal from the fire with the help of sticks. The *lei* was a large *p'ou*. The *li* was known, and the *li-ting*, a combination of the two types of tripods. The *ku* was a trumpet-shaped vase; so was the common *tsun* which was much stouter than the *ku*; and there was also the *kuei*, a tureen with or without a pair of handles. It looks as if the *kuei* was originally a *p'ou* with a very wide mouth.

A certain directness of purpose lends these vessels an air of seriousness and sincerity. Their several parts are always massive, and admirably fitted for their jobs; except for the *ku,* all these types are heavy, sturdy, and without any pretense at elegance. Clarity of structure was the ideal, and it was aided and stressed by the arrangement of the décor. The results were sometimes works of great vigour, and even monumentality.

BRONZES WITH PLASTIC DECOR

An observant student will have noticed that all the bronzes described had one feature in common: the décor was always flush with the vessel. Distinctness of design, the main concern of many generations, was finally achieved by a sharp separation of pattern and background. It was discovered that it could be achieved in another way, by rendering it plastically.

The time when the change from a graphic to a plastic décor took place can be determined with the help of the *t'ao-t'ieh*. It happened after this monster was being represented with powerful jaws that curl inward, and with horns in the shape of a recumbent C. This, of course, must not be interpreted to mean that older shapes did not occasionally turn up; they did, but seldom, and then usually together with those innovations just mentioned.

Along with the shift from an incised representation to one in relief went other changes. The sprightliness of line, so charming in bronzes like the *chia* (fig. 12), is entirely gone in the earliest works of the new style, and with it went the freshness of the preceding epoch.

A *kuei* in the Art Institute of Chicago shows the new characteristics very well (fig. 13). The horns of the *t'ao-t'ieh* have gone limp. Ears were known earlier; now they become increasingly frequent. The relief is one of a single layer from which only the eyes and the central ridge protrude.

A few words must be said about the handles. The oldest *kuei,* those with an incised décor, have handles that are covered either with a scale pattern, or with the engraved picture of a bird. An animal head is placed at some distance from the vessel. With the relief décor came another type of handle: the plastic animal head with an upturned snout is moved closer to the rim which is touched by the broad, flat horns. From the handle hangs a rectangular piece which carries the legs and tails of the bird whose wings are represented upon either side of the handle in more or less pronounced relief. This type of handle was retained until the early decades of the Chou epoch.

The somewhat sluggish forms of the *kuei* in Chicago can be found in a great many bronzes of all types. However the old sprightliness of form and design was soon regained. In a *yu* in the Freer Gallery all the technical and artistic difficulties that might have arisen are completely mastered (fig. 14). It has a tenseness that was unknown in even the best specimens of former times. The structure of any vessel is now generally emphasized by horizontal division and a clever use of flanges. Flanges appear everywhere; they grow in size and importance. They are chiefly responsible for the jagged appearance that is to be so characteristic of Chinese bronzes for some time to come.

This effect is due not only to the flanges; the décor itself juts forth in bold relief. On the *yu,* there are three layers. The horns, for instance, are no longer flat but slightly concave, with the pointed tips sharply upturned. This form was probably taken over from the animal heads in the round that were placed on handles and shoulders, and which had been treated so at an earlier time (cf. fig. 12). From such heads came also the eyebrows which appear rather late in representations of the *t'ao-t'ieh.*

Then followed a period in which the plastic accessories so gained in weight and size as to overpower the vessel that bore them. It is as though an irrepressible force had surged from within, seeped through the walls and seams, and thrown up design and flanges. The various motives of the décor are always vigorously modelled; the horns of a *t'ao-t'ieh* or other animal leave the ground and shoot out into space. In such cases it was no longer considered necessary to set off the design by a roughened background; for the first time in the history of Chinese bronzes the ground was left blank and smooth. In other cases the foil of tiny meanders was kept. The small *yu* of the famous Pao Chi set, in the Metropolitan Museum of New York, illustrates the new tendencies very well (fig. 15).

Upon the two *yu* from Pao Chi the *t'ao-t'ieh* is replaced by an array of birds.

THE BRONZES

For centuries the *t'ao-t'ieh* was almost ubiquitous; it adorned the most prominent parts of ritual vessels and weapons. Now, in the time of the ornate style, more and more bronzes were decorated with other motives such as birds, spikes, and closely packed vertical ribs.

This does not mean that the *t'ao-t'ieh* and the host of minor fantastic animals that accompany them were discarded. On the contrary, it was at this very period that they received their most savage forms. Too savage, in fact, to be as convincing as their ancestors were. A short time later, all these animals were treated in a playful fashion. They were turned into elaborate creatures with frills of little hooks that were anything but awe-inspiring. A *fang-i* in Chicago is a very significant work of that phase (fig. 16). The exuberant vitality that had found expression in bronzes like the Pao Chi *yu* (fig. 15) has now subsided. The solid flanges were dissolved into rows of hooks, and the same spirit of levity, gracefulness and elegance may be found in the vessel itself and in its ornaments.

To these late works of the ornate style can be ascribed a definite date. A few vessels of this style bear inscriptions which either mention the kings Wu (1027-1024 B.C.) and Ch'ēng, or persons who were related to them and must have lived at their time. One of these bronzes is the four-legged *ting* in the Nelson Gallery in Kansas City (fig. 17). Its décor consists of such characteristic elements as fields of vertical ribs, spikes, large hooked flanges, and horns in the round on the animal heads that serve as capitals of the legs. The inscription of this *ting* says that it is "King Ch'ēng's vessel." Though this leaves some doubt as to whether the bronze belonged to Ch'ēng himself, or was cast after his death for sacrificing to him, several good reasons are in favour of the first view; one is the absence of the qualifying "sacrificial" from the noun "vessel." Ch'ēng was the son of Wu; he reigned in the last quarter of the eleventh century B.C., according to the chronology based upon the "Ancient Bamboo Books" which evidently has greater claims to being correct than the "traditional" chronology.

There is no doubt that the late ornate style extended into the first decades of the Chou dynasty. But there is also no doubt that its roots are deeply sunk in the art of the Shang. Its types, its motives, its forms, and its means of representation were developed in many centuries of hard and incessant work. This work had been done under the Shang. The ornate style is the last and perhaps the most charming product of Shang art.

THE BRONZES

WESTERN CHOU

It has often been asserted that early Chou art was but a continuation of Shang art. From a purely historical point of view, this is true. Under Ch'ēng Wang's reign a number of bronzes were cast in the ornate style, and that style is essentially of Shang character. Yet it was under the same king that a new and radically different style came into being. It would be more correct to say that Shang art did not perish with the change of dynasties, but died the moment the Chou were firmly established.

Even if the overthrow of the Shang by the Chou were not a known historical event, some sort of revolutionary change would have to be inferred from a comparison of the bronzes. Seldom in history has a break in the political situation been so distinctly reflected in art.

A *yu* in the Victoria and Albert Museum of London is as different as possible from earlier vessels of the same type (fig. 18, cf. fig. 14, 15). Gone are the jutting accoutrements of flanges, the over-all décor, the strong relief of the ornaments and the jerky rhythm of the whole. The vessel has a simplicity of structure and a quiet nobility of line unknown in former times. The décor is restricted to three very small friezes around the lid, the shoulder and the footring. They are so inconspicuous as not to endanger the newly discovered beauty of a plain smooth surface; yet large enough to enhance it by contrast, and to mark the vital parts. The handle now invariably connects the small lateral sides, thus revealing in full the comely silhouette.

There are many bronzes in this severe style: *tsun, ting, kuei,* and *chih,* a tall beaker. Some of them carry inscriptions dating them in the time of Ch'ēng Wang. Vessels of the severe style must not be confounded with bronzes of Shang date that present a superficially similar appearance. There is ample evidence that bronzes with an over-all graphic décor were accompanied by simpler ones that were either plain or decorated with one or two small friezes only. However, their types, their form, the motives and the technique of their décor, always mark them for what they really are: the modest by-products of the elaborate style then ruling.

Though utterly different in form and décor, and in their interrelation, the function of the bronzes remained the same under the Chou as under the Shang. It would be a mistake to attribute their changed appearance solely to varying religious beliefs, or to differing tastes. Both were involved; they were only the realization in two different spheres of the same cause, a new attitude toward this world and the world beyond.

The most astonishing phenomenon is the vanishing of the *t'ao-t'ieh* at ca. 1000 B.C. Nothing is known about the ideas it stood for. The inscriptions do not mention it. The name was first used by Lü Pu-wei (d.232 B.C.) when he described what he believed to be a *ting* of Chou date. It is, however, probable that the *t'ao-t'ieh* played an apotropæic rôle, i.e., it had to ward off evil spirits from the objects that bore its image. The cicada was very likely a symbol of resurrection; dragon and bird are often said to be emblems of fertility and fecundity; but no definite proof is available.

Of the large flock of real and fantastic animals that adorn Shang bronzes, the Chou kept only the dragon and the bird. Along with this sharp reduction in motives went an equally sharp reduction in types. After one or two generations, the *tsun*, the *ku*, the *fang-i*, the *kuang*, the *chia*, the *chüeh*, the *chio*, the *lei*, the *p'ou*, and the four-legged *ting* were no longer made. A strange case is that of the *hsien*, a steamer consisting of a *li* with a large pot on top of the tripod. The *hsien* is the only instance where the *t'ao-t'ieh* was retained; it appears on the *li*, and generally in strong relief on a smooth background. Very often it is scarcely recognizable. The pot, however, is always decorated in the typical "modern" Chou style. Many *hsien* show this discrepancy. A few disastrous failures might have cast discredit upon *hsien* which did not have at least the eyes of a *t'ao-t'ieh*. For this is, very tellingly, the only part that finally survived.

The Chou are often presented as less cultivated than the Shang. This verdict is certainly not borne out by their art. Simplicity of form does not imply a simple mind, or indicate a lower state of culture. The noble restraint of early Chou bronzes makes Shang vessels appear by comparison exuberant and flamboyant; it also makes them appear barbarous in form and spirit.

It looks as though for some time the artists were exclusively concerned with creating simple, clear, and balanced forms, and that little effort was spent in inventing appropriate patterns for the few narrow friezes. At the beginning, they are often filled with motives of earlier periods, provided these motives are subdued in character. After a short time the severity of line softened, form became limp and languid, and the parts merged more readily than before into a whole. It was then that birds with enormously long, sweeping tails, and dragons in sinuous curves filled the few registers (fig. 19). The vessels grew broader. They became more relaxed and comfortable than their taut and tense forerunners.

The tempo of that evolution was apparently quite lively. A *yu* cast under Kung Wang (fig. 20) looked very different from that illustrated in fig. 19. To that period, the fourth quarter of the tenth century, a great many vessels can be ascribed. They no longer rely on the beauty of sheer bronze; their walls are again covered with an over-all décor. Its motive is always the same: large birds with their heads turned back, their tails raised, and large plumes streaming from their crests. Through their size and position they convey an impression of richness, and, through their curved lines, of movement. It is a movement that is strictly confined to its own quarter, in the

THE BRONZES

literal sense of the word. This new décor finally appears on all types, such as on the *ting*, the *kuei*, the *yu*, and the *chih*.

It will be scarcely necessary to point out the difference between this over-all décor, and that of the Shang bronzes. The decorative unit is the quarter of a vessel; formerly it was more often the half. But now it is filled with a single large theme, coherent in form and fluent in line; there is a perfect correspondence between the contours of the design and those of the vessel. Any earlier bronze seems to be built of elements that pay little or no heed to one another, when compared with these works of the late tenth century.

Whatever may be said in praise of Early Chou art, it cannot be credited with great inventiveness. Original motives, such as the large bird with the upraised tail and the sinuous dragon, were created only toward the end of that period. The other designs, such as bird and dragon, had been taken over from the Shang. A particular motive, the "confronted dragons" that were a favorite Shang pattern (cf. fig. 12, 14), led an obscure life during Early Chou. By the end of the tenth century, its meaning was evidently no longer understood. It disintegrated; the parts no longer formed a unit, but became independent. What is more, these split forms of mouth, horns, nose, eyes, and ears were combined into a new pattern. Were it not for the presence of eyes and ears, lying lonesome amid the remnants of their former self, it would be impossible to make any sense of this new ornament.

A chalice-shaped vessel in Boston has a small frieze with such a design (fig. 21). The process of cleavage that had led to its making must have been concluded at the beginning of the ninth century, for at that time such broken up dragons are ubiquitous.

All this became important when the artist took up the pattern, eliminated the elements reminiscent of its animal origin, and rearranged it into something that was going to be the most typical motive of the ninth century. It usually has the shape of two recumbent interlocked G's. It serves exclusively as a filling for the small friezes around the lids, shoulders, and feet of vessels, as on the imposing *kuei* of the Loo Collection (fig. 22). This bronze is a work of the ninth century, and remarkable for a number of interesting features.

This *kuei* has retained many traits of the preceding style. Here is the broad and limp form of the vessel; the over-all theriomorphous décor; the handles transformed into animals, an invention of the late tenth century; and the little animal head with spiral horns in the centre of the upper frieze which is identical to one in the same place on a *kuei* with a décor of large birds, in the Freer Gallery. The large animals on body and socle are not birds, but dragons. They are of a peculiar species: they have wings, feet, turned back heads, and streamers flowing from their noses. In fact, these creatures are nothing but the familiar large birds with upraised tails of the tenth century converted into dragons. New are the flattening of the relief, its sharp edges, and the use of comparatively broad bands of even width. New, too, is the pattern that marks the merging of two dragons in the centre of the belly. It looks like an eye with four prongs. It is as frequent on bronzes of this period as are the interlocked G's.

It is also found on a *kuei* with lid in Kansas City (fig. 23). This type, which was a favourite of the ninth century, had been known for a long time, at least from the very beginning of Chou. Under the hands of later generations it underwent considerable changes. The parts that Early Chou masters had left plain received a horizontal fluting. Datable vessels show that these flutes appeared first under Mu Wang; under his successor, Kung Wang, they were accompanied by sinuous dragons in their friezes. The evolution of this type of *kuei* can be traced without great difficulty, for the animals that top the handles were subjected to many metamorphoses until they reached their final form with flaring ears, curled snouts, and coiled tongues. One such *kuei* is dated the 27th year of an unspecified king who in all probability was I Wang II (d.858 B.C.). The *Kuei* in Kansas City belongs to a group of four (B 117) with identical inscriptions, dated in the third year of a king who must be Hsüan Wang (827-782 B.C.). It was therefore cast in 825 B.C.

The limp, sagging form of the vessel, the flutes that cause a glimmer of light, the flourishing handles and the three upturned feet that lift the whole from the ground indicate a new attitude toward form. It aims at the negation of weight and at the destruction of clear and definite surfaces. At the end of the ninth century, this tendency led to a décor of dragons in very high relief. It appears especially on the *hu,* large vases with lids. For the first time in the history of Chinese bronzes the elements of a décor are not simply strung in files, but wound around one another. Another and very effective way of dissolving the ground was to render the design with raised contours. The majority of bronzes thus treated, especially the *hu,* the *kuei,* and the *ting,* were ornamented with a pattern that was invented in the ninth and lived on to the eighth century. It is an endless undulating band that is knocked slightly out of direction when ascending and descending. The interstices are filled with scales or kidney-shaped elements, and two hooks; sometimes with a pair of dragons whose tails merge. This design is usually accompanied by files of horizontal and vertical scales.

All these innovations in motive and style are found on a *kuei* in the Loo Collection (fig. 24). Its most striking features are the magnificent handles. They are protoma of dragons, and truly baroque in form. It was a new and typically baroque idea to add a small feline animal locked by fangs and claws to the chest of the dragon. It made form more complicated and helped to divert attention from the vessel itself. This end the artist evidently had in mind; he wanted to express a centrifugal force emanating from the container. The hypertrophy of handles and crown and the care

THE BRONZES

bestowed on them direct the spectator from the vessel to its accessories. It is no longer the lucidly built form that counts, but the movement of the décor. Even the square socle is now covered with a design that leads around its corners.

This style reached its apogee in two enormous *hu* from the famous find of Hsin Ch'ēng, in Honan. These magnificent vases are more than one meter high. They are lifted from the ground by two felines. Similar animals climb up on either side, their heads turned back, crowned by broad openwork crests. The bodies of these "tigers" are perforated; as a matter of fact they are made up of interlaced bands that are treated *à jour*. Both vases have tall thick necks and comparatively small sagging bellies. They show a complete and utter disregard of well-balanced form. Seen from a moderate distance, the simpler *hu* looks as though its upper parts were covered with tiny plastic curls in no apparent order. Their only function seems to be the roughening of the surface. When scrutinized, they turn out to be minute dragons and other elements, rendered with raised contours. The base of the lid is covered with a square pattern of two intertwined dragons. It is repeated with the help of a die, in an almost imperceptibly low relief. The flaring crown is formed by interlaced dragons in openwork.

The second *hu* is even more bizarre (fig. 25). The supporting "tigers" and those serving as handles are richer in appearance. Winged dragons wriggle at the four corners; smaller dragons fighting leopards protrude from the centre of the front and back. From mouth to foot the vessel is covered with an interlacing of long thin dragons in moderate relief. Their bodies are covered with a diminutive cicada pattern. It would take up too much space to describe all the details. Suffice it to say that the little square pattern of entwined dragons appears on the foot. The crown of the lid consists of two rows of petals formed by thin interlocked dragons in openwork. It is surmounted by a crane with outspread wings. The figure is in the round and shows no trace of that geometrization to which every animal had been subjected up to this time.

The two *hu* and a few more bronzes from Hsin Ch'ēng represent the final stages of an evolution that had started with the creation of the severe style under Ch'ēng Wang. With them the second great cycle of ancient Chinese art came to its logical end.

THE BRONZES

THE HSIN CH'ĒNG STYLE

So profound was the impression made by the sophisticated bronzes from the Hsin Ch'ēng hoard that most scholars think of them alone when that name is mentioned. In reality, most of the bronzes found there are very different in form and décor; they are the very opposite of the flashy *hu*. Ornamentation is so subdued as to be scarcely noticeable; it is absolutely subservient to form which, in its turn, is always comprehensible in all its parts.

The bronze find of Hsin Ch'ēng falls into the same category as those of Li Yü and Chin Ts'un. The three of them do not represent closed groups. The objects display a variety of styles, with one style predominant. A close scrutiny of forms and décors reveals, however, that these various styles constitute a sequence.

The oldest group of bronzes from Hsin Ch'ēng definitely resemble works of the late ninth and early eighth century; then follow those bronzes that cluster around the two *hu,* described in the preceding chapter. Then came that radical break in style I just pointed out. The connecting link between works of the flamboyant, atectonic style, and works of the simple, tectonic style is a small square pattern of entwined dragons. It occurred on the two *hu,* and became the principal motive in the next phase. It is so frequent and so characteristic that I propose to call it the Hsin Ch'ēng pattern. It looks like this:

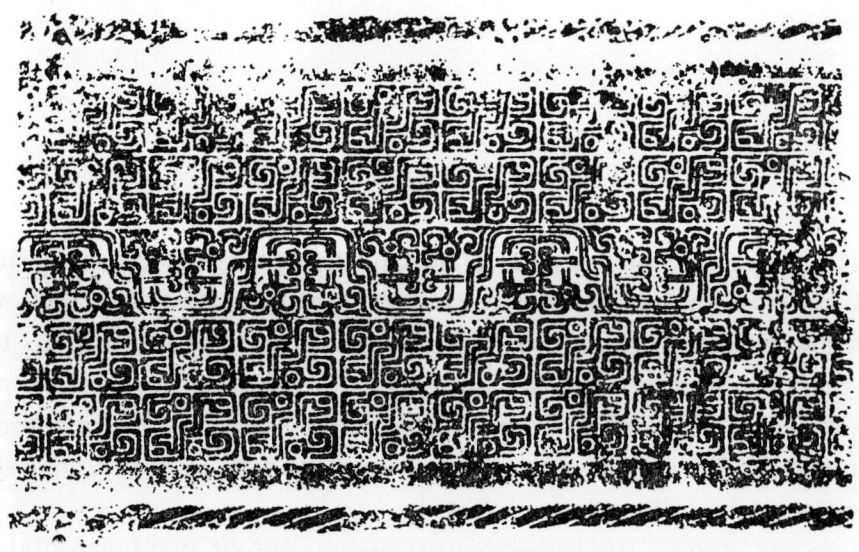

X. THE HSIN CH'ĒNG PATTERN

There were many variations of it, and these differed widely in size. On some of the bronzes in the new tectonic style they are so small as to be scarcely visible. Such is the case with a *fu* in the Art Institute of Chicago (fig. 26). This bronze is identical with several *fu* of the Hsin Ch'ēng hoard. A *fu* is a covered tray of

41

rectangular form. The upper part is the exact replica of the lower. The *fu* from Hsin Ch'ēng are built of clear-cut sections with sharp edges. Four dragon heads of moderate size on the handles, and six small ones along the rim seem to be all that exists in the way of decoration. The walls appear plain and soft; only the closest examination shows that they are covered with a minuscule variety of the Hsin Ch'ēng pattern.

The trend toward clear tectonic forms can be traced back to the end of the ninth century. It was particularly the *ting* that heralded the coming of a new style. Such *ting* have often hemispheric bodies and no décor at all, or only a very small frieze under the rim; they always have plain bulbous legs instead of curved legs; sometimes they are topped by the heads of horned animals, a common feature of the heavily decorated *ting*. Yet the baroque style evidently had to exhaust all its possibilities before the tendencies toward a simple form and a restrained décor could become victorious.

It is true that form is now always simple; but it is seldom beautiful. A great many bronzes of the Hsin Ch'ēng style, especially the *ting,* show a strange disregard of balanced and harmonious proportions. It is possible for an enormous body to sit on dwarfed legs which by now are again capped with animal heads. The lid may be almost flat and is sometimes provided with three upright rings. Another characteristic of the Hsin Ch'ēng style is the use of a rope in slight relief as the border of a frieze and of triangular blades with curved sides which hang from the lowest frieze. As time went on, these blades, or leaves, became more curvilinear, almost heart-shaped.

THE LI YÜ STYLE

Though it is uncertain how long the Hsin Ch'ēng style reigned during the seventh century, it is certain that it reigned over a vast area. Bronzes of this style were used from Shansi to Shantung, and from Chili to Anhui, as their inscriptions testify.

From the Hsin Ch'ēng style sprang another which has much in common with it, but is sufficiently distinct to deserve a designation of its own. It was first brought within our ken by the bronzes that were found near Li Yü in northern Shansi. It may reasonably be called the Li Yü style.

This style also divides the bodies of vessels into one or two horizontal registers, and does so very often by a rope in relief. The friezes are always filled with files of independent dragons, or with an endless pattern of interlaced dragons. Both were produced with the help of dies, and are minute in elevation. For this reason the effect is always very restrained. It never detracts from the vessel and its form, which is usually more pleasing than that of a work in the Hsin Ch'ēng style. Legged

THE BRONZES

bronzes, such as *ting,* have animal heads on top of their curved legs. These rather elaborate heads resemble those on similar vessels from Hsin Ch'ēng so closely as to make their intimate connection quite evident.

The main difference between works of the two styles lies in the size of the dragons. In Li Yü they are comparatively large and flat, with thin smooth contours which enclose a filling of very small volutes and triangles. Dragons with an interior pattern were already known in Hsin Ch'ēng, e.g., on the large *hu* (fig. 25).

All this, however, refers to the fully developed styles of Hsin Ch'ēng and Li Yü. A few works exist showing the gradual transition from one to the other. Among the most precious finds from Hsin Ch'ēng are two plaques in gold sheet. They are covered with goodsized interlaced dragons, whose bodies are rendered in smooth contours and filled with narrow oblique striæ.

XI. Design of Gold Plaque from Hsin Ch'ēng

The very same dragons occur on a *ting* in the Art Institute of Chicago. They are arranged in files on a work which any student of Chinese bronzes would call a simple piece in the style of Li Yü. Even such striking details as the small bars connecting two adjacent animals and the curious "plain faces" are here found again (fig. 27).

The same museum possesses one more bronze that proves the close relationship of Hsin Ch'ēng and Li Yü. It is a *hu* whose walls are divided into four friezes; they are alternately filled with a variant of the Hsin Ch'ēng pattern and with typical Li Yü dragons.

A *ting* from Li Yü, now in the Louvre, shows the new style in its prime (fig. 28). It is a work of great beauty and excellent workmanship. The upright rings on the lid are here replaced by marvellously modelled ducks. The heads and breasts of these birds are covered with innumerable little dots that give the effect of a rather coarse granulation. Even more impressive are two recumbent sheep with wriggling serpents that are placed on the lid of a four-legged *ting* from the original hoard (fig. 49).

The mock granulation appeared also on the dragons of the main décor after the style was well established and aimed at greater wealth of form. The little dots were then restricted to some parts of the head, usually the snout. A large basin in Chicago is adorned with such dragons (fig. 29). It also carries another new element, the braid. This is always rendered in relief, and the effect is very striking in contrast with the flat décor of the friezes.

Another pattern appears at about the same time. It consists of a central head, usually bovine in character, from which bodies spread in either direction. Like the banded dragons in simple file, the motive is repeated alternately in an upright and a reversed position.

It will have been noticed that the dragons of the Li Yü style are covered with small volutes. Wherever an outline changes its direction, a volute or a bent hook is apt to appear. They do not obtrude because they are as flat as the rest of the design.

After some time, however, this reserved and quiet style changed. Form grew strangely restless. The curved parts, such as the jaws, noses, ears, and wings of the animals were rendered in a higher relief. A subtle yet important transformation ensued. Where formerly the straight line predominated, curved elements now take the lead. And where formerly a single and extraordinarily shallow layer of relief sufficed for all, two and three layers are now needed for the curved parts.

The tendencies and achievements of this mature phase of the Li Yü style come out very clearly when a magnificent basin in the Freer Gallery is compared with the basin in Chicago (fig. 30). The theriomorphic character of the décor is easily deciphered. This, however, holds only for the ornamentation of the central frieze. The interlaced winged dragons on the rim with their dancing rhythm and undulating movement are difficult to make out. A short while afterwards, as the bell in fig. 31 shows, the interlaced dragons were transmuted in a whirling mass of plastic bands and spirals. In some places, such as the oblong fields of the walls, the animals were recognizable; in the registers of the handle this is no longer possible.

Finally, the décor throws off even the slightest pretense of a zoömorphous character. It is made up of an inextricable maze of little volutes and feather-like elements which have no objective meaning whatsoever. This stage was reached by 550 B.C.

THE BRONZES

THE HUAI STYLE

THE year 550 B.C. is the date of an event recorded in the inscriptions of several bells, called the Piao bells after a clan which is also mentioned in them. The tops of these bells are covered with the spirals and feathers into which the dragons of Li Yü had been transformed. In form, motive, and aim, bronzes so decorated are very different from the Li Yü bronzes. It is appropriate to designate this new style by a name of its own. It may best be called Huai style, after the river Huai, near which the first works so decorated were found.

The pilgrim's bottle in Chicago is a work that shows the new style at its best (fig. 32). The flattened body is divided by plain bands into square sunken fields; these fields are covered with the typical Huai pattern. In this particular case one even gets the impression that the vessel has been latticed, and the interstices backed by another sheet of bronze.

In the first quarter of the fifth century, the Huai pattern had already lost much of its neatness and precision. This is proved by the famous basin which was made for Fu-ch'ai, king of Wu, who reigned from 495 to 473 B.C. (C 183).

However, there are some bronzes which continue the Li Yü style in a very peculiar way. Their décor is negative; i.e., the design is left plain, and the background is filled with those geometric elements which, in Li Yü, had been used to cover the bodies of dragons. Design and background are always flush with each other. This principle had already been known and applied in Li Yü. The lids of the *ting* (fig. 28) and the four-legged *ting* (fig. 49) were decorated in this manner. Yet most of the vessels that are exclusively decorated with such a negative ornamentation are of later date; they are more or less contemporaneous with the works of the Huai style.

It is a fallacy to think of any style as dying suddenly and being replaced by its successor. There are always and everywhere artists who, by inclination, education, or lack of spirit cling to the old. They are undoubtedly persuaded that they are upholding tradition. Their efforts run parallel to those of their fellow artists who set out for new aims. It would be rash to assume that their work is always doomed to fail. It did not in this case.

The decorative system of the bronzes with negative ornament was as legitimate an offspring of the Li Yü style as was the system of the Huai style. Most of the motives of the inverse décor are those of the preceding period; namely, interlaced dragons. But these animals were given a long pointed beak instead of a curled nose and a comparatively thin body. In some cases new motives were invented, or old ones so transmuted as to pass for new ones. Such is the case with some designs on a pair of *hu* in the Loo Collection (fig. 33). The walls are divided into eight narrow registers of which four carry an inverse décor. The design is very complicated. It is derived from a rather fanciful pattern which, in its turn, had resulted from a disintegration of the Li Yü dragons. What appears on this *hu* is purely geometric and has as little meaning as the Huai pattern. The other four registers are filled with rows of a small oval element. On close inspection this turns out to be a bird's head with an enormous curved beak. Though small in size and rendered by the means of this period, the affinity with the birds' heads of contemporaneous Scythian art in southern Russia is unmistakable.[2]

The bird's head — always the highly characteristic one with a large curved beak — occurs again and again in works of this period. It may mark the joints of two felines which serve as the handle of the type of bell called *po*; or the outer border of a mirror whose field is covered with the typical Huai pattern may outline such a head.[3]

The mirror itself came to China at this time. It has long been known that the Chinese mirror was but a variant of the Scythian mirror. In addition, the short Chinese sword which also appears at this time is plainly derived from the Scythian *akinakes*.

The borrowing from the Scythians was done with a certain fervour in the sixth century, but it had started much earlier. Max Loehr found a curled animal, a Scythian motive *par excellence,* on a bell of the type *po*. Even such an extraordinary peculiarity as the "ring foot," i.e., the substitution of a ring for a paw, is faithfully represented.[4] To judge by its style, this *po* must have been cast in the seventh century. In fact, a few things that turned up in Hsin Ch'ēng, and a great many in Li Yü were of foreign origin: the demarcation of joints by volutes, the simple rope, the crocheted rope, the braid, the twisted ribbon and mock granulations.

THE CHIN TS'UN STYLE

THE smooth parts of the pilgrim's bottle (fig. 32) are not uniform in material. They are inlaid with copper; the contrast between its red and the silver of the bronze must have been very beautiful when the vessel was new. Inlay of turquoise in bronze had flourished under the Shang, but had died with that dynasty. For about half a millennium, the casters used bronze alone; if they wanted to make a vessel very luxurious, they hammered thin sheets of gold over it. Not before the sixth century did inlays of alloys other than bronze occur; at first it was used in inconspicuous places, later more prominently. A square trough with convex tapering sides, in Toronto, is covered with the Huai pattern; under the rim is a design of oblongs inlaid in gold, copper, malachite and turquoise.[5]

XII. Inlaid Design of the Trough in Toronto

The inlay is rather thin, and its effect somewhat poor. Yet the vessel is important because it belongs to a fairly large group which displays the same combination of Huai pattern and an inlay of thin, straight lines and little bits of turquoise. Such works can be roughly dated to the first half of the fifth century B.C. But many bronzes use these thin inlaid lines alone. A given surface was usually divided into narrow sections, and these were filled with patterns which run parallel to the borders. A *hu* in the Ohta Collection is thus treated. The steplike pattern is a little feeble (fig. 34). The use of semiprecious and strongly coloured stones is here of as little help as it was in the case of the trough in Toronto.

These were the humble beginnings of a style which was to create the most sumptuous vessels in the times to come. Its motives were always purely geometric, simple at first and very complicated at the end. The technique of inlay was new. The aim was also new: the creation of an even surface, intricate in design, gorgeous in colour, and dazzling in effect. The objects finally look as though covered with heavy, luxurious brocades in gold, silver, red, blue, and green. Fundamental to this development is a profound change in the idea of what decoration ought to be. It is now conceived as a splendid coat spread over an object; formerly it was always of a piece with it. By virtue of intention and means, this is a new style. It should be called the Chin Ts'un style, after the site where most such bronzes were discovered.

The first attempts in the new style were anything but promising; the lines were too thin and too few, and so were the stray bits of coloured stones. But line was soon made heavier, though not uniformly. The décor consisted of horizontal and vertical lines of varying thickness, interspersed with leaf-like shapes and tenuous spirals. It was always static and strictly symmetrical. Diagonal lines, at first used very sparingly, began to play an increasingly important rôle. Finally the whole décor was tilted. An urn in the Loo Collection shows these two successive stages on one and the same vessel (fig. 35). The décor of the neck is more old-fashioned than that of the body. It is not enough to point out that in one case a horizontal and in the other a diagonal order was applied; form has become richer, more variegated and complicated; where the horizontal ornament is spread out in one plane, the diagonal décor is arrayed in two imaginary layers, and according to the rule of movement and counter-movement.

THE BRONZES

This style with its predilection for tilted angular patterns reached its apogee before the last decades of the fourth century B.C. So much can be safely concluded from a square vase, called *fang,* in the University of Pennsylvania Museum in Philadelphia (fig. 36). Its inscription refers to an event of 314 B.C.; but it is very likely that it was engraved some time after the casting.[6]

The walls of the famous vessel are inlaid with malachite and covered with a very involved design of lozenges. It is symmetrical along a vertical axis; but the order is so sophisticated and so difficult to make out that the impression is one of irrationality in composition, and of unbridled fantasy in invention.

What followed was the replacement of symmetry by asymmetry, of rigidity by fluency, of the straight line by the curve. The décor began to stir, to move, and finally it rushed forth like water breaking through a dam.

It is quite fascinating to trace this change of attitude. I shall do so by comparing the friezes of two identical pieces. The task and the decorative elements that were used were the same. The first example is the main ornament of an axle mounting in the Museum of Far Eastern Antiquities in Stockholm.

XIII. Design on an Axle Mounting

Between two friezes of oblique double T's whose upper and lower beams end alternately in small and large volutes is a broad register filled with two zigzags. In reality, there is only one zigzag line, inlaid in silver. The zigzag which seems to overlap the silver one is made by the outsides of the adjacent triangles. The genuine and the mock triangles are alternately upright and inverted, and form such planimetric elements as triangles and lozenges which are embellished by thin spirals. Though all these patterns are slightly off the median axis, the effect is nevertheless a rather static one.

The small frieze in the centre of the second axle mounting is again made by such triangles as are described above; but everything is transmuted in form and function. The accents are put on differently. The result is a design that seems to surge forward and snap back. It is full of tension and dynamic force. There is the same spirit in it as that which makes the winged and horned dragons above and below

48

XIV. Design on an Axle Mounting

this frieze wheel around as if they were trying to burst through their confines. It is also very characteristic that no straight line or right angle appears in the whole décor; there is always a curve to lead the eye in endless motion.

There exist hundreds of small objects such as handles, sockets of weapons, fittings of chariots, finials of poles, and belt hooks, all of them showing this change from the rectilinear to the curvilinear and from the static to the dynamic. The change sometimes affects the plastic core itself; an object may be twisted, with its parts imperceptibly flowing into one another. Two finials of poles, the older one in the Art Institute of Chicago, the more recent one in the Fogg Museum in Cambridge, illustrate the change very nicely (fig. 37, 38).

To the late stage of this style belongs a small *hu* in Chicago (fig. 39). The décor, inlaid, or rather hammered on in gold and silver, consists of large sweeping curves which run on incessantly. There is no centre and no axis, either for the several friezes or for the whole. A characteristic feature of this decorative system must be mentioned: a form may disappear behind the border to emerge at some distance and continue its course.

Such a deliberate complication would have been impossible in the earlier stages of the Chin Ts'un style. However to an artist of the former Han dynasty it was the natural way to decorate the registers of the magnificent *hu* that is now in Chicago (fig. 40).

This is a work of extraordinary refinement. One can almost see the artist letting his needle dance in graceful curves over the surface, and applying silver and the palest of golds to set off his drawing.

THE BRONZES

The end of this elegant style with its love for moving volutes of an almost floral quality can be approximately dated in the middle of the first century A.D. Then graceful tendrils appear as the décor of some lacquer boxes, bowls, and dishes which have been discovered in Chinese tombs of the Lo-lang district in Korea.[7] These lacquers are sometimes dated, the latest date being 69 A.D. There can be no doubt that these were among the last products of this gracious style.

Before this survey of the development of ancient Chinese bronzes draws to a close, one more thing must be discussed briefly. The reader may have formed the opinion that ritual vessels were the only works produced from Shang to Han times. This is most decidedly not the case. The ritual bronzes were selected because they were the most important objects; as such, they were the main concern of artistic effort. But they never stood alone. For every one ritual vessel there were a hundred other things made: implements; weapons; trimmings for architecture, furniture, and chariots; utensils for personal use. These things were not all of bronze; some were of wood, of jade, of bone, or of ivory. If they were decorated, their ornaments were the same as those found on contemporaneous vessels.

MIRRORS

MIRRORS are perhaps the most charming and delightful products of ancient Chinese art. As pointed out, they appear first in the seventh century B.C.; i.e., in the time when the Li Yü style flourished. This date is also attested to by literary evidence.

It is, of course, only the back of a mirror that was adorned. A few specimens can be assigned to the seventh century. It seems, however, that the making of mirrors did not become widespread before the sixth century B.C.

Among the earliest mirrors rank those round and square ones that are decorated with two bears' heads. The heads are flanked by paws with three claws (fig. 41). The rest of the surface is covered with rather large bands that end in hooks and volutes. The bands are filled with striæ or with spirals; their contours are slightly raised, and the centres of the volutes protrude quite noticeably. The style is intermediate between Li Yü and Huai, and such mirrors can be dated to the first half of the sixth century.

The mirrors that followed are unmistakable, for they are covered with the Huai pattern. In most cases it serves as a foil for a variety of motives. A few of them are rendered in moderate relief; they represent such animals as dogs and deer in a remarkably realistic manner.[8] But most mirrors have a geometric design, such as the slanting T, the zigzag lozenge (a lozenge with broken sides), or little circles surrounded by four leaf-shaped elements. Others are adorned with bold drawings of fantastic animals (fig. 42). The *élan* and facility of invention make one forget the disregard of anatomical probability.

In all these cases the outlines are raised, with the space within left smooth or even slightly concave so as to catch the light and make the contrast with the rough background more striking. It is this type of mirror that shows Siberian influence. That there was an exchange between the two countries is proved by a typical Huai mirror that was excavated near Tomsk, in Siberia; it is now in the Hermitage in Leningrad.[9]

Mirrors with the Huai pattern must have been made from 550 B.C. to about 450 B.C. Thus far, the mirror closely followed the ritual vessels. From the middle of the fifth century it seems to have struck out for new forms.

True enough, a few mirrors are known that are decorated in the typical Chin Ts'un style. The Freer Gallery possesses an excellent specimen of this kind. The famous mirror in the Hosokawa Collection belongs to the same category (fig. 43). The three complexes of volutes that divide the roundel are of the same nature as those on the design illustrated in fig. XIV.

But these are exceptions. The overwhelming majority of mirrors cast after the rise of the Chin Ts'un style are not inlaid. Their *fond* is covered with extraordinarily fine patterns of slanting and interlocked T's, zigzag lozenges or simple lozenges. These patterns are often filled with tiny round, triangular, and square spirals, and the interstices with minute mock granulation. These elements were obviously derived from Huai mirrors. In fact a few pieces exist which show the transition and transformation as neatly as one could wish.

The patterns are in a relief that is but a fraction of a millimeter high. They were, of course, applied with dies; but this does not detract from their being miracles of craftsmanship.

Most important, however, is the effect produced by these patterns; the mirrors seem to be covered with a finely woven fabric. This is the same aim that stimulated the artist of the Chin Ts'un period to cover a vessel with inlays of gold, silver, and precious stones. The mirror casters treat the *fond* exactly as if it were coated with a patterned cloth upon which was placed the flat or scalloped rim, the ring around the centre and the several zoömorphous or geometric motives. The patterned background does not pay the slightest regard to them; it emerges from under the rim on one side, and runs under all the tectonic and decorative elements, to disappear under the rim on the opposite side.

These decorative elements are animals and geometric designs. The animals are usually dragons with long curved tails and flabby snouts. The body of such a dragon is often replaced by a purely geometric form (fig. 44). In some cases very ingenious combinations of lozenges and swinging curves were provided with legs. A clear distinction between representation and ornament was not made.

THE BRONZES

It was this type that led finally to a change in style. The flat ring around the central knob was made a little more conspicuous by parallel lines. The roundel is now replete with volutes in swift motion. It is often impossible to decide whether these tendril-like elements are of a zoömorphic or geometric nature. The whole décor looks like a delicate lace placed upon fine grit, for the *fond* is still covered with extremely fine spirals and triangles. The little granulated lines have gone.

It would be futile even to try to describe the patterns formed by these intertwined elements. There are hundreds of them; they are all very elegant and pleasant in the perfect rhythm with which they dance around the centre, moving forward, halting, retracing a step or two, to go on with fresh vigour.

In the next group the interlacement of dragons and volutes is rendered differently. They are no longer flat in themselves, but are dissolved into two or three thread-like parallel lines. In this group the large circle around the centre often carries an inscription. Karlgren pointed out that the inscriptions date these mirrors definitely after 213 B.C. In that year, writing was standardized on the basis of the Ch'in script. Since many of these inscribed mirrors hail from the part of China which was until 223 B.C. the main province of the kingdom of Ch'u, and since Ch'u had a different form of script, the inference is that such mirrors were cast after 213.

This is important; for at the beginning of the first century A.D. the style had changed again. The outer rim was then broad and so raised as to let a mirror look like a shallow dish. These mirrors are heavy, sometimes rather thick. More significant is the replacement of the light movement of the ornaments by a static, symmetrical arrangement of the decorative elements. A new pattern, the saw-tooth, ran inside the rim; it was commonly accompanied by the finer comb-tooth pattern. A big, round knob had replaced the tiny, fluted one of previous epochs. It was surrounded by an eight-pronged star, a quatrefoil, a square, or a number of nipples. The background was now always plain.

A special type is the TLV mirror, so called because the geometric parts of its décor have the shape of those letters (fig. 45). Their arrangement shows a striking similarity with ancient Chinese sundials, but their specific significance on mirrors is as yet unknown.[10] This type of mirror appears as early as the second century B.C. It is subjected to the same changes of style as the other types. At the beginning of the first century A.D. the square in the centre enclosed twelve nipples, usually accompanied by the signs of the duodenary cycle. On the outside of the square are eight nipples in groups of two; they stand for the eight periods of the Chinese year. Between them are rendered in outline the four animals that are the symbols of the four quarters: the Sombre Warrior (Tortoise and Serpent) in the north; the Green Dragon in the east; the Red Bird in the south; and the White Tiger in the west. It seems that such a mirror was believed to be a magic instrument that put the cosmic forces at the service of the owner.

THE BRONZES

Other mirrors have motives that are definitely Taoist. Their character is borne out by the inscriptions, which are always in the nature of felicitations.

Among the heavy mirrors of the first century A.D. the "New Dynasty" of Wang Mang (8-23 A.D.) is often mentioned; other pieces of the new style were discovered in Chinese tombs in Korea that contained dated lacquers; some mirrors are dated, one in the year 6 A.D. All these mirrors lack the fineness and grace of the earlier specimens.

There can be little doubt that an old and graceful culture came to an end at the beginning of our era. It lived on a little longer in the delightful and capricious décor of a few lacquers. But this was the last flicker of a dying flame.

CONCLUSION

HE who looks for continuity in the evolution of ancient Chinese bronzes will find abundant positive evidence. Important as was the change from the graphic to the plastic rendition on Shang vessels, the stock patterns remained identical. The same can be said of the severe style of the Chou. Many pieces exist which display every variety of transition from the ornate style. Many characteristic designs of the ninth century bronzes were derived from those of Early Chou. The bronzes found at Hsin Ch'ēng form a continuous row, with one end abutting on the art of the early eighth century, the other on Li Yü. The gradual transformation of Li Yü into the Huai style can be observed on many works; and a number of typical Huai bronzes carry a décor in the incipient Chin Ts'un style.

This continuity reveals itself, of course, only when the correct sequence of styles is established. These styles are the visible expression of the decisive periods in the history of ancient Chinese art. Any attempt at ordering and articulating that history must take cognizance of and start with them.

The first period comprises the art of the Shang from the beginnings of the graphic to the dissolution of the ornate style. It will be remembered that the latter style outlived the Shang dynasty, though only for a short time. The development of Shang art took its natural course, from the simple to the complicated. Shang bronzes clung tenaciously to the principle of an over-all décor. At first this décor did not impair the structure of the vessel; at the end, its excessive luxuriance almost drowned it.

The second epoch starts with the creation of the severe style, apparently under Ch'ēng Wang when the Chou regime was firmly established. It lasted to the time when such bizarre works as the two *hu* of Hsin Ch'ēng were cast. In other words, a new cycle started on a new basis with very simple tectonic forms and ended with complex atectonic forms. At the beginning, structure counted most, and decoration very little; at the end, structure was deliberately obscured by an exaggerated décor.

What is called Middle Chou is nothing else than the second phase of this evolution. It came to its end in the eighth century B.C.

The third period began with the Hsin Ch'êng and ended with that phase of the Li Yü style in which the animal décor in high relief had become unrecognizable. The Huai style with its preference for lucidly constructed vessels, and its emphasis on a sharp division of form and décor, was an attempt at regaining a new basis of design. This was found not by the Huai but by the Chin Ts'un style. With its rise started the fourth important period. A characterization of this style was given a few pages ago, and can be dispensed with here.

These epochs correspond roughly to the main divisions of political history. That the first period covers the reign of the Shang dynasty needs no explanation. The second period lasted as long as the Chou rulers executed their power *de facto*. The third period corresponds roughly to what is called the Period of the Spring and Autumn Annals which lasted from ca. 722 to ca. 481 B.C. This was the time when the Chou kings had become helpless and the feudal princes were all powerful. Approximately the last seventy-five years of this period saw the rule of the Huai style. It does not coincide with any important political event; but it does coincide with the most fateful event in the history of Chinese thought, the life and work of Confucius (551-479).

The fourth period includes the political Period of the Warring States (ca. 481-221), the Ch'in (221-206), and the Former Han dynasty (206 B.C.-8 A.D.).

This looks reasonable enough. It would be ludicrous to expect the changes in style to happen at the exact time of the great political upheavals. But it is agreed that Chou culture was something very different from Shang culture; it is natural that this difference should find expression in art. Too little is known about the culture of the feudal epoch to offer a similar explanation. In the field of art, the break with the past was radical. The same might well be said of political thought.

In the fourth period, art remained totally unaffected by such grave events as the unification of China by the Ch'in. Another remarkable fact is that the art of the Former Han dynasty is radically different from that of the Later Han dynasty (25-220).

SCULPTURE

SHANG TO HAN

FOR almost a millennium and a half the making of ritual vessels was deemed the foremost task of art. These vessels were of an importance that exceeded everything else. They were indispensable for the correct performance of sacrifices to the spirits of Heaven, of ancestors, of hills and streams, and to the God of Earth. The conviction was deeply rooted that on properly conducted sacrifices depended the welfare of the state and the individual: peace and order, the fertility of the soil, and the fecundity of women and cattle. And such was the mentality of the ancient Chinese that greater importance was laid upon the act of worship than upon the worshipped.

As I have pointed out, there was no urge to imagine and represent these spirits and deities in the shape of man or even animal. I doubt whether any animal, real or fantastic, that can be found on a ritual bronze, stood for them. They are demons, some protective, some apotropæic; some plainly direct the attention of the worshipped to the wishes and hopes of the worshipper.

This holds also for the figures in limestone that have been excavated near Hou Chia-chuang. Some of them are easily identified as a turtle, a frog, and an owl; another may have been intended to represent a tiger in a kneeling pose.[11] It is reported that human figures were also found, though none has as yet been published. They probably resemble the figure of a squatting man discovered in the first campaign at An-yang.[12] Like the owl, it has a deep groove at the back. This means that such figures were attached to beams, probably as bases or capitals. Moreover, they are covered with the same ornaments as the ritual bronzes.

In fact a number of ritual vessels in animal shape exist which resemble these stone figures very closely. A few receptacles in the form of an owl are known, and the earliest of them, in the Holmes Collection in New York, comes very near to the limestone owl.

The most famous of these zoömorphous bronzes is the large Camondo Elephant in the Louvre (fig. 46). The animal is almost a meter long. The head, body, and upper parts of the legs are covered with a sunken décor that dates the work very early in the Shang epoch. Such a work was thought of first and foremost as a vessel. As such, it contained food to be offered. The contents had to be safeguarded; therefore it was adorned, as any other vessel, with the usual décor. That the vessel was given the shape of an elephant was probably due to the belief that this was more efficacious than the mere insertion of a little elephant in the general ornamentation. A few bronzes thus decorated have survived. The elephant was probably the strongest animal known to the Shang; it is not fanciful to assume that it became an emblem of strength.

Another problem is that of form. The animal is rendered in the most summary fashion; only a general form was apprehended. The several parts are not distinguishable: they flow slowly into one another. Yet the whole figure is subject to rigid symmetry. A plane laid along the spine would divide the object into two identical halves. This is Lange's famous Law of Frontality. It reigned with an iron hand in ancient Chinese art.

There remains the question of why those figures of animals in the round which were not vessels were also covered with the usual ornaments. The answer is: for their protection. The chief task of a décor was to ward off evil forces that lurked everywhere. Ornamentation was the armour which practically every object required.

Some of these early animal sculptures display a striking squareness. They seem to be cut from a rectangular block, with the edges left more or less intact. The sculptor had become conscious that the outlines of a form change their direction, and he brought these changes into their most impressive aspect. This is the beginning of a process of differentiation which was to go on for a very long time. The phenomenon has nothing to do with the law of frontality. It has its perfect counterpart in two-dimensional representation. On the *chia* (fig. 12) the plastic solution may be seen in the head on the handle, the graphic one on the vessel itself. This differentiation caused the breaking up of the whole into several parts distinctly set off from other parts, which receive ornamental themes of their own.

The reason for this procedure was, of course, the desire for better understanding; only he who knows the components will comprehend the whole. The results of this more advanced attitude were figures that look much stiffer than those of an earlier stage where a vague concept had sufficed the artist. A pair of enormous tigers in the Freer Gallery demonstrates this very impressively (fig. 47). They lack even the faintest trace of that suppleness so characteristic of their kind. In fact, an elephant in the same museum, considerably later than the Camondo elephant, has much more of it; and an elephant is not exactly a supple animal.

The tigers can be dated to the late tenth century B.C., by dint of the ornament on their shoulders and legs. It was shortly afterwards that the artists succeeded in integrating into a whole the component parts they had so crudely isolated. This stage is illustrated by the well-known recumbent buffalo in the Pillsbury Collection in Minneapolis (fig. 48). The décor is rather similar to that of the tigers; it is rendered a trifle more softly. The head is turned to one side at right angles. The hindquarters and shoulders are no longer sharply outlined, though traces of the older attitude can still be discerned in the arrangement of the décor.

SCULPTURE

It is a long way from this buffalo to the recumbent sheep with serpents on the four-legged *ting* from Li Yü (fig. 49). These tiny animals are masterpieces of subtle observation and consummate craftsmanship. Their pose is very complicated. The forepart is raised, the hindquarters lie relaxed with the legs folded under the body. The left foot is placed on a wriggling snake. The head is lowered. This artist made some incredibly perspicacious observations, such as that the spine stands out sharply in the raised forepart and the soft belly is pressed aside when the animal lies on the ground.

These sheep — really only one, repeated twice — are exceptional in every respect. The ducks on the three-legged *ting* (fig. 28) do not quite equal them. A few bronze vessels in the shape of dog-like animals, also found in Li Yü, cannot vie with them in quality.[13] They correspond exactly to what one might have expected at this stage. They do not go very much beyond a figure of the eighth century, such as the little elephant in the Oeder Collection.[14] The bodies of all these animals are covered with the same ornaments found on the bronze vessels of their time. However, the sheep and ducks were represented without any decorative addition, but entirely for their own sake and in their own right.

This was not the case with the large dragon in the Stoclet Collection in Brussels (fig. 50). It is a most remarkable work. The chest and the forelegs rest on one level of the ground while the hindlegs are placed on a much lower level and at different angles. This and the tense muscles of the hindlegs suggest an original pose in which the animal heaved itself up to look over some kind of barrier. The effect of awakened suspicion and menacing watchfulness is admirable. Yet the artist saw fit to cast a net of fine ornaments over the dragon; there are large and small spirals in slightly raised outlines, upon a ground of short strokes. I do not think that the wish for greater magical efficacy was the reason for doing this. It was rather that delightful mixture of decoration and representation that replaced the body of a dragon by a geometric pattern on contemporary mirrors (fig. 44). The décor, which is so subdued as not to endanger the image, permits at least a rough dating. The same means — raised outlines, smooth intervals, and short strokes — are used on a few mirrors ornamented with interlaced angular elements.[15] Such mirrors cannot be later than the third century B.C. Moreover, the dragon with the long flabby snout makes its first appearance on mirrors that immediately followed the Huai mirrors, i.e., after ca. 450 B.C.

It was during the sixth century B.C., a time for which there is ample evidence of contact with the outside world, that the Chinese for the first time ventured to represent man in plastic isolation. The figures invariably depict a man kneeling on the ground and holding a small tube in his outstretched hands. A second tube is

SCULPTURE

in front of his knees, and it is safe to assume that something, probably a torch, was inserted in these tubes.

These figures are very awkward. The heads are large, almost as broad as the bodies; the shoulders, very narrow and sloping; the arms, two stumps without any indication of elbows. Quite a number of these statuettes exist, all showing the same style. In other words, their primitiveness is not due to any individual lack of talent; indeed this was the form under which man was apprehended.

It is but the most general conception of a kneeling human figure that is converted into form. The parts are not differentiated; they melt indistinctly into one another. The head, which was considered the most important, is therefore disproportionately big. This definitely primitive apprehension of form has much in common with that responsible for the Camondo elephant. One wonders why his experience with the representation of animals stood the Chinese sculptor in no better stead. One can only guess that he was confronted with a task for which he was singularly unprepared; and he had to start anew.

The Bidwell servant (fig. 51) is the only one of this group whose socle is decorated with interlaced dragons. The pattern is evidently derived from the Li Yü dragons and contemporaneous with the Huai style, which dates these figures to the end of the sixth or the beginning of the fifth century B.C. This date is borne out by a beautiful *p'an,* a bronze dish supported by three little human figures, in the Art Institute of Chicago. The outside of the *p'an* is covered with the Huai pattern; the small men, clad in typically central Asian coats, are treated in the same manner as the kneeling servants.

The primitive attitude did not last long. A few other statuettes of kneeling men show that the artists had worked hard to arrive at a better understanding and at a clearer form (fig. 52). They were but partially successful. The viscous cohesion of the parts is not quite overcome; the law of frontality still reigns supreme. Though the figures are better proportioned, they are far from perfect. The heads are still as broad as the bodies. In other respects, the changes are remarkable. The heads rest on thin necks and are effectively set off from the square and strong shoulders. The arms are no longer placed somewhere between neck and waist, but emerge from the right place, are longer, and bent at the elbows. The faces are not flat, as formerly, but subtly modelled. The cheeks protrude and the eye-sockets recede; the mouth is clearly outlined and there is a small, well-shaped nose. The same holds for the details of the costume, such as the cap and the belt hook. The latter is important because it settles the question of where and how such agraffes were worn. It also provides a clue to the date. These spatula-shaped hooks are usually inlaid with obliquely set angular lines in gold and silver; they belong therefore to the first phase of the Chin Ts'un style.

Both groups have a more or less noticeable disregard of proportion. It is entirely absent in some statuettes, which are so bold in invention and so complex in form that considerable time must have elapsed between their making and that of the kneeling servants. Outstanding among them is a group of two wrestling boys, in the Spencer-Churchill Collection.[16] The two boys are standing in front of each other with their legs apart and bent, their right hands clasped, their left hands on each other's hips. Each head is turned to the left. In fact the two figures are identical. By the simple and ingenious device of casting the same statuette twice and joining the two, a symmetrical and well-balanced group was attained. The young men are summarily modelled, but with a fine insight into what is essential in a human figure. Every joint is bent, and thus artistic articulation coincides with natural articulation. This was an enormously important achievement.

Another work is even more intricate than the wrestlers. It is a boy dancing on a toad (fig. 53). He balances on his right leg. The left leg is lifted, and so are his two arms. The body turns at the hips; the right shoulder is raised, the left one lowered. The constantly changing directions of limbs and torso and the fluent form convey the impression of swift and easy movement. This group is no longer composed in parallel planes, as were the wrestlers. Very decidedly it takes diagonal recession into account.

To the same category belongs the silver statuette of a nude, obese child that came to the Fogg Museum with the Winthrop bequest. The dragging weight and deforming effect of excessive fat are extraordinarily well observed. The figure bears an inscription of little interest but for the fact that it tallies with other inscriptions from Chin Ts'un which have been pronounced "anterior to the unification of script" which was ordered by Ch'in Shih Huang Ti in 213 B.C. In other words, these mature works are not later than the third century B.C.

The same attitude toward form was responsible for such complicated groups as the hill censer in the Holmes Collection in New York.[17] Censers of this type have lids representing a fabulous mountain landscape with tiny figures of men and animals. Everything seems to be in motion, even the landscape. The idea of representing a hunt in a setting of mountains by plastic means is a typically baroque one, and baroque is the execution. This goes, of course, for the whole group. A little figure seated on a crouching feline lifts the heavy censer with his right hand; the body is turned slightly to the left, the head is thrown back. The boy smiles at the fabulous bulb as a magician would smile after a startling performance.

The boy on the toad may be a propitious emblem of longevity. The hill censers represent one of the three "Isles of the Blessed" which float in the "Ocean of Grey Jade." These were places of paradisiac existence which all people hoped to reach some day. Such motives were drawn from the myths, legends, and tales that had been known for a long time. It was apparently not before the Former Han dynasty that these fairy lands and their inhabitants became the subject matter of sculptors and painters. They tell of a profound change in attitude toward the aims and function of art, for in all these works the symbol has been replaced by the allegory.

SCULPTURE

A few animal statuettes remain to be mentioned. The horse in the Nelson Gallery in Kansas City relied almost exclusively on the beauty of its unbroken silhouette and on large, smooth surfaces of bronze (fig. 54). Only one view counts, that from the side. It reveals what the artist wanted to make known: the long unbroken contour from head to tail, the heavy body, the long neck, and the short head. Body and neck look as if inflated; only where the legs emerge was some delicate modelling done. To represent the jaw, the sculptor even had recourse to graphic means; he used a thin, plastic line. Yet the whole horse is monumentally conceived, though it is only 21 cm. high. It is of more recent date than the horse found in the Chin Ts'un graves, with its utter disdain of proportion, but it has retained something of the same quality; the neck is still too long and the head too small. On the other hand, the horse in Kansas City has nothing whatsoever in common with the horses that can be dated to the first three centuries A.D. It must be even older than the large horse in stone that guards the approach to the tomb of Ho Ch'ü-ping, who died in 117 B.C.

Much more widely known are the statuettes of bears. These animals are represented either squatting on their haunches with their clumsy drollery and deceptive jolliness admirably well brought out; or sitting with their forelegs wide apart and their mouths opened in a growl, thus giving a convincing picture of enormous strength and slow but ferocious temper. The best of the seated bears are a pair in the Gardner Museum of Boston (fig. 55). The complicated pose is mastered with astounding ease. The modelling is summary, but correct. When limbs, body, and head merge into a whole, it is something radically different from the vague unity with which plastic representation had started (cf. fig. 46). The asymmetry of composition, and, as a result, the invitation to look at such figures from more than one side, places these bears alongside the boy who dances on the toad.

TOMB FIGURES FROM HAN TO WEI

These bronze statuettes, or groups involving several figures, animals, and even landscapes, differ in the most striking fashion from the few monumental sculptures in stone which have survived. The best known of these are the large animals that flank the way to the grave of Ho Ch'ü-ping, one of the most brilliant generals in Chinese history, who died at the age of twenty-four in 117 B.C. At the emperor's command his tomb was erected in the Wei valley. Of its guardian animals only one is standing, a large horse towering over a prostrate man.[19] The man represents the traditional enemy, the Hsiung-nu, against whom Ho had fought in six campaigns.

This is a group of two figures, but no action is depicted. Horse and man are as stiff as if touched by a magic wand. Only the lateral view is important and meant to be seen. From the front, the horse's chest is ludicrously broad, and so is the head of the stricken enemy between his forelegs. There is not the slightest deflection from a central axis; the figures seem to be compressed between two parallel planes. Once more it is only the general form that counts, and, therefore, mass as such. This mass is timidly approached and never broken up. There is very little modelling done; in fact only a few attempts were made by crudely incised lines to indicate the ribs and the sinews of the legs. The ribs run in the wrong direction, and the sinews are only approximately where they should be. The only part that received more than a superficial treatment was the head. It is built of a few sharply outlined planes. The figure of the Hun is disproportionately large in relation to the horse, and his head is much too big for his body. The figure is not rendered in the round, but in relief. A crouching horse and a crouching buffalo from Ho's tomb have the same uncouth form.

This rather shocking primitiveness is not a unique phenomenon with stone figures of large size. A number of them, mostly men, are known from Honan and Shantung, and all of them display the same massiveness. The two guardians at Tēng-fēng in Honan, who can be dated to 118 A.D., have enormous heads, extremely narrow shoulders and bodies, and short, thin arms.[20] The square pillars of stone out of which they are sculptured are scarcely touched; the edges are barely rounded. No attempt was made to fuse front and side views. The guardians of the tombs of the Kings of Lu near Ch'ü-fu in Shantung can be dated to between 75 and 146 A.D.[21] They do not differ from the primitive figures in Honan.

All these statues of men and animals share the same characteristics: they are all guardians; they are monumental in conception, large in size, and extraordinarily crude in form — things that were at that time very un-Chinese.

In fact, it has long been seen that the idea of monumental statues in stone with the function of guardians of sanctuaries or tombs is of West Asian origin. It is also known that the nomads of central Asia, so fluctuating as to racial composition and so uniform in thought, beliefs, and art, had taken over the idea and the forms of such monumental guardians. The earliest works of this kind, undoubtedly fashioned after Near Eastern models, go back to the seventh and sixth century B.C. Such figures spread all over the northern parts of Europe and Asia, from East Prussia to China. When Siberian herdsmen today erect poles with the roughest indication of a human face at the graves of their dead, they are only continuing what their ancestors did for more than two thousand years.

The impact of that nomadic culture upon China can be felt everywhere. Its influence can be traced back to the seventh century; in the sixth, it is obvious. From the beginning, these nomadic peoples not only passed on their own motives, but foreign ones as well. Thus the "compound eye beads" of glass had reached China; they can be traced from early La Tène graves in France to the tombs of Chin Ts'un in Honan.[22] Under the two Han dynasties such objects as hooks and plaques for belts show the most striking dependence upon foreign forms. Especially those adorned with animals interlocked in furious fight often come so close to their nomadic models as to make correct attribution very difficult. They may have been made in China, in the Ordos region, or in Minussinsk. But it is not only forms that migrate; ideas, too, wander. Thus the idea of setting up figures of men and animals was carried to the East by the Scythians, the Sarmatians, and Hsiung-nu. The torchbearers (fig. 51, 52) are very likely the first evidence of such an infiltration of foreign ideas. It is very probable that Shih Huang Ti emulated his nomadic foes when he set up the twelve statues of gigantic barbarians in bronze.

What has remained of such sculptures is, as pointed out, very crude. So crude, in fact, that stone masons rather than artists seem to have been entrusted with their making.

From the second century A.D. on, enormous stone lions were erected to guard the tombs of the mighty. This, too, was a western Asiatic custom which reached China at that time. The oldest monument of this kind is the collapsed lion of the Wu tombs, near Chia-hsiang in Shantung. It was set up at about 147 A.D.[23] The powerful head, neck, and chest are very cleverly contrasted with a supple and slightly curved body. Lions are unknown in China, except those animals that were brought as tribute and kept in zoölogical gardens. The sculptors did not rely on the immediate observation of a live lion, but on representations they had come to know. Thus, the welt-like ridge that stands for the mane was taken over from Achæmenian Persia which, in its turn, had received it from Assyrian sculpture. Another Iranian trait is the faint traces of wings on the shoulders. The large rectangular mouth, with its corners drawn down very deeply, is an exaggerated version of Greek and Hellenistic forms. These forms probably reached the Far East at different times. By the second century A.D. they were fused into something distinctly and unmistakably Chinese.

Winged felines of a more or less fantastic character appear everywhere from Ssŭch'uan to Shantung. They are always impressive for their size, and often for their quality. Among these the winged chimæra at the tomb of Kao I near Ya-chou in Ssŭch'uan (209 A.D.) ranks foremost.[24] It is the model of those monsters that conquered the whole of China: a head with an open mouth, feathered whiskers on a strong, curved neck; a goatee touching a mighty, bulging chest; wings on the shoulders; short forelegs; a pliant, arched body; and hindlegs that are much higher than the forelegs. These animals are always represented as striding along, with both legs of one side moving in the same direction. The wings look like streamers, and such streamers also cover the flanks, the back, and the hindquarters. This type reigned supreme till the middle of the fifth century. It was then replaced by a standing animal.[25]

The most striking phenomenon, however, is the unchallenged tyranny of the curved line over form. Every part is subjected to it. The whole is composed of beautiful curves that contrast with and complete one another. They move swiftly, then come to a sudden halt, only to start off in a new direction. It is a manneristic art. Form is pressed into a preconceived pattern of linear beauty (fig. 56).

This phenomenon is not restricted to monumental sculpture. It can also be observed in mirrors where it is even more pronounced. Some dated specimens make it probable that this manneristic style reached its height during the third century A.D.[26] In painting, it can be traced back to the second century. The engravings of the Wu tombs, of which I shall speak later, display it unmistakably.

This attitude toward form is extremely significant, especially in the domain of sculpture. Tridimensional form so dealt with appeals to the optic rather than the tactile sense. These sweeping curves that rise and fall can be perceived and enjoyed by the eye alone. The subjection of the plastic form to the visual sense is a highly characteristic trait of Chinese sculpture. This is a different phenomenon from what is called the optic nature of baroque sculpture, which was also known to the Chinese. What is meant here is most apparent in the archaic stage of Chinese sculpture; the borders of forms at this point have an irrepressible tendency to arrange themselves in linear patterns which have a beauty all their own, but often do violence to or are quite independent of tactile experience.

BUDDHIST SCULPTURE

WESTERN Asia brought about the first revolutionary change in Chinese sculpture. Southern Asia instigated a second change. The agent was Buddhism. When Buddhism came to China in the first half of the first century A.D., many factors worked for a friendly, even eager acceptance of it. Spiritual restlessness leading to skepticism had taken hold of the educated. The masses had suffered even more than usual from the endless financial and political crises that shook the land from the latter half of the first century B.C.; for them, there had never been anything that deserved the name of religion. Buddhism offered both classes the spiritual consolation for which they yearned.

Yet Buddhism might not have taken root in China but for the Kushān and Parthian missionaries. Iranians both, they were active, energetic, and fired by a truly apostolic zeal to go out and preach the gospel of the Enlightened One.

The conquest of China by Buddhism is nothing other than the victorious advance of South Asia to the Far East. It is well known that this event profoundly affected Chinese religion and philosophy.[27] It is not always realized that in the field of art the impact was as fateful.

When Buddhism came to China, it had a long history behind it. It had developed a definite ritual with definite needs. Temples, monasteries, statuary, paintings were

SCULPTURE

now indispensable to the proper conduct of religious life. This was a fact of extraordinary importance. Buddhism, in other words, brought to China new ideas about the function of art; namely, that art had to serve the divinity.

Sacred edifices in stone and plastic representation of the deity in the shape of man are the expression of this attitude. It was the attitude of India and all the countries which fell under her influence. It was the offspring and modification of western Asian ideas, which ruled from the Mediterranean to the Hindukush, from the third millennium B.C. till the advent of Islam. Of whatever race the peoples living within these limits of space and time, they saw in art but the means to proclaim the power of the state, embodied in the sacred person of the monarch.

FIFTH CENTURY

THE earliest recorded date of the encounter of China with Buddhism is 2 B.C. In that year, a Chinese official, Ching Lu by name, heard an envoy of the Kushāna recite some Buddhist scriptures. By 65 A.D., Buddhism already had adherents in the province of Kiangsu. This is the more startling as Kiangsu lies on the coast of the Yellow Sea. Into the same region leads another report about a certain Chai Yung, who had appropriated the taxes of three counties and used them to erect a temple and to regild a statue of the Buddha. This happened toward the end of the second century. Other records speak also of the east and of the south. In 226 A.D. Hsün Hsü ordered twelve Buddhas and Bodhisattvas to be cast in gold; the Secretary of State Ho Ch'ung (282-364) donated seven groups of Buddhas. These statements led some scholars to believe that Buddhism and Buddhist art came to China by way of the sea. It is probable, almost certain, that this route was taken by some missionaries. But what has survived of early Buddhist art from southern China does not show the slightest trace of influence from any quarter of India.

The Freer Gallery in Washington possesses a gilt bronze statuette of the Buddha dated to the year 451 A.D. (fig. 57). According to the inscription, it was made under the Sung dynasty, i.e., in the south. The Buddha sits with interlocked legs, and hands folded in his lap, in the pose of meditation. The legs are hidden under the monk's robe that covers both his shoulders. His head is disproportionately large, his body slim, with narrow, sloping shoulders. The *ushnisha,* the excrescence on top of the skull indicating extraordinary intelligence, is very pronounced; the eyes are half-closed, with protruding lids. The pleats of the garment are rendered by parallel ridges; on the chest they are symmetrically arranged in U-shaped curves. A flat halo is behind the head; a large mandorla in the shape of a pointed leaf encloses the whole figure. Upon it are three tiny seated Buddhas; the rest is filled with kidney-like patterns and bordered by a fringe of flames.

Enough is known about the various forms under which the Buddha was represented at various times in various parts of India to assert with conviction that none of them had suggested or inspired this type. That it was a type can be deduced from another statuette, from the former Tuan Fang Collection, which is dated to the year 437 A.D.[28] It also came from the south and resembles the piece in Washington very closely.

It is somewhat surprising to find that the prototype of these Buddhas comes from the region of Khotan in the southwest corner of central Asia. The Khotanese type has the same narrow face, the slit eyes, the large *ushnisha,* the same mouth and nose, and the leaf-shaped mandorla. The pleats of the garment, however, are asymmetrical as they are in the art of northwestern India, or Gandhāra.[29] The symmetry of the folds on the statuettes of 437 and 451 is a simplification or "correction" of something the Chinese did not quite understand. The Khotanese type must have reached southern China in the fourth century at the latest because in the fifth century it was replaced by a very different type in the southern part of central Asia.

At the end of the second century A.D., Khotan was known to Mou Tzŭ, who lived in the extreme south of China, in fact in what is today Tonking, as an important seat of Buddhist learning. Documents found in Niya, one of them dated 269 A.D., speak of Chinese officials vested with authoritative powers governing the region of Khotan.[30] It is very likely that a wave of influence from Khotan had reached northern China at the same time.

If Buddhist sculpture of the Khotanese type existed in northern China, it was destroyed in the severe persecution of the new faith which lasted from 444 to 452 A.D. When Buddhist art began to flourish with renewed vigour in the sixties of the fifth century, it drew its inspiration from a different quarter.

The large standing Maitreya in bronze in the Metropolitan Museum illustrates this very well (fig. 59). The pose is very free; the coming Buddha stands with legs slightly apart, and outstretched arms bent at the elbows. The monk's robe clings to the body, which is tall and slender, narrow in the hips, and broad in the shoulders. The head is full and oval. The ridge and nostrils of the nose are well defined, as is the curved, smiling mouth. The eyes are half closed, with heavy upper lids. Hair and *ushnisha* are covered with large waves and volutes, the meaning of which is not quite clear. The webs between the fingers are, like the *ushnisha,* one of the auspicious birthmarks of a Buddha. The long ears are those of a noble Hindu when he has discarded his heavy, dragging earrings.

Most remarkable is the treatment of the garment. Its folds look as if they had been applied to an originally smooth surface. They often end in sharp points; sometimes they are split and look like forks. They are rather symmetrically arranged on the chest and the arms. The sagging part between the legs is less distinct. Upon each leg appear hanging curves; they are also found on the undergarment. An inscription dates the statue 477 A.D.[31]

Rarely in the history of sculpture can the origin of certain forms be so exactly

SCULPTURE

located as in this case. They had been taken over lock, stock and barrel from the clay and mud statues of Kuchā in central Asia. The particular style of representing a garment had developed there as a rather unsuccessful attempt to imitate the mature stucco sculpture of the Kushāna in northwestern India and Afghanistan. The only material available in these parts of central Asia was a mixture of clay, mud, dung, and chopped straw; this played a rôle in bringing about these strange forms. Such works were discovered in many sites ranging from Kuchā to Turfan. Chinese Buddhists and sculptors in the second half of the fifth century looked upon them as Buddhist statuary *par excellence;* they took them as models and endeavoured to copy them as faithfully as possible. They did so in clay and mud, as in the early caves of Tun-huang; in stone, as in the cave temples of Yün-kang and Lung-mēn; on hundreds of stelæ, and in bronze.

These cave temples themselves had been taken over from Kuchā, not from Gandhāra or India. The idea of imitating a temple in living rock was, of course, Indian. The Chinese became acquainted with it not by direct contact, but through central Asia.

This borrowing from Kuchean art probably goes back before the year 444 A.D.; for there exists a little bronze statuette of a standing Buddha bearing that date which displays all the characteristic features of Kuchean sculpture.[32]

SIXTH CENTURY

TOWARD the end of the fifth century the Chinese artist began to alter according to his own ideal the forms he had received from the west. The large, fat, and round heads became tall and narrow; the shoulders, which were sometimes unnaturally broad and square, became very slender and sloping; very often there seem to be no shoulders at all. The body, which could always be seen under the transparent garments of Kuchā, disappeared under ample robes. The *appliqué* folds were transformed into flat pleats with long parallel lines. At the same time, the free and loose poses of standing and seated figures were replaced by rigid and stiff ones that strictly obey the law of frontality. Along with all these changes goes a very definite reduction in plasticity. Some stelæ, when seen from the side, show only the heads in high relief, with the rest of the figures almost flush with the background.

In other words, the Chinese were creating a style of their own, a truly archaic style of sculpture. The process can be traced step by step because there are enough dated monuments. It came to a successful end in 500 A.D. Of course, quite a few stelæ and bronzes were done in the old central Asian style after that date; but they do not prove more than what is true in every country; namely, that there were conservative artists and patrons. By 520 A.D. even these exceptions have disappeared.

The new type of Buddha has a striking resemblance to that of the two statuettes

SCULPTURE

of 437 and 451 A.D. This does not mean that the south had gained supremacy over the north. It only means that this type was far more congenial to the Chinese taste than that of Kuchā which had been forced upon China from the outside. The new representation of the garment has nothing in common with the solution of the early southern works.

Very soon it became evident that the Chinese sculptors were only mildly interested in the human body. Those of Kuchā had been, though with little success; to the artists of Gandhāra and India, the representation of the human figure was the chief concern. The Kushāna apprehended it as an organism whose several parts prepared for and supported one another. The Hindu sculptor regarded it as a sort of mechanism constructed of parts with definite functions. The Chinese artist did not probe so deeply. His attention was arrested by the spectacle of garments draped over the figure of man. At this early stage the head, hands, and feet emerge from these masses of cloth. The heads are composed of clear-cut parts; at the beginning these parts stand side by side a little uncompromisingly; later, toward 520 A.D., they are held together by a rhythm that bends the contours of eyebrows, lids, nose, mouth, and head into corresponding curves.

But most of the sculptor's thought and inventiveness go into the arrangement of the robes; the hems are attended to with special love. By 510 A.D. a definite linear pattern is found: hanging curves with oblique lines at either side. Along with it goes a very outspoken centrifugal rhythm. The garments fall from the shoulders in many concave curves that stop abruptly, but each is always a little farther out than the preceding one. The silhouette resembles a tree with drooping boughs.

This peculiar style is sometimes called "Northern Wei style" because it flourished under that dynasty (386-535). The term is not very fortunate, for this style reigned only for one generation, from about 510-540. Monumental works of enormous size were subjected to its rules as well as very small bronze statuettes.

The religious zeal that made people erect stelæ, donate statuary for the cave temples, or cast bronzes for altar pieces must have been fervent and widespread. The results were not always pleasant. The range in quality is very wide, and it is quite natural that mediocre works outnumber the good ones. Too many pieces that are plainly the well-meant but inadequate products of stone masons have landed in our museums. Many of them are dated, and their historical value is then beyond dispute. Their artistic value is often nil. The uninformed person will derive from them notions about the character and quality of Chinese sculpture that are as false as those he would receive were he to judge European sculpture by works that had been collected from cemeteries.

The Maitreya in gilt bronze in the University Museum in Philadelphia is one of the finest and latest works of this archaic style (fig. 58). It is dated to the year 536 A.D. — fifty years younger than the Maitreya in New York (fig. 59). The two statues mark the final stages of two successive styles. The Maitreya of Philadelphia displays all the typical traits of the younger style: the rigid pose; the stress laid upon drapery; the cataract of sharply cut pleats; the jerky rhythm; the centrifugal tendency in composition; and the resultant serrated silhouette.

The absolute symmetry of the garment is a late feature. Works of the tens and twenties are much freer, and may even have an acentric arrangement of softer and more pliable lines.

The most sumptuous works of this style are the two altarpieces in gilt bronze in the Metropolitan Museum of New York. One is dated 524 A.D.; its companion is perhaps a few years younger.[33] Both are invaluable because they reveal the peculiar attitude of that period toward sculpture. It is one that has a burning interest in sharply defined parts, but goes on to accumulate them in such a way as to bring about an effect of restless, leaping movement.

This love of sophisticated linear themes, the composition of the whole by small, sharp, and clean-cut parts, the use of light and shadow having little to do with tactic experience, finally led into a *cul-de-sac*. The break with this ideal came in the forties of the fifth century.

A statue in the new style, such as the Buddha in the museum in Toronto, is different in every conceivable respect from a work of the preceding epoch (fig. 60). One is struck by the simplicity of the contour, and the power of the plastic mass. The pleats are very few in number, and incised with double lines as symmetrical hanging curves. The pattern of the hems, subdued as it is, is the only link with the fluttering and splashing forms of the preceding phase.

This statue is conceived as a plastic work, with emphasis on a closed mass. It is no coincidence and not due to chance that quite a few statues in the round of this period (ca. 550-560) have survived. The archaic style had a strong and almost irrepressible desire to lean its figures against a wall, or a mandorla that served the same end. That so few folds were represented, and those which were in so shallow a manner, sprang from the wish not to endanger the newly won plastic core. But there is not the slightest indication of a human body under the stiff and heavy garments. It was the same with the Maitreya of 536 A.D.; though in every other respect the two works differ as much as possible.

More beautiful and charming than the Buddhas and monks of this period are the Bodhisattvas. They are usually represented with a nude torso and a skirt-like garment, the dhotī; it hangs from the waist and has folds in double lines. The bodies swing forward in a subtle curve. The heads, at least in the finest works such as those in the Louvre and the museum in Munich, are small and narrow. The half-closed, downcast eyes and faintly smiling mouth evoke an angelic beatitude which is unforgettable. This expression compares very advantageously with the vacuous smile that the sculptors of the previous period invariably bestowed on their figures.

Closely related to these statues is the wonderful but slightly later Bodhisattva

SCULPTURE

in the Meyer Collection in Philadelphia.[34] It is a companion to the three famous statues in the University Museum in the same city. They all come from a rock temple near Nan Hsiang-t'ang in northern Honan. They are the most majestic sculpture China ever created.

The monk who holds a lotus bud in both hands admirably personifies the superhuman power invested in him (fig. 61). The figure is more than life-size. The pose is erect; practically the whole effect of grandeur and monumentality is derived from the closed mass of the robe, in which straight vertical lines predominate. They are deliberately contrasted with the horizontal forms of the shoulders and forearms. The superbly proud head is almost square and rests upon a strong neck. Here again it is the way in which head, neck, and shoulders are set off from one another that produces the effect of magnificent dignity. One has only to compare this statue with that of fig. 59 to realize that this anonymous sculptor was an artist who knew all about the inherent possibilities of his style and made the best of it.

He was not quite so successful with his Bodhisattvas (fig. 62). The ribbons streaming from the tiara, the locks of hair on the shoulders, the shawl draped around them and tied in the centre, the pleated dhotī and the heavy jewelry taxed his ability very much. He solved these problems by rendering most of these elements with great restraint. Only the long chain and the breast plaque were more boldly treated than the rest. Each form is sharply outlined, and this led in the lower parts to a profusion of lines, all of them arrayed in rigid symmetry and strict verticality. The wavy contour of the hem, like that of the monk, is all that remained of the richer pattern of the previous period. Yet the intention to keep the plastic masses intact is quite evident. When the sculptor ventured a little farther away from the core, as he did in his modelling of the jewelry, he probably did so because he knew what was going on at the same time in western China.

This style, whose greatest works are the statues from Nan Hsian-t'ang, ruled unchallenged in Chili, northern Honan, and part of Shansi. It developed out of a style that was a definite and deliberate refutation of the florid archaic style.

In Shensi, however, that archaic style gave birth to one that set out in a different direction. A younger generation of sculptors also wanted a closed, compact core for their statues. They tried to achieve this end by reducing the plasticity of the surface. But they covered this core with an abundance of details, and added broad shawls on either side. As time went on, all these elements became increasingly round, a weighty load that almost dragged down its wearers. It certainly stifled any effect of greatness.

These statues share with those of the east the subtle forward bend of the body. Seen from the side, they describe a very mild S curve. Some of them are definitely top-heavy. The most beautiful and characteristic of these monuments is the gigantic Bodhisattva Avalokiteśvara (Kuan-yin) in Boston (fig. 63). Viewed from the side, the figure is incredibly flat and leans dangerously forward.

SCULPTURE

Another characteristic of this style is the slight sideward bend of the body. The axis of the Kuan-yin in Boston follows, in reality, a scarcely perceptible spiral. Though in some works the whole burden of the body seems to rest on one leg, with the other set lightly on the ground, a clear and definite formulation of this important pose is never arrived at. Here are a few more specific traits: the full heads of Bodhisattvas are covered with heavy and elaborate tiaras; the eyebrows are rendered by an incised line, and an incised semilunar line marks the chin; the three folds of the neck, prescribed by Indian tradition and rarely represented in earlier times and in the east, are carefully indicated; the statues are always placed on a round lotus that is inserted into a square socle with four little lions at the corners.

By 560 A.D. this western Chinese style was not yet fully developed, by 580 A.D. it was about to die. Much sculpture exists in which the eastern and the western styles are curiously blended. It is seldom pleasant to look at. Stocky of figure, clumsy of make, it is obviously the work of artisans who had heard but not quite understood the message.

In the east, a remarkable change came over sculpture about 570 A.D. The figures became rigid in pose and the shallow relief was still more reduced. On the statues, large plain surfaces appeared; details were suppressed as much as possible.

The Bodhisattva in Kansas City is a perfect example of this new attitude toward form (fig. 64). The masses are scarcely differentiated, and deliberately so. When compared with one of the Bodhisattvas from Nan Hsiang-t'ang, it will be observed that the dhotī is quite plain. No folds interrupt it. Where there are pleats, as in the piece hanging over at the top, they have an unmistakable tendency to form a pattern that has nothing to do with reality. Jewelry, formerly heavy and impressive, is either discarded altogether or curtailed to a few thin and inconspicuous chains. The same holds for the dangling shawls: they have dwindled to a few stiff ribbons.

The heads are either perfect ovals, or rectangles with softened corners, as in the previous decade. The several parts of a face stand out more sharply because they lack a common rhythm. The finely curved lids have disappeared: the half-closed eyes are mere slits. There is little doubt that the unmitigated clash of lines, their abruptness, and the resulting hardness were considered beautiful.

This is evident when such statues are seen strictly from the front, as they should be. Torso and legs are taken as a large unit without any articulation. Sometimes a statue reminds one painfully of a bowling pin. On this mass the arms, with sharply pointed elbows, are fastened at awkward angles. The fact that the dhotī invariably ends above the ankles makes these figures no more pleasant.

The bleak austerity of such statues was certainly deliberate. This seems to call for an interpretation in terms of expression; namely that the austerity of form was intended to suggest an austerity of feeling; that this resolute turning away from anything that might be beautiful indicates a spirituality that does not measure by earthly standards.

Such an explanation appears to be supported by the fact that the T'ien-t'ai sect of Buddhism was founded in 575 A.D. by Chih-k'ai (538-597), at about the time when the first works of the new style made their appearance. This sect made the concept of *bhūta-tathātā* the basis of its speculations. *Bhūta-tathātā* (Sanskrit, "Suchness") as understood by the T'ien-t'ai school has a rather striking resemblance to Schelling's "absolute Intelligence" (*absolute Vernunft*), or to his principle of "Indifference of Nature and Soul, of Object and Subject." Every phenomenon, spiritual or physical, exists solely by virtue of the *bhūta-tathātā*.

It is not of great significance that the first figure in this austere style was made five years before the founding of the T'ien-t'ai sect. The doctrine might well have been known and expounded before that event. More important is the fact that these philosophic (rather than religious) ideas had little chance to be easily understood and widely accepted. It is known that they were not. Moreover, the seat of the school and its spiritual centre was on Mount T'ien-t'ai in Chēkiang, far to the south, whereas the centre of the new style of sculpture was in Chili and northern Honan. This is not all. Many of its Buddha figures, such as the enormous statue in the British Museum which is dated 585 A.D., are called Amitābha in their inscriptions.[35] A relief in the Freer Gallery, an excellent work of this style, represents Amitābha as Lord of the Western Paradise (fig. 65). This relief comes from Nan Hsiang-t'ang, and must have been executed between 570 and 585 A.D.

The "Pure Land" school, with its teaching of life after death in the Western Paradise under Amitābha, had unquestionably found many adherents in the second half of the sixth century. To judge by the representations of the paradise, existence there was not understood as a state of perfect knowledge, but as the fulfillment of very human wishes: its inhabitants lived in large palaces and airy pavilions, rested under shady trees, sat around ponds, and were entertained by girl musicians and dancers. One had only to have implicit faith in Amitābha to be reborn in that paradise.

No other sect of Buddhism offered more consolation to the poor and distressed than the Pure Land school, and no other sect made better use of the arts. The paradise was depicted in every possible way as the most enchanting and desirable place; transcendental bliss was interpreted in terms of terrestrial beauty and material happiness.

I have discussed the two main Buddhist sects of the sixth century and their teachings in order to show the fallacy of explaining works of art solely in terms of expression. The T'ien-t'ai doctrine seems to fit perfectly that peculiar ideal of beauty embodied in all sculpture of the austere style: yet it cannot have

SCULPTURE

had anything to do with it. In the relief in the Freer Gallery every single figure is as forbidding in appearance as any other work of this style; yet the whole is ostensibly intended to represent the pleasures of luxurious life. The two little figures taking a dip in the pools at either side quite convincingly reveal the spirit in which the whole was conceived. They do not represent the souls reborn in paradise; these are the tiny men seated on lotus flowers in the central pond.

The extreme linear style that reigned in the eastern regions from about 570 to about 590 A.D. must be regarded as a deliberate and radical attempt to obtain pure and simple plastic form. The trend toward this goal became apparent as early as the fifties. It was led astray in Shensi. But it looks as if by 590 A.D. the austere style was victorious on the whole front.

In the nineties form underwent a subtle change. The famous bronze altar in Boston representing Amitābha and his attendants and dated in the year 593 A.D. cannot be properly understood without a knowledge of what was going on in the two preceding decades.[36] The poses are still very stiff; but now at least one Bodhisattva bends his head to one side, and the old monk does the same to read a manuscript. All these figurines are strikingly crude in make. Amitābha is the only exception. He, too, lacks coordinating rhythm, and is, therefore, as ungainly as his companions. But the folds of his robe are given in long parallel ridges. The same device, plastic lines that look like strings laid upon a smooth surface, was used on a few earlier works, such as the Amitābha of 585 in London, and one of 577 in Toronto. But there the intervals between two lines were so large as to make them insignificant. Here these ridges are strong and comparatively close together. It is a new means of representation, one which points to the future.

What a large statue of this style looks like can be seen in the seated Buddha made of dried lacquer in the Metropolitan Museum.[37] He has the same round head with hard and sharp features, the same sloping shoulders, the same thin and angular arms, the same arrangement of the garment that falls from the left shoulder across the body to the right knee in long, uninterrupted curves. Here again it is not the body but the robe which holds the interest. All this changed in the seventh century.

SCULPTURE

SEVENTH TO NINTH CENTURY

WHEN, in this book on Chinese art, such terms as archaic, classic and baroque are used, it is because they are familiar to anyone versed in the history of Greek, Roman, and European art, and denote very definite kinds of apprehending form. These same kinds of apprehension can be observed in the Far East, where they appear in the same order and sequence as in the West.

A word of warning is necessary however. These terms do not imply an identical, but only a parallel evolution; they must be taken not in an absolute, but in a relative sense. In other words, archaic Chinese sculpture stands in the same relation to classic Chinese sculpture as archaic Greek sculpture to classic Greek sculpture. Although a surprisingly large number of problems presented themselves at about the same stage of the development, and their solutions often resemble each other, the attitude toward the visible world was fundamentally different. Yet this does not exclude the fact that the West and the East moved in the same direction.

Toward the middle of the seventh century, Chinese sculpture reached its classic stage. The word must not be taken as a verdict on quality; it denotes a phase in artistic apprehension in which the ideal of the perfectly clear, articulate form rules supreme. In sculpture, with its main themes of man and animal, partial form, firm and immovable within its contour, is combined with other such forms into a total figure that, as a consequence, possesses an unsurpassable lucidity of appearance. It is of decisive importance that the relation of the parts to the whole is now controlled by a deeper insight into their interdependence than ever before. In the twenties and thirties of the sixth century every element vied for attention without regard to the total effect. To avoid this danger, the artist sinned by default in the last quarter of the same century: the parts were submerged in large plastic units, the details suppressed, or relegated to mere ornaments.

On this basis the sculptors of the seventh century had to start. The problems they had to solve were these: to loosen those uncouth masses of bodies and garments, to soften their crude and forced tectonic rigidity, and to make flexible their stiff contours.

By 620 A.D., new solutions had been found for the Buddha and the Bodhisattva. The changes in the representation of the Bodhisattva are especially striking. Before that time, it will be recalled, the lower parts of this figure were a closed compact block. Now the dhotī is rendered as a thin, almost flimsy piece of cloth that clings so closely to hips and legs as to reveal these essential parts of

SCULPTURE

the body in full. In addition, head, torso, and limbs are modelled in simple, easily apprehended contrasts. Stress is laid upon the natural points of division, the joints, where one organic part ends and another begins. All this means that now Chinese sculpture took an interest in the human body. It was no longer arbitrarily articulated as before; artistic articulation coincided with the articulation of nature. For the first time in the history of Chinese art a figure stands free, at ease, with relaxed limbs. Every movement is counterbalanced by another, according to the rules of contrapposto.

This change in form is often attributed to a strong wave of Indian influence. Those who hold this opinion point to Hsüan-tsang, the great scholar and pilgrim who returned to China from India in 645 A.D., after an absence of sixteen years. He brought back with him scriptures and copies of the most holy and venerated statues in Buddhist India. Fortunately the list of these statues has been preserved.[38] They were mostly statues of the Buddha. Enough is known about Indian sculpture to form a good idea of what they must have been like. None of the Buddha statues made after Hsüan-tsang's arrival shows the slightest resemblance to any one of them. In 620 A.D., nine years before Hsüan-tsang's start, the new style was already flourishing.[39]

It cannot be denied that the new type of Bodhisattva, with his legs showing under a diaphanous dhotī, looks much more "Indian" than his predecessors. In fact there existed something like an international type of Bodhisattva in the seventh and eighth century A.D. It reigned from Nepal to Sumatra and Java, and from central Asia to Japan. Indian Bodhisattvas sometimes stand in a pose called *tribhaṅga* (Sanskrit, "thrice bent"). This pose is sometimes regarded as the model of the contrapposto in contemporaneous Chinese Bodhisattvas. The situation is, however, much more complicated. Such figures existed in India and central Asia for a very long time; in fact they may be found in the earliest caves of Tun-huang, made when the copying of Kuchean art was at its height. But during the archaic period Chinese sculptors stubbornly ignored them, and continued to do so until the seventh century. When they took up the theme at that time, it was because it squared with their own intentions, which were arrived at in the natural course of evolution.

The end of the seventh and the beginning of the eighth century saw the classic style in full bloom. In these few decades a great many statues were created that belong to the finest works ever done in China. Prominent among them is a pair of Bodhisattvas in the University Museum in Philadelphia (fig. 66). After what has been said a short while ago, it will not be necessary to analyze their style. But a few more things must be mentioned. One is the way in which the garment is rendered by plastic ridges of small elevation. They were known, as has been pointed out, as early as in the seventies of the sixth century; but now they explain not only the garment, but also the structure of the body under it. Moreover, they

SCULPTURE

are now lines of enchanting beauty and unsurpassable clarity. The joints, the cardinal points of the human body, are so stressed as to let the figures appear to be of an order which is clearer, more lucid and more inexorable than that of nature herself. These statues give a well formulated answer to any question that might be asked.

The quest for absolute clarity sometimes led to an overemphasis on tectonic structure. The two Bodhisattvas in Philadelphia display a slight and rather charming stiffness of pose. Other works did not always keep within these limits. A seated Bodhisattva, one of a monumental triad in the Art Institute of Chicago, is certainly clear in build. Each part is set off from the other in the most impressive way, so much so, indeed, that the effect of the whole seems to suffer a little from it. The resulting stiffness is exaggerated in the photograph reproduced in fig. 67. It was taken from an incorrect angle: only a strictly frontal view reveals form and function at the first glance. The awkward and disturbing foreshortening of both arms then disappears; and the figure is suddenly beautiful.

There is little doubt that in the decades around 700 A.D. Chinese sculptors were possessed by a strong determination to build up their figures with sharply defined parts. They preferred a little rigidness to making concessions in this respect. This was their ideal of beauty and it was binding, regardless of motive and religion. Taoist sculpture abode by the same rules. The magnificent statue of T'ien Tsun, dated 709 A.D., now in the Field Museum in Chicago, proves that very convincingly.[40] The same holds for the tomb figures in clay, whatever their subject matter. The horse (fig. 69) belongs to that category. It is a masterpiece, truly monumental in conception and perfect in execution. The beautiful shape and noble spirit of this animal were never better understood and represented than in the first few decades of the eighth century. When this work is compared with the horses from the tomb of emperor T'ai Tsung (627-649), of which two are housed in the University Museum in Philadelphia, the difference in form is the same as that between two Buddhas of these periods.[41]

The eighth century saw the loosening of the severe tectonic system and the softening of the definite lineament. Behind it stood the wish for a more thorough integration of the parts into a whole. An excellent example of what the younger generations aimed at is the large relief of two Bodhisattvas from a stela in the Metropolitan Museum in New York (fig. 70). The pose is very relaxed, almost lazy. The bodies move gently to one side. The parts merge where they formerly had been broken up to make clear their different functions. As the most decisive result, the tension with which older figures stood or sat has disappeared.

Here one has a right to speak of fluent and beautiful contours. But above all line has given up its old intransigence. It defines form with less exactness, and is no longer an insurmountable barrier to eye and hand. It is characteristic that this master was prepared to part with the great discovery of the early T'ang sculptors, the plastic ridge for representing folds. These figures are conceived as coherent wholes, but on the basis of what the previous generations had achieved. The square, fat faces are typical of the eighth century.

Though excellent in quality, the New York stela is rather conservative in the interpretation of its subject matter. Other artists, especially those working for the cave temples of T'ien-lung Shan in Shansi, were evidently determined to tackle the problem of the human body in rest and action. One of the most famous of their works is the Rockefeller Bodhisattva.[42] The statue has unfortunately lost the head and both arms. But what is left is enough to secure for it a unique place in the history of Chinese sculpture. The body swings out rather violently to its right, so that the left hip is considerably higher than the right one. The shoulders are thrown back, the right one more than the left; the right leg is placed farther back than the other. In other words, this Bodhisattva is represented as striding forward impetuously. The axis of his body is bent in a helical twist. This interest in recession and the exaggerated movement are new. Yet the statue is still conceived in terms of a principal frontal view; all the other aspects leave something to be desired.

The treatment of the garments, too, shows that the break with the past was not complete. The pleats are rendered by thin plastic lines in hanging parallel curves. But the nude parts are far more subtly modelled than those of the Bodhisattvas in Philadelphia and Chicago.

A standing Bodhisattva from one of the caves of T'ien-lung Shan has come to Boston (fig. 71). The head with its full moonface is a little heavy. The body is modelled with more firmness than anyone discussed so far. Shoulders, arms, breasts, thorax, belly, hips, and legs are clearly outlined. Yet the figure is not merely an assemblage of these parts, but an organic whole. The wish for perfect clarity had led the artist to abandon the ridges as means of representing drapery. The body appears almost nude under the clinging "wet" robes.

The further development is best illustrated by a seated Bodhisattva from Cave XVII of T'ien-lung Shan (fig. 68). In pose the figure is identical with that of fig. 67. But what was there hard, definite, and uncompromising, is now soft, melting, and relaxed. The erect carriage of the Chicago Bodhisattva has given way to one which is more natural, gracious, and flexible. The difference amounts almost to that between a mechanism and an organism. This is not a verdict on quality, but a statement about the aims and achievements of Chinese sculpture at the beginning of the eighth and at the beginning of the ninth century. Only after the constituent parts had been defined as to form and function could they become integrated. It will be noted that the late artists go much farther in this respect than their forebears. This fine and delicate modelling of the torso would have been impossible at any earlier period. Form can now flow imperceptibly into an adjacent form, and only

SCULPTURE

this makes it possible to give some of these faces their soft, melting, and somewhat longing expression.

The change from the high classic to the mature classic style took place within the years 700 to 850 A.D. The terrible civil war which tore China between 755 and 763, reduced her population from fifty-three to seventeen millions, and shattered the civil, social, and economic order, did not affect the normal evolution of art.

NINTH TO ELEVENTH CENTURY

In 847 A.D. the Japanese priest E-un Sōzu (798-871) returned from China and brought with him five wooden statues from the temple Ch'ing-lung in Ch'ang-an. The figures are kept in the Tōji in Kyōto.

The five statues are almost identical in form and attitude. They are seated on five different animals: a lion, an elephant, a horse, a peacock, and another bird. These are the animals of the five Dhyāni-Bodhisattvas Samantabhadra, Vajrapāni, Ratnapāni, Avalokiteśvara, and Visvapāni.

Bodhisattvas and animals are appallingly stiff. There is a lack of subtlety and grace that makes them look almost primitive. Line is hard and sharp: the several parts do not merge. There is practically no unity of composition. Large planes have supplanted the delicate modelling of earlier works. The only thing that connects these figures with those made but a few decades ago is the representation of the shawl that runs across their chests. The shawls are rendered as they were on the languorous Bodhisattvas from T'ien-lung Shan. Otherwise everything is so different in style and spirit as to suggest a radical and revolutionary break.

These five Bodhisattvas form a second section of a *"maṇḍala* in two parts," namely, the *garbhadhātu* (Sanskrit, "Matrix Element"; the material world), that is complementary to the *vajradhātu* (Sanskrit, "Thunderbolt Element"; the spiritual world, or complete enlightenment).

These are practices and concepts peculiar to a branch of Buddhism called Tantrism. This word is derived from Sanskrit *tantra*. Originally it means a warp, then a thing that runs through something like a warp, an order, a system; finally it came to mean the system of a textbook, and the textbook itself. Above all, the term is applied to textbooks dealing with ritual. Such books deal with what might be called the practical side of religion. They contain directions about how a deity must be worshipped, about prayers, gestures, and meditations, about daily and exceptional rites. *Tantra,* in other words, deal above all with "technique"; they contain advice about the effective use of the mechanical apparatus of a religion.

Tantrism, therefore, is the conviction that through the correct performance of definite, fixed rules the ultimate aim, salvation, can be reached automatically. It is commonly ignored that the term designates a procedure rather than a religion;

Hinduist Tantrism exists as well as Buddhist Tantrism. The latter, however, is more widely known.

Of course Tantrism is magic, though magic in a sublimated form. It was possible only on the supposition of a complete analogy and interdependence of microcosm and macrocosm, since both spring from a common eternal and universal ground. Such ideas were natural to Brahmanism and Hinduism. They were, at least at the beginning, foreign to Buddhism. They found entrance only after the concept of *śūnyatā* (Sanskrit, "the Void"; nonsubstantiality) became the central concept of Mahāyāna Buddhism. *Śūnyatā* underwent many changes of meaning in the course of time; originally a purely negative concept, it ended by being a positive one, synonymous with *tathāgata-garbha* (Sanskrit, "The Womb of the Tathāgata": the Buddha); i.e., the common ground of all phenomena. The similarity to the concept of *ātman* in Brahmanic metaphysics was seen and discussed by the Buddhists themselves.

By its very nature, Tantrism had no use for the arts. It was not exactly iconoclastic; but it despised the setting up of sculpture and paintings. As a help in meditation it permitted *maṇḍala,* i.e., charts or maps upon which the names of the *vīja* were inscribed in Sanskrit. *Vīja* means seed, and a word out of which the image of a deity rises in meditation, as a plant emerges from its seed. It was but a concession to human weakness when the *vīja* were supplanted by the images of the deities themselves. Though they already belong to the world of illusion, they must be kept as simple as possible. They differ only in gestures and attributes: hence the monotony and uniformity of such representations. The question of whether they might be good or bad as works of art never arose; they were either correct or false. This was decided by the initiated. The priest became the last judge in these complex matters.

It was only in the eighth century that this Buddhist version of Indian theopanism got a firm foothold in China. It was mainly due to the work of two priests, to Amoghavajra (705-774), one of the profoundest thinkers of Buddhism, and his teacher Vajrabodhi (642-732). But it took one more century till the impact of Tantrism on Buddhist art became apparent.

Chinese sculptors had just begun to represent the human bodies of their Bodhisattvas as flexible organisms, to represent a movement as involving more than just the limb executing it; to represent emotion and to depict the different textures of cloth and flesh. Now they were told that all their efforts counted for nothing; if anything, an image was to be the manifestation of a seed word, and as such something of an *Urform.*

This demand necessarily led to a grave conflict. In the intellectual and religious centres, such as the capitals, mature and living form was rapidly replaced by stiff and petrified formulæ. They were arrived at by a radical and deliberate simplification. This new style was an intellectual product, not an artistic one. It was a sort of neo-classicism. It did not appear, as neo-classicism always does under normal con-

SCULPTURE

ditions, when all the perceptual and representational possibilities of a very mature style were exhausted, but was imposed on Chinese art from outside, for reasons that had nothing to do with art, and at a most inopportune moment.

The five Bodhisattvas of the Tōji were among the first works of this new style. Another product is the Bodhisattva in the Wannieck Collection (fig. 72). A greater contrast to the Bodhisattva from T'ien-lung Shan is scarcely possible. The figure is completely wrapped in its garments, and stands stiffly with folded hands. Yet it represents the same being as the statue with the almost lascivious pose.

The Wannieck Bodhisattva is a strange blend of old and recent forms. The folds of the broad shawl drawn tightly around the body are treated as are those of the Bodhisattva from T'ien-lung Shan (fig. 68). The arrangement of the garment below that shawl is reminiscent of that on the Bodhisattvas from Nan Hsiang-T'ang (fig. 62); the position of the arms, their contrast with the long verticals that contribute so much to a monumental effect, is almost identical with those of the monk from the same cave (fig. 61). This must not be interpreted to mean that the sculptor knew these specific works; but he undoubtedly was acquainted with works of that style and was inspired by them. In other words, these artists were conscious of the past and of the effect of certain forms. In the works that had been created in the sixties and seventies of the sixth century, they found the problems set by their spiritual leaders more or less satisfactorily solved, and followed them.

The stiff poses and sharp-edged contours were somewhat softened in the following period. An excellent work of this time is the gilt bronze Bodhisattva in the University Museum in Philadelphia.

It was impossible however to keep sculpture from completing its cycle. The adherence to forms of the sixth century became superficial. The sculptors faithfully carried on such irrelevant things as the scrollwork and files of pearls in diadems and necklaces, but ignored the essential traits; viz., the block-like, closed mass and unswerving verticality of body and garment. This means that sculpture had recovered from the first shock and was trying to get back on the road to baroque forms and ideals. It did not return to the point where it had been forced to leave it.

The new tendencies are best illustrated by the magnificent Bodhisattva in the Metropolitan Museum (fig. 73). The body swings gently to the right. The movement is extraordinarily subtle and fluid. It is as different from the stiff pose of the Wannieck Bodhisattva as from the violent contrapposto of the T'ien-lung Shan Bodhisattvas. The lower parts are clad in a dhotī of heavy material; though it is not transparent and does not cling to the legs, their position and function are clearly apprehended. What is more important is that the weight and texture of the cloth is rendered with a mastery not yet encountered in Chinese sculpture. The section where the heavy fabric is draped over the petals of the lotus socle, dimly revealing their shapes, is exquisite.

With such works as this, neo-classicism reached its apogee. To arrive at a proper

SCULPTURE

understanding of its aims and achievements, a comparison of the New York Bodhisattva with the two figures in Philadelphia (fig. 66) is very helpful. In both cases, a distinct and beautiful line carries the burden of representation. But here is the first difference: in the younger work, line follows a long, quiet and uninterrupted course; the older solution with its shorter rhythm and frequent repetitions seems to be composed of independent themes. Classic sculpture articulates the body and makes the garment serve this aim also. This articulation is not missing in the neo-classic work, but it is no longer stressed.

It was not necessary to do so because the problem of apprehending the human body as a coherent organism had been solved during the eighth century. As a result, line has now an incomparably greater liberty; it moves freely over the caesuras in a continuous movement, binding the several parts into large coherent units.

The same observations can be made when a classic Buddha such as the fine torso in Boston is compared with one of the neo-classic epoch, such as the Buddha of 1032 A.D. in the Freer Gallery.[43] Here again the structural values of the body are not worked out. The lines of the robe stream unhampered over chest, arms, and legs. In the drapery of the socle a phenomenon can be observed that was to be expected: the recurrence of the classic ridges.

TWELFTH TO SEVENTEENTH CENTURY

The Buddha of 1032 A.D. is a very provincial work. Still cruder are the stelæ and figures of men and animals that flank the avenues of approach to the tombs of the emperors Jēn (d.1063 A.D.) and Ying (d.1067 A.D.).[44] They are so bad in quality and abominable in workmanship as rather to obscure than to illuminate the course Chinese sculpture took in these times. The only exceptions are two stelæ with phœnixes over a landscape. The birds and the elements of the landscapes are either deeply undercut or rendered by drilling and gouging. The surfaces of the stones are dissolved into an oscillating maze of light and shade. It is impossible to make out a single form. What counts is the movement of the light, and this means of course a purely visual apprehension.

These two stelæ herald the coming of a new phase in Chinese sculpture, namely, the baroque phase. Unfortunately, very few dated monuments exist, and they are often of little value. The cast-iron Lokapāla (Sanskrit, "Guardian of the World") of 1097 A.D. in Ch'in Tzŭ (Shansi) is almost as crude as the figures along the roads to the imperial tombs mentioned above.[45] The four Lokapālas on an octagonal pillar in the Hall of the Nuns of the temple Shao Lin in Honan are evidently transpositions of paintings into relief. One of them is dated 1125 A.D.[46]

More instructive are the reliefs on the large "Pagoda of the South" in Fang Shan, Chili.[47] They must have been executed about 1120 A.D., and are identical

SCULPTURE

in style with the two large Buddhas in white marble that came to California with the Munthe Collection.[48] These Buddhas are heavily built, with square heads, curled hair that looks like a wig, broad noses, and over-small mouths. Their monks' robes are admirably rendered; one sees that they were made of a heavy, pliable material. The cloth draped over the socles, with a pointed apron-like centre flanked by frills of small pleated folds, is almost identical with that on the statue of 1032 A.D. The folds in the centre are rendered with soft double lines. There is little doubt that the makers of these statues belonged to a school which looked back upon a long history: it was already at work in the sixth century. Though the sculptors stuck to such traditional devices as the double line, the total effect of these two Buddhas is very different from that of any older work. They show a feeling for volume, weight, and texture that former statues did not possess.

A new tune is set by two works that fortunately are dated. One represents the fifth Lohan, Nakula, playing with a mongoose. The figure is dated 1158 A.D.[49] The Buddhist saint sits on a rock; his right leg is pendent, his left rests flat on the seat. His body is slightly turned and recedes diagonally. Above the figure rises a mountain landscape with a wanderer and a tiger.

The decisive feature of such a plastic composition is the unity of socle, figure, and canopy. They are inextricably united. The eye is forced to leap from one cleft form to the next; from the holes in the rocky seat and the fissured garment to the deep shadow behind the figure and the rough landscape. There is another feature that is new. In former times it would have been impossible to render the head and chest of a figure in quiet, smooth planes while the rest was torn up into oscillating pieces of light and shade. The head is thus made a leading motive. The ideal of an all-round clarity was no longer binding. The Nakula is a typically baroque work. So is the seated Kuan-yin in wood of the Tonying Collection which is now on loan to the Dalton School in New York. It is dated 1168 A.D. (fig. 74).

Kuan-yin seated on a rock, with one leg propped up and one arm resting on it, while the other arm supports the body and the second leg hangs down, became the favourite theme of Chinese baroque sculpture. It was the motive *par excellence* for representing the Bodhisattva Avalokiteśvara as the main figure of a trias.

It is understandable that this motive fascinated the sculptors. The discrepant axes of body and limbs; their different functions; activity and tension side by side with rest and relaxation in one and the same figure; these were the chief problems that had to be solved. A long row of monuments show that the wood-carvers tried their hands at them again and again.

The Kuan-yin of 1168 faces the spectator squarely. Stiffness in the figure is still evident. A thinly concealed system of horizontals and verticals is responsible for this. When representing the shoulders and arms, the hanging leg and the socle, the artists relied very much upon this contrast. The rocky socle in its present shape is perhaps more asymmetrical and recessive than it was originally. But it is quite in keeping with the ideals and intentions of the epoch when this figure was created. It is, at any rate, much better than the puristic way in which such figures are displayed in the museums of America and Europe. To place them on bare boxes does them incredible harm; they can only come to life in their proper surrounding, which is one that takes up and completes the movement in the figure.

The Kuan-yin in the Art Institute of Chicago (fig. 75) is one of the best that have survived. Such difficult problems as the plausible and convincing rendering of the relaxed muscles of the abdomen, or the function and correct position of the left arm, which keeps the body upright, are admirably solved. It is the great achievement of this as of any other baroque art, that it incorporated the most subtle observations in its works without endangering their unity. The way in which the heavy chains in varying positions are represented is but one case in point.

There is a fluidity in the garment that was formerly unknown. The gap between the outspread legs presented a very difficult problem, and many solutions were tried. In this case the sculptor relied on the old formula of hanging plastic curves. It is the only spot where his inventive power slackened.

The Chicago Kuan-yin has preserved its old colouring, and this alone would secure it a prominent place among its fellow statues. Chinese sculpture was originally always painted. But different times had different views about the aim of such colouring. Archaic stelæ must sometimes have looked like exotic butterflies pinned to multicoloured cardboard. In classic times painting served the ideal of perfect clarity. Now painting and sculpture have joined forces to produce something that could vie with nature, if not surpass it. The yielding softness and glowing lustre of human flesh, the gloss of silk and shimmer of brocade, the hard glitter of gold and precious stones, and lastly the gleaming eyes between their deeply undercut lids; all these things create the illusion that Kuan-yin in flesh and blood has descended to hear the plights of the worried.

A few words must be said about expression. Though all these Kuan-yins show compassion and sympathy, every one of them seems to differ from the other in intelligence and temperament. These qualities can be plainly seen in their faces. They are no longer variants of a single type as were the Bodhisattvas of classic times.

Along with these seated Kuan-yins go the standing figures of Bodhisattvas. A pair of them in the Museum in Toronto is especially important as they were dedicated in the year 1195 A.D. (fig. 76). They come from a temple in southern Shansi. The heavenly beings were imagined as powerful figures with almost square faces, with elaborate tiaras upon their heads, clad in gorgeous dhotī and bedecked with jewels. The bearing is portly, the expression, at least in this case, one of a mild and slightly bored interest in suffering mankind.

In these figures and their like the knife penetrates far into the plastic core, cutting out deep furrows for the shadows and creating high ridges that catch the light. A constant struggle goes on between these two, in the fissures of the robes as well as on the swelling surface of the nude parts. Works like these live in and by light.

Between these somnolent valkyries of compassion and sagacity and the elegant Kuan-yin of 1282 in the Metropolitan Museum (fig. 77) must be placed many statues that vary from half to over life-size. The Bodhisattva in New York is lighter in form and movement than the two figures in Toronto. The heavy masses of flesh and cloth have disappeared. The facture is more subtle, and the taste more refined. This statue was carved under the Yüan dynasty (1271-1368). It does not show any difference in kind from works of the late Sung dynasty. Many wooden figures that generally pass as "Sung" in our collections were actually done under the Yüan. Especially those statues whose garments display a charming contrast of large smooth planes with a ripple of folds at the edges, must be attributed to the first decades of that dynasty.

The course Chinese sculpture took in the fourteenth century is not difficult to chart. I have just mentioned the eddy of folds along the hems of some early Yüan statues. After some time the garments as a whole were in an uproar. They flutter around the figures, which are often represented as stepping forward with one hip thrust violently to one side and the body inclined to the other.[50] This same tendency and the same style can be observed in the reliefs of the Nan K'ou pass which are dated 1345 A.D.[51]

Such turbulent draperies and exaggerated poses can be found in many wooden statues. They were all carved with the idea that form had above all to suggest movement. They are the products of the mature, even the over-mature baroque. They do not always avoid the danger that lurks in every baroque art; namely, that a highly complicated apparatus was at the disposal of artists who were not able to fill the grand form with grand ideas.

On the whole, this last phase of the Chinese baroque produced a loud, superficial, and theatrical art. A few exceptions exist, one of which is the seated Kuan-yin of 1385 A.D., an anonymous loan to the Metropolitan Museum (fig. 78). It is one of the extremely rare cases where the name of the sculptor is known. He was Fēng Hsiao-chung. His Kuan-yin has a certain powerful coarseness. There is a notable simplification of form; all the curls and flourishes have disappeared. A few cuts divide the torso. Not a trace is found of the delicate modelling by which the standing Kuan-yin of 1282 excels, and which can be discovered even in works of the first half of the fourteenth century.

Fēng Hsiao-chung must have been a sculptor of some repute, since he is called in the inscription a *tai-chao,* a title usually reserved for outstanding artists in the Imperial Academy. He also either belonged to or had founded a family of sculptors. His son helped him in the carving of the New York Kuan-yin. Two other members of the family, Fēng Chih-pao and Fēng Li, are mentioned in an inscription of 1429 A.D. as the casters of a Taoist group in the Museum in Berlin.[52]

The group consists of a male figure seated upon a lotus socle placed on the back of a tiger. But for the typical Taoist crown, which looks like a little lotus flower, the whole might easily pass for the Bodhisattva Wēn-shu upon his lion. In fact, there can be no doubt that Wēn-shu was transformed by this slight addition into T'ai I, who, after a long and variegated career, became the patron of travellers and officials.

This bronze group was done in a new style, which was fully developed by 1429. It is a linear style that aims at closed plastic masses: it restricts the treatment of surfaces to a minimum. Folds are rendered with as little modelling as possible, often by incised lines only. The pose is again stiffly erect and rigidly symmetrical. Another trait must be pointed out: the forehead seems to flow down into the nose.

All these characteristics can be found on three life-size Bodhisattvas in Toronto (fig. 79). When the Kuan-yin of this group is compared with that of 1385 A.D., it seems almost impossible that such a radical change should have taken place within one generation. A few works exist that were executed during these three or four decades. They show a gradual hardening in pose and drapery, a reduction in the volume of the details — the thin, absolutely symmetrical chains are more characteristic than anything else — and a freezing of any movement.

The tall, five-pronged crown is due to Nepalese influence, which played a moderate rôle in Chinese Buddhist art of that time. Literary sources speak of a Nepalese sculptor, Aniko by name. He was born in 1244, was called to Tibet in 1260, and came to China in the following year. He had a Chinese pupil, Liu Yüan, who came to him to "study Indian art." Both became so famous that Kublai Khan created a special office for them. Their main activity fell between 1270 and 1318 A.D.

This was the time when the Kuan-yin of 1282 was carved (fig. 77). There is not the slightest trace of Nepalese influence in it. It can be discovered, however, in the rock sculpture of Fei Lai Fēng, near Hang-chou, some of which are dated 1282 and 1292 A.D.[53] And above the purely Chinese reliefs of the Nan K'ou pass is enthroned a Tibetan Buddha. It is obvious that Tibeto-Nepalese art met with the same fate as Tibeto-Nepalese Buddhism: it was a stranger in a strange land.

Sufficient dated monuments have survived to permit reconstruction of the history of Chinese sculpture in the fifteenth century. Toward the end of it, there was evidently a strange predilection for cast-iron figures. Practically all of them are very crude.

The youthful type of Bodhisattva, as seen in the figures of Toronto, prevailed throughout this epoch. Toward the end of the century, their smooth faces were a little enlivened by wrinkles added to their eyes. Insignificant as this may appear, it indicates a turning back to the baroque ideals of Sung sculpture.

One of the extremely rare works of quality that have been preserved from this

SCULPTURE

time is the head of the Taoist deity Pi-hsia Yüan-chün (Princess of Coloured Clouds), alias Shēng-mu ("Holy Mother"), the tutelary goddess of the T'ai Shan, one of the holy mountains of China (fig. 80). The piece with its characteristic headdress of birds is in the Art Institute of Chicago. This perfectly oval, youthful face is typical of the fifteenth century.

From 1500 onward Buddhist sculpture openly tries to follow the baroque models of the thirteenth century, though of course the intervening periods left their mark. The iron Kuan-yin illustrated in fig. 81 is a characteristic work. It is dated in the year 1511 A.D. There is little feeling for proportion in most of these figures. The head is usually too large, the body too long, the legs too short. The stiff and symmetrical folds, as they are seen here on the shoulders, occur again and again. The thirteenth century did not know this sort of pleat; it was a heritage of the fifteenth century.

This coarse revival of the baroque lasted throughout the sixteenth century. Its works are quite numerous: they are commonly labelled Sung in our museums.

In the following centuries the sculptors freely took ideas and forms from the past, often presenting them in strange and unexpected combinations. Perfect craftsmanship led to a sleekness which is quite characteristic of their products. They are nice, pleasant to look at, but rather empty. A Kuan-yin of 1624 in the Metropolitan Museum is a good representative of such figures (fig. 82). It is quite obvious that knowledge, skill, and routine are poor substitutes for creative power.

PAINTING

SHANG TO FORMER HAN

IN a strictly technical sense, painting was known in China from neolithic to modern times. The alleged invention of the brush by Mēng Tien (220 B.C.) was probably an improvement of the tool then in use.

The Shang had the walls of their tombs decorated with paintings whose patterns were certainly those found on their bronzes. More recent works, especially lacquers, show that the current designs were merely executed in a different material.

From this point of view, the sunken ornamentation of early Shang bronzes is the most ancient relic of Chinese painting (cf. fig. 11). Indeed, by using one's imagination, it is not difficult to form an idea of what the walls of a room looked like when covered with such motives in green, red, and yellow. These were the pigments discovered in the funerary chambers of the Royal Tombs near Hou Chia-chuang; the outlines were probably drawn in black.

Such paintings are usually called symbolic when the stress is laid on subject matter, or stylized when on form. Not much is gained by these terms: it must be understood that they do not designate simply two different aspects of one and the same thing. A bat, e.g., is a symbol of good luck; as such it was painted in the most impressionistic manner in about 1500 A.D. No less ambiguous is the word "stylization." Those who use it are often apt to forget that a drawing by Rembrandt is as "stylized" as one by an Egyptian painter. "Omission of the accidental, and reduction of an object to its basic form" is a definition of stylization that fits widely different works. The reason is that different times have different ideas about what is accidental and what basic.

In this particular case "stylization" is brought about by representing practically every motive in terms of approximately right angles. In other words, ancient Chinese paintings, as preserved in the décor of Shang bronzes, is the result of that very early apprehension of form in which only changes in the direction of outlines are discriminated and represented in the most impressive manner: at acute angles. As everywhere else, line lost its intransigent angularity and became more flexible as time went on.

It was not before the seventh century, the time when the Li Yü style flourished, that Chinese art began to depict animals with a semblance of nature; not instead of, but alongside, the old theriomorphous symbols. Fragments of a basin from Li Yü in the Louvre have the *fond* adorned with sunken drawings of running dogs, tigers, bucking rams, leaping stags, frogs, turtles, and fish. All the mammals are seen from the side, with one fore- and one hindleg only; frogs, turtles, and a kind of catfish are seen from above, the other fish from the side. A definite principle is plainly adhered to: it is always the most extensive and therefore most informative view that is chosen for representation. If that side stands at right angles to the ground, the animal is rendered in pure elevation; if it is parallel to the ground, the animal is given in pure plan. This principle applies of course to the representation of any object. It was not an invention peculiar to the Chinese, but was known wherever man began to clarify and order his visual experience in visual terms.

In Chinese painting this principle ruled supreme for almost a millennium. There were considerable changes, but none violated it. On the fragment from Li Yü the animals of earth and water were placed side by side without any regard to their respective sizes and species. There is no such thing as a composition, for they were severally conceived. In one case only a running dog faces a ram; this may have been an accident, but the effect is that of a depicted action.

Action, however, was without any doubt the chief theme of the pictures in inlay upon a basin in the Freer Gallery (fig. 83). These hunting scenes are of the kind that lend themselves to stimulating description: chariots camouflaged with branches deceive the bear or tiger; a man attacks a tiger or a buffalo with a short sword; archers shoot straight into the air at flying cranes; a hunter performs a flying tackle to catch a goose; two men have come to grips in the heat of the hunt. Such descriptions make one frequently forget that all these forms are represented in pure elevation; that there is no indication of ground, and not the slightest suggestion of the third dimension, still less of space. It is interesting to note that the four-legged animals are always rendered with one fore- and one hindleg, but that man, with the exception of one type of kneeling archer, always has two legs and two arms. On close inspection these hunting scenes are not so chaotic as they appear; they form rather complex units, which are repeated over and over again.

The Louvre possesses a vase with similar hunting scenes interrupted by narrow friezes where men offer libations or beat drums. In these quiet and sedate scenes, men and objects are placed upon a base line. The plastic braids and the animals' heads of the handles on the basin of the Freer Gallery date it to the sixth century. The vase in the Louvre may be a little younger. Such hunting scenes were inspired by similar representations in Caucasian, Hallstadt and Ordos art. The connecting link was what is rather vaguely called Scythian art.

A new world was discovered by the Chinese when they turned from the representation of static symbols to the depiction of movement and action. The stimulus may have come from outside, but it was avidly taken up and completely appropriated. The scene of the Hosokawa mirror (fig. 43), where a rearing tiger attacks a horseman, when compared with any similar group of the basin in the Freer Gallery,

PAINTING

will show how far the Chinese had gone; here, as on at least one other mirror of that time,[55] the furious animal is represented with a twisted body, and the horse is slightly foreshortened. It is true that these are exceptions that remained, for the time being, without consequences. It is also true that something of this kind might have been expected of an art that had produced the boy dancing on the toad.

The further development of painting shows a curious and charming blend of decoration and representation. Forms that stand for one thing unexpectedly change their function; time and again scrolls turn into fantastic animals or tails of animals into scrolls. There is also ample evidence that such scrolls, which had become more luscious and rich as time went on, were interspersed with tiny figures of men and animals, and that these scrolls were transformed into a kind of *rocaille*. They serve in a new capacity, as a background of rocks and trees to Taoist saints who stand around conversing, listening to music, and patting the heads of tigers or riding on their backs. These scenes appear on a mirror that was once in the Loo Collection; it can be dated to the second century B.C.[56]

The same unreal and charming atmosphere, like that of a fairy tale, can be found in other "pictures" that adorn two tubes in bronze with inlays in gold and silver. They were discovered in Korea and brought to Japan. The most interesting of them is in the Imperial Academy in Tōkyō; its four sections show "landscapes" in which animals chase one another. In one frieze a hunter mounted upon a horse in "flying gallop" turns in the saddle to shoot at a pursuing tiger.

XV. SECTION OF AN INLAID TUBE

The irregular band, with its strange excrescences, that meanders diagonally across the surface is what has become of the old volutes. Imagination and fantasy have associated them with the contours of hills. They are so arranged as to frame

PAINTING

the main scene. The small intervals between them are filled with thin spirals; these are the tendril-like offshoots of the ancient volutes, and may be taken now for plants or flowers.

The lightness of touch, the ease of design, the facility with which movement is rendered, the eurhythmic composition that seems to have been achieved without effort — all this tends to make one forget that this was an art still unacquainted with the third dimension and space.

Pictures of this kind probably adorned the walls and palaces of the great under the Former Han dynasty. It is even possible to reconstruct their palette, for this very style has survived in some painted lacquers excavated in Korea. They come from Chinese tombs of the ancient Lo-lang district. The latest date of a work of this style is 69 A.D. Pale yellow, pink, and a subdued green were used against a background of glowing red, black, or dull dark green. The effect was always a gorgeous one. The *élan* with which the various motives were painted very often borders on sloppiness. It might be objected that such lacquer paintings were executed by artisans in workshops and studios like the famous Shang-fang atelier with its four branches, one of which was in Ssŭch'uan; and that the inscriptions speak of a very advanced division of labour. All this may be granted; but the few paintings from a tomb near Lo-yang which are now in the Museum of Fine Arts in Boston show that this light touch and slovenliness of make are characteristic of this style (fig. 84).

These paintings are borne by large brick slabs that form the walls and tympanum of a tomb. The slabs were first covered with a white ground that did not stick too well, and then painted on both sides. Upon the tympanum is a scene depicting a tiger and a bear about to fight, with other animals held back by armed men. The other pictures represent men and women in various activities taken from everyday life. A messenger with his banderoled staff reports to his superior, whose face is a marvellous blend of consternation, anger, arrogance, and stupidity. The man next to the messenger listens with downcast eyes, in an attitude of modesty which seems to be not quite genuine. In another scene two young girls glare at each other; a girl rushes upon them, her arms outstretched in a soothing gesture.[57] Most amusing is a third scene: two wily foreigners in the trousers and Phrygian caps of Iranians have succeeded in showing their merchandise — jewelry — to the ladies of the house. One of them lets a string of pearls dangle from his hand. A lady argues and pleads with a gentleman, evidently the husband, to buy them. Her gestures could not be more entreating. Nor could those of the husband be more eloquent: he personifies stern refusal. Nowhere was the cruelty of husbands better depicted, or their crude contempt for the finer things that move the hearts and minds of women.

All these figures are put side by side in file. They are executed with a facility that often comes close to carelessness. Line is sometimes incredibly supple, especially in some male heads; it is not even, but increases and decreases in breadth as more

PAINTING

or less pressure was applied to the brush. This gives the line a certain dynamic quality, and suggests spontaneous creation.

This same free and dynamic handling of line can be found in the painted décor of a box from the tomb of a certain Wang Hsü in Lo-lang, which contained lacquers dated to the years 45, 52 and 69 A.D. This square box is covered with very thin tortoise-shell; under the shell are depicted four scenes, with a large quatrefoil in the centre. In each of the two upper corners sit two ladies who are harangued by what appear to be spirits. On either side at the bottom stand two men, evidently of high rank; between them kneels a fifth man in an attitude of excited pleading. All persons are placed on baselines, and drawn with free, loose, swift strokes of varying thickness. The same style is used to paint a tiny picture of Hsi Wang-mu, the Queen Mother of the West, upon the lacquer dish of 69 A.D. This piece came from Ssŭch'uan to Korea.

FIRST TO FIFTH CENTURY

THE break in style that is apparent in the bronze mirrors at the very beginning of the first century A.D. occurs in painting toward the end of it. A few dated monuments exist that differ very much from the paintings discussed so far. It is true that these monuments are not pictures executed with brush and colours, but engravings of such pictures in stone. The aim was obviously to make them more durable. The identical intention had led to the same technique artists of Bœotia and the island of Chios in the fourth and third century B.C. Such engravings were a substitute for painting; they are found on pillars in front of tombs, or on the walls of offering shrines for the dead.

The earliest dated pillars are those from Nan Wu-yang in Shantung, of 86 to 87 A.D. They set the pattern for the more elaborate pillars of the second century, such as those from the tombs of the Wu family near Chia-hsiang in Shantung. These pillars, erected in 147 A.D., guard the entrance to the graves of Wu Pan (d.145 A.D.), Wu K'ai-ming (d.148 A.D.), Wu Liang (d.151 A.D.), and Wu Jung (d.168 A.D.). At least three offering shrines stood there.[58] Even the names of the artists are known; they were Li Ti-mao, Mēng-fu, Wei K'ai, and Sun Tsung.

Still intact is another offering shrine with engraved walls, that of Hsiao T'ang Shan. It was standing when visited in 129 A.D.

The offering shrines were open at the front. Their walls were divided into registers. The three shrines of the Wu family which can be reconstructed show an increasing order and coordination of these friezes. The tops, usually triangular in shape, are filled with representations of gods and spirits; then follow long rows of heroes; below them come large scenes, which, on the side walls, depict a battle of charioteers and horsemen upon and around a bridge, or the vain attempt of Shih Huang Ti to recover the sacred tripods of Chou from a river, an incident that happened in 219 B.C. On the rear walls appear what have been called receptions; one or two men are introduced to a high dignitary on the ground floor of a palace. This is a scene that takes place in the world beyond. I think it probable that it depicts the reception of the deceased.

Such scenes had adorned the palaces of the great in the second century B.C. This can be gleaned from a famous poem by Wang Wēn-k'ao (first half of second century A.D.) in which he describes the wall paintings of the Ling-kuang palace. This palace was built between 154 and 129 B.C.

Though differing considerably in the treatment of form, the engravings from Nan Wu-yang, Hsiao T'ang Shan, and the Wu shrines belong to the same stage of apprehension. In each case, form is so outlined as to offer its most informative aspect, the lines within the contours playing a comparatively subordinate rôle. In human and animal figures alike a gradual change from a halting to a jerky rhythm of line can be observed. The animals in motion from the Hsiao T'ang Shan and the Chia-hsiang shrines have been famous from the time they became known. They are amazingly vivid and expressive, though they do not surpass those on the inlaid bronze tubes from Korea. As in the latter, the horses are rendered in a pose called the "flying gallop" (cf. fig. xv). This phenomenon has given rise to many speculations, because the same device was known only to Minoan and Scythian art.[59] It must be pointed out that animals other than horses were depicted with fore- and hindlegs outstretched in the air, in "flying gallop," as early as on the basin of the Freer Gallery (fig. 83). This pose is eminently suggestive of rapid movement, and probably for this reason it was given to animals such as horses which do not move in this way except when clearing an obstacle. Compared with the animals, the human beings of those stone engravings are rather stiff, like marionettes, whether represented with timid correctness as in Hsiao T'ang Shan, or with exaggerating mannerism as in the Wu shrines.

Men, horses, chariots, palaces, and trees are strung along a base line which is nearly always visibly drawn. When missing, it is easily restored, except in those cases where the confusion of a battle was to be indicated. The modern spectator of such scenes is inclined to interpret them in terms of space. The fact that houses, chariots, or a bridge are always given in pure elevation should warn him against it.

The *Battle on the Bridge* was repeated three times in the Wu shrines. The motive was complicated because it required a representation of the water, the bridge, the firm ground on both banks, and the combatants in their chariots or on horseback. The composition is always the same. The bridge is rendered in elevation. It frames a flight of birds; below the birds are boats with fighting men; on either side of them are fishermen and herons. The boats, of course, appear in elevation. The intention was to show that the bridge rises into the air over a body of water. Riders and

PAINTING

chariots not attached to the outlines of the bridge are scattered over the remaining surface.

Even more instructive is the scene of the attempted recovery of the Chou *ting* from Hsiao T'ang Shan (fig. 85). The river banks and the square fields of the surrounding countryside are rendered in plan; the men on land and in the boats in elevation. The lines of the river banks and the upper lines of the fields serve also as base lines for the workingmen and spectators. This simultaneous use of plan and elevation, and the actual fusion of the two in the cases just pointed out, is not a specifically Chinese solution. It was known to many peoples at various times; in fact, it is the only possible way for any art that ignores the third dimension to deal with such problems.

It is interesting to observe that in one or two cases objects were represented as extended, that is, three-dimensionally. But these are isolated phenomena, and become general only at the beginning of the third century A.D. A few engravings from the tomb of Kao I (d.209 A.D.) near Ya-chou in Ssŭch'uan show the usual motive of chariots accompanied by a few horsemen and footmen. The wheels of the chariot are set at different levels; its body has side-lines that run parallel to the tangent of the wheels. The base line is replaced by a base plane.

This important change in apprehension did not happen at once, but step by step. Upon a second set of slabs from Hsiao T'ang Shan are depicted a palace with a tree beside it and a banquet. The same motives were treated on the Wu engravings, and there the house was, of course, always given in elevation. Here the front of the palace still clings to a base line; a side is added to the front at an obtuse angle. The base, rafters, and top beam of the roof of one side run strictly parallel to each other.[60] In other words, the house is conceived as an extended body with four parallel sides. In this case the principle of parallel perspective is applied; it demands that horizontal and vertical lines be represented as such and that the depth lines which run obliquely at any chosen angle also be parallel. However, it took many centuries before a strict and orderly system was worked out. An object so represented always appears to be seen from an elevated point of view. This is typically Chinese, whereas parallel perspective is not.

On the slab from Hsiao T'ang Shan, the sides of the house stretch out into emptiness because to the right of it a man, a horse, and a tree are arrayed along the same base line as that on which rests the front of the palace. It is quite obvious that these new observations were made on single, isolated objects. Evolution was slow, the result of laborious work. This was a time when artists went soberly over their problems, insisting on honesty and visual logic, abhorring the facile vagueness with which their forbears had been satisfied (cf. fig xv). By investigating and solving these basic problems they laid the foundation upon which the proud structure of Chinese painting was to rise. The same spirit drove Hsü Shēn (d. 120 A.D.) to write his *Shuo Wēn*.

PAINTING

To get an idea of what original painting at the time when the Wu slabs were engraved looked like, one must turn to the figures that adorn the sides and the lid of a lacquered basket discovered in a late Han tomb in Korea.[61] This painted basket that gave the name to the grave has rightly become famous; but it must be borne in mind that it, too, is but a mass product. The persons depicted are paragons of filial piety (fig. 86).

In the third to the fourth century, manneristic formulæ give way to more objective representation. The sprightly silhouette disappears, and the lines in the interior of a figure become more important. The most striking result of this change is that man and animal seem to move less abruptly, more gracefully, and more convincingly.

This new sober line, representation of the third dimension and even of space, can be found in the engravings on the walls of Chu Wei's shrine near Chia-hsiang in Shantung.[62] Because Chu Wei had defended Lo-yang against the pretender Liu Hsiu in 25 A.D., the shrine and its pictures have been attributed to the first century A.D. This is an impossible date. In subject matter and style these engravings are considerably more mature than those of the second set from Hsiao T'ang Shan which, in their turn, are more recent than the Wu slabs. The Chu Wei slabs must be placed in the fourth rather than the third century, for their figures are closely related to those in the scroll *Admonitions* by Ku K'ai-chi (321-379), an old copy of which is in the British Museum.[63]

The Admonitions of the Instructress to Court Ladies was, in its original state, a handscroll with eleven scenes illustrating short didactic sayings inscribed beside them. The scroll in the British Museum contains only nine such pictures.[64] It is an old copy, probably of the T'ang period, and has been repeatedly repaired and repainted. On the whole, it seems to be a faithful reproduction of the original, one of the most famous works of Ku K'ai-chi.

The connection between text and illustrations is rather loose. In fact it is sometimes forced, and one gets the impression that the painter often illustrated the lofty sayings with his tongue in his cheek. His interest in the human body in rest and motion was, however, real and genuine. He arranges his persons in well-balanced groups. He succeeds in making clear their spatial relation and in depicting emotion as mirrored in the human face. Ku K'ai-chi certainly earned the praise his contemporaries bestowed upon him, for he was a genius who led his generation a long way on the road to a greater command of pictorial expression.

There are two toilet scenes with one and two persons, respectively, illustrating the world-wide wisdom that it is more important to improve one's soul than one's looks. A slightly irritated and agitated husband explains to his naive wife the unreasonableness of jealousy: "No one can endlessly please. Affection cannot be for one alone; if it were so, it would end one day in disgust." The possibility that the lady might act upon this statement about human nature was not considered.

A complicated picture like that of the emperor Ch'ēng (32-5 B.C.) riding in

PAINTING

a palanquin and talking to the virtuous Lady Pan must have appeared a miracle of perfection to Ku's contemporaries (fig. 87). Everything is in it: the varied poses of the jolly bearers who move swiftly along; the litter with its large framework of mosquito netting; the admirable vividness in the expressions of the two main persons. The emperor, already moving, calls back through a little side window to the lady to come with him; Lady Pan stands in dignified silence. She had refused to ride with the monarch "lest she detract his thoughts from the affairs of state." The subtle humour of the painter made him seat another girl at the emperor's side; thus Lady Pan's highmindedness does not convince as much as she would like.

Throughout the scroll the garments are rendered with fine, even lines in graceful curves; no background is indicated, though figures and objects appear to be placed on a gently ascending base plane; and the palanquin, like the bed in another scene, is constructed with the help of parallel perspective, as a sort of hollow cupboard holding one or two persons.

But Ku K'ai-chi failed miserably when it came to representing a scene in the open. The subject matter is a hunter aiming at a tiger with a cross-bow. The event is evidently imagined as taking place in a mountainous landscape. The hunter is rendered in the scale used throughout the scroll. He kneels on the imaginary ground and faces a mountain that rises from under the lower edge. The animals upon this mountain are very small. This makes the archer gigantic in size, and, for lack of a common plane, hovering in the air.

It is precisely in this respect that the final scene of the Lo Shēn scroll in the Freer Gallery differs from the *Admonitions*. This work illustrated a poem about *The Fairy of the River Lo,* written in 222 A.D. by Ts'ao Chi.[65] Unlike the *Admonitions,* the several scenes follow each other without interruption by writing. This painting also claims to be the copy of a work by Ku K'ai-chi, because an entry in the Ch'ien Lung catalogue attributes a picture of the same content to him. A little monochrome painting on the window of a ship in this scroll suggests the Sung epoch as the date when the copy was made.

The scenes are laid along the banks of the Lo where the young poet met the fairy, fell in love with her, and lost her when he refused to follow her into the water. The topography is indicated by a strip of little mountains and trees that run along the lower edge, occasionally giving way to open water. At certain spots mountains and trees rise a little, thus bringing an episode to a close. Here, too, is a series of more or less disconnected situations, with only the scantiest hints at a landscape, and none at space.

In the concluding scene a most important innovation can be observed. A gentleman, presumably the poet, sits in the open on a dais, attended by two servants. The dais is rendered, as may be expected, in parallel perspective. The tiny hills and mountains and a row of trees are so arranged as to run roughly parallel to the sides of the dais. Thus a "space cell" is constructed within which the group of three is placed. It is true that the proportions of men and their surroundings are still arbitrary; but this does not alter the fact that here landscape was for the first time rendered spatially.

The space cell was constructed as if it were a hollow rectangular body. That this was the form under which space was conceived and represented is borne out by a number of works that must be dated to the second half of the fifth and the first half of the sixth century. They are found in the cave temples of Tun-huang on the border between China and central Asia.

FIFTH TO SEVENTH CENTURY

IN Tun-huang more than a hundred caves were decorated with wall paintings from the fifth to the thirteenth century. Thanks to the extremely dry climate, these frescoes, all of them Buddhist in subject matter, were miraculously well preserved when Pelliot had them photographed.[66] They are an invaluable thesaurus of Chinese Buddhist painting for the second half of the first millennium A.D.

One of the oldest caves is Cave 110. In it, among other paintings, is one illustrating the *Ruru Jātaka*. A *jātaka* is a pre-birth story; that is one about events that have happened to the Buddha in a previous existence. Since every oriental is an avid listener to stories, these tales were an important instrument for propagating and strengthening Buddhism, and illustrations of them are found wherever this religion had taken root. In the *Ruru Jātaka,* Gautama was born as a golden gazelle. One day he saw a man struggling in the water of the Ganges. He was a wastrel who had decided to drown himself after he had dissipated his fortune. The gazelle saved him; he thanked the animal and went away. At the same time, the king of Benares, a great hunter, had promised a high reward to anyone who could lead him to a golden gazelle he had heard about. The profligate did so; when the king poised his arrow, the animal began gently to reproach the wretch who had brought the king. When the monarch heard the story, he wanted to kill the ungrateful scoundrel on the spot. But the gazelle interfered in his favour, uttered some profound and pertinent words, and withdrew.

The painting illustrating this *jātaka* fills a narrow frieze, in the format of a Chinese hand scroll. The principle of composition used is that called continuous narration. Successive scenes are presented within the frame of one picture. The object of the artist is to give the clearest possible account of the different phases of a tale, and to it he subordinates the pictorial unity of space and time. In this mode of representation, the actors appear whenever their presence is required. The principle was known to the Chinese, for the *Lo Shēn* scroll had made use of it. There is no ground for assuming that it had been brought to their knowledge from outside.

PAINTING

But in Cave 110 the story runs from left to right, instead of from right to left, as Chinese scrolls do. This was without doubt due to central Asian influence. This influence is even more apparent in the treatment of human figures. They are as un-Chinese as possible, not only in costume but also in style. The prominent parts of their bodies, especially their faces, have highlights in white. In other words, they appear modelled in the round with the help of light and dark tones. The resemblance to Kuchean painting is as striking as that of contemporaneous Buddhist sculpture with Kuchean sculpture. This interpretation of form in terms of plasticity has, of course, nothing to do with religion. It was the Indian attitude which had been carried to China by Buddhism, and for exactly the same reasons which I have mentioned in the chapter on sculpture, the Chinese painters took it up. It went directly against the innate perceptual character of the Chinese, who does not incorporate his tactile experiences into his painting, as the West and India did. The reason for this cannot be discussed here. It would lead into a consideration of the psychology of peoples, and finally into metaphysics. Suffice it to point out that the Chinese never understood the phenomenon, even when they imitated it; whenever such modelling is found in a Chinese painting, it is certain to have been caused by foreign influence.

Overwhelming as Kuchean influence then was, the painter of the *Ruru Jātaka* revolted on one point: he told his story in terms of space. Kuchean painting did not know space; it worked with the principles of plan and elevation; its landscapes are but aggregates of landscape elements so rendered. The Chinese artist transposed these elements into his own language by setting the little mountain ranges in rows that enclose sections of space. A generation later, when the *Vyāghrī Jātaka* was illustrated on a wall of Cave 135, in the shape of a scroll cut up into three equal parts, the same device was employed; in addition, the story now reads from right to left.

The vast landscapes that are found on the walls of the cave temples in Tun-huang down into the eighth century turn out on close inspection to be nothing but aggregates of such space cells. The mountain ridges meander over the picture surface without any apparent order; yet they create innumerable irregular space cells, large or small, in which action takes place. Improvement lay in quite another direction; the artists were chiefly concerned with such problems as representing men, objects, and animals in a plausible and correct scale within their cell.

Roughly contemporaneous with the frescoes of Cave 135 in Tun-huang, but incomparably better in quality, are the engravings on two coffin slabs in the Nelson Gallery in Kansas City (fig. 88). These slabs can be dated with confidence to the twenties of the sixth century A.D. They are reported to have come from a grave in the region of Lo-yang that contained a tablet with a eulogy to a Lady Yüan-shih, dated in 522 A.D.[67] In style, these engravings are identical with those of an offering shrine in the Museum of Fine Arts in Boston which bears the date 526 A.D. The Kansas City slabs show examples of filial piety, motives that had belonged to the

PAINTING

stock of Chinese painting since Han times. The stone reproduced here illustrates the stories of Yüan Ku, of Kuo Chü, and of the legendary emperor Shun, from right to left. The three episodes which have no other connection than a moral one, play in an ideal landscape; there are windswept trees, some tall and slender, some old and gnarled; a bubbling brook where fallow deer come to drink; pheasants floating in the air and clouds drifting in the sky; fantastic rocks in the foreground and soft hills in the distance. The rocks separate one cell from the other. Within such a cell two episodes of the same story are usually depicted.[68] It would take up too much time to relate all these tales. One may suffice. It is the story of Yüan Ku, the filial grandson, illustrated at the right end.

An old man, too sick to move by himself, was a heavy burden upon his son and daughter-in-law. Since he would not die, they decided to take him out into the woods and leave him there to his fate, which was certain death. The grandson, a young boy, remonstrated with his parents, but was told to keep his own counsel. A stretcher was quickly made, the grandfather put upon it and carried away. This is the first episode depicted. When the old man was put down and his son turned to go, he saw the boy carrying the stretcher. He told him to leave it, since it was no longer needed. "But it will be," replied the boy, "when you have grown old." Whereupon the grandfather was carried back. The conversation between father and son, with the grandfather listening, is the second episode represented.

It is illuminating to compare this treatment of the story with that which it received upon the painted basket. There, a single figure only, that of the filial grandson, was represented (fig. 86, the third figure from the right). He is just one member of a long gallery of filial paragons.

The Kansas City slabs reproduce the work of a truly great artist. His inventiveness in composing the various scenes, the firmness of his drawing, the angular grace with which he imbued everything mark him as a genius. The gem-like hardness of line and its peculiar rhythm were not his alone; they are characteristic of his generation, as is evinced by the wall paintings of 538-539 A.D. in Cave 120/N in Tun-huang.

One will do well to bear in mind the representational possibilities of the fourth to the sixth century, especially when ancient painters and their works are described in glowing terms. Thus, a certain Tsung Ping is recorded to have roamed the country, climbed mountains, and, when old and ill, to have painted them on the walls of his house. One can get a fairly correct idea of what they must have looked like merely from the dates of his life, 375-443.[69]

PAINTING

SEVENTH TO NINTH CENTURY

ONE of the most important themes of Buddhist painting was the representation of the Enlightened One with his entourage of saints, in a monumental group. This type of picture, where a number of persons stand together without performing any action, was unknown to the Chinese before the advent of Buddhism. The earliest examples were, of course, profoundly influenced by Kuchean painting, in form as in composition. Even in Cave 120/N, when form was rendered in the characteristic style of that period, the several figures were symmetrically distributed over the picture surface, without any indication of a common base for them. It is safe to assume that the artists worked in the second half of the sixth century to represent these closed groups in terms of space, for in the first half of the seventh century such solutions were general. In Cave 77 a configuration consists of a Buddha in the middle, with two Bodhisattvas in a front row and two monks in a back row. The spatial relation is now clear.

A good example of the new solution for this theme is found in Cave 118/A, dating from about the middle of the seventh century. The figures, all of them on lotus socles of their own, are placed in a single plane. This was done deliberately, to enhance the effect of order and clarity. The cæsuras between the Buddha in the centre and the groups on either side of him, which are taken together as closed units, serve the same purpose (fig. 89).

The almost statue-like effect of such compositions was little to the taste of the Chinese. Shortly afterwards they began to weave a few more spatial elements into them. The ideal solution was found in frescoes like those of Cave 146, which can be confidently dated about 700 A.D. There the main persons, the Buddha and his two Bodhisattvas, are shifted to the middle ground; the other figures are so arranged as to converge in the background. The attendants furthest away stand behind the Buddha. The whole fresco is so constructed as to form a triangle if it were transposed into plan. The desire for a lucid tectonic composition was so strong at this time that even Amitābha and his Western Paradise were pressed into the schema (fig. 90). In keeping with the texts, the paradise is a cool pond with lotus flowers as thrones for the re-born enjoying the bliss of Amitābha's presence. In the background, two mountains descending toward the centre close the stage.

What has been said about the style of sculpture around 700 A.D. applies to painting as well. The same problems were solved in the same ways. Such an enormously difficult task as letting the body of Amitābha appear under a diaphanous robe is exquisitely and admirably accomplished.

In style and subject matter this paradise of Cave 146 is almost identical with a fresco in the Kondō of the Hōryūji in Nara. The wall paintings of the Kondō are the work of an excellent Chinese artist who emigrated to Japan. This is a phenomenon which will be observed time and again: famous solutions of certain themes spread with incredible speed to the extreme outposts of the Chinese orbit.

Such a tranquil configuration, however, does not seem to have had much appeal to the public as an ideal picture of the Western Paradise. It wanted a more explicit description of its joys and wonders. By the beginning of the eighth century, the painters of Tun-huang had returned to the type of the relief from Nan Hsiang-t'ang (fig. 65). That work was surely based upon a picture. The paradise is a luxurious garden with three pools, trees and pavilions. The side lines of the pool in the centre converge, and so do the side lines of the pavilions at either end. Such converging orthogonal lines not infrequently occur on stelæ from the beginning of the sixth century. They were at that time not the result of acute observation, but rather an attempt to obtain perfect balance and a hieratic symmetry by treating one half antithetically to the other. This was no longer the case with the relief from Nan Hsiang-t'ang. There the device was used to produce a spatial effect. It was not consistently applied. The artist simply repeated the formula of the central pond when he drew the other two pools.

Such unsystematic application of perspective means persisted well into the eighth century, when representations of the paradise became richer in appearance. They usually have a large palace behind Amitābha, and this is rendered with converging side lines, of which the lower ones ascend and the upper ones descend. A building at one side always has an exact counterpart on the other side. Their various depth-lines meet at a series of points which form a central axis. In other words this perspective construction knows not the vanishing point, but a vanishing axis. In these self-contained, strictly symmetrical paintings, it always coincides with the central axis.

Inconsistencies in the use of this method abound. It happens time and again that a pavilion in the middle ground is represented with one rising and one falling side line, and one farther back in space is rendered in exactly the same way. This means that an imaginary horizon was assumed only for single objects, but not for the sum total of them. It was not before the second half of the eighth century that a sort of solution for this problem was found. In the famous *Paradise* of Cave 139/A, all orthogonals below a horizon which is assumed to run through the front eaves of the central building ascend; all above it descend. Yet even here the rails of the two lateral pavilions rise (fig. 91) and the sides of the central palace, which one would expect to appear as horizontal lines, fall sharply.[70]

The representation of the human figure also underwent profound changes in the seventh century. As pointed out, these were identical with those described in the chapter on sculpture. There was an absolute uniformity of style, due to an identical apprehension of form. The human body seems to have gained in weight and volume: it is well articulated, with emphasis on the joints; and it is represented with a line that had gained in clarity, strength, and beauty.

PAINTING

This linear and tectonic art reached its apogee in the frescoes of the Kondō. Details of these wall paintings evince an incredible charm and vigour of line, and a clear, lucidly constructed form.

A few fragments of frescoes from Cave 139/A of Tun-huang are now in the Fogg Museum in Cambridge, Massachusetts. They display the same exactness of line, though that cave was decorated during the second half of the eighth century. One piece shows the old monk Kāśyapa, a favourite disciple of the Buddha, and his inseparable companion, together with a Bodhisattva and two Lokapālas (fig. 92).

The contour of Kāśyapa's head consists of rather short lines that do not always touch each other. In Cave 118/A and the frescoes of the Hōryūji, line ran evenly and without such interruption. This new handling of line gave form an energy and a vigour which was formerly unknown. Before long, these strokes were to vary in thickness, and the effect of dynamic strength was then very striking. Though the new technique was not universally used, it was fully developed before the middle of the eighth century. The painter who depicted a Buddhist saint surrounded by dignitaries and monks in Cave 54 of Tun-huang, was familiar with it and used it to great advantage.

It will be recalled that this line of varying strength had been known to Chinese painters at the beginning of the first century A.D., but fell into complete oblivion. In calligraphy, however, it played an important rôle on account of its expressiveness. The rediscovery in the eighth century of what may be called the modulated line was of great importance. The even line had encompassed form like an iron wire; it made form appear rigid and immovable. The modulated line suggested movement and action and, therefore, life. With its appearance the range of representation was incredibly broadened. Such emotions as joy, delight, pride, anger, despair, and sorrow were now depicted with a convincingness heretofore unknown; and physical action also gained.

It would be tempting to credit one of the great artists with its invention. Yen Li-pēn (600-673), the most famous figure painter of his time, did not know it, to judge from the copies of works ascribed to him. The scroll with the *Thirteen Emperors,* now in the Museum of Fine Arts in Boston, is often attributed to him; groups 7 to 13 of this scroll are regarded as scarcely retouched sections.[71] The figures are, however, so poorly drawn, so out of proportion, so stiff and awkward in movement, so mask-like in expression as to make it difficult to believe in the authenticity of the work. Another scroll in the same museum, the *Collation of the Classics,* is a Sung copy of an original by Yen Li-pēn.[72] In both paintings line is thin, hard, and even.

It is the same in the copy by Hui Tsung (1082-1135) of Chang Hsüan's *Preparation of Silk,* also in Boston.[73] Chang Hsüan was active between 713 and 742 A.D., and won much fame for his paintings of ladies and their activities. The

PAINTING

copy is much better than that of the *Collation*. As there, and as on practically every painting that goes back to an original of this time, the figures are placed on the silk without any indication of background. Exceptions are the badly damaged fragments of pictures recovered by Sir Aurel Stein from the Chinese graveyard of Astāna, near Turfan. Since the conquest of Kuchā in 648 A.D. by the Chinese, Chinese culture had spread to that territory; and many monuments of purely Chinese character have been discovered there by the English and German expeditions. The tombs of Astāna were those of Chinese people, and dated inscriptions place them in the last decade of the seventh and the first decade of the eighth century. On the two fragments mentioned, a tree is placed behind a row of standing ladies and their servants.[74] The treatment of form is the same as in the scroll depicting the *Preparation of Silk*, with the important difference that what is a little timid in the copy is free and spontaneous in the provincial originals.

Ladies and trees also are the theme of six panels that form a screen, in the Shōsōin. This Shōsōin, or store-house, was erected in 756 A.D. to shelter the objects of the imperial household which were given to the Tōdaiji in Nara by the widow of the emperor Shōmu. In the framework of the screen, Japanese papers with the date 754 A.D. have been discovered. The date of these panels, which were to be filled out with coloured feathers, is therefore well established. The ladies, and especially the rocks and trees, were rendered with swift, free lines which grow a little stronger here and there.[75] Yet form is still held firmly by an even line in the series of portraits of famous Buddhist ecclesiastics in the Tōji of Kyōto. They are the works of Li Chēn, created about 800 A.D.[76] One of them, that of Amoghavajra, the great apostle of Tantrism (cf. p. 78) is somewhat better preserved than the rest. Amoghavajra sits on a dais, with clenched hands and a head of striking appearance because of its high dome, its strong nose, its fanatical eyes, and its weak chin. He was evidently not a man of this world. The faint indications of shadow in the folds of his monk's robe, lacking in the other portraits, must be taken as a subtle hint of his central Asian origin. Through these portaits Li Chēn reveals himself as a good painter who clung to tradition as his firm and solid basis.

The greatest painter of the century was Wu Tao-tzŭ (700-760). His contemporaries called him a genius, and later generations have never challenged this verdict. As happens so often, his admirers felt his superiority, but became a little vague when they tried to describe his works. What struck them was that his figures seemed to be more alive than those of his predecessors and fellow artists, and that the persons and animals of his larger compositions were drawn with what we call correct perspective diminution.

Nothing has survived of his *œuvre*, save a few engravings on stone of some famous works.[77] Rubbings of them must have been widely known. There are, of course, hundreds of paintings with his name attached for no better reason than that they were considered to be done in his style, or that their subject matter was

101

PAINTING

one for which Wu had become renowned. During his lifetime Wu had already won a high reputation through his treatment of Buddhist themes; and one of his most admired works was the Parinirvāna, or the *Death of the Buddha*. This painting was repeated in a thousand versions in China and in Japan. Practically every museum of Far Eastern ethnography, at least in Europe, has a more or less free copy of it. They all represent the deceased, wrapped in his monk's robe, lying on a couch, with his head turned to the left. The locality, the Sāla grove near Kusinārā, is indicated by a row of these trees that practically closes the scene at the back. The Buddha is surrounded by a crowd of gods, heavenly beings, men, and animals. They display a wide range of mournful emotion, from controlled grief to unchecked despair, in their expressions and their gestures.

One copy of this famous work, which must have been made within a very short time of Wu's death, has come down to us. It filled the lunette of the Kinnarī Cave at Kumtura, near Kuchā, and is now in the Völkerkundemuseum in Berlin. Since a very characteristic style sprang up in central Asia at about the middle of the ninth century, this painting, which is purely Chinese, must have been executed before that date. In fact there is every reason to believe that it was painted in the second half of the eighth century.

The Kumtura fresco is not a masterpiece, but it contains enough to make one understand why Wu was called divine. Among the mourners at the right side are a few heads that are exquisite studies in human character (fig. 93). There is a gentleman with the threadbare beard of the Chinese; he laments loudly, but with dignity. Next to him stands an old monk, emaciated, toothless, and a little feeble-minded; he holds his folded hands to his quivering lips in a gesture of utter despair. At his side is an Iranian with a hawk's nose and a rich flowing beard; his expression admirably suggests that he rather feels than understands the sad event. Below him is a full-blooded monk who abandons himself to grief with gusto; he cries out and strikes his forehead with his right hand in a gesture that is as vulgar as it is expressive.

As a painter of horses Han Kan (ca. 710-760) was almost, though not quite, as famous as Wu. An original work of his is now in the collection of Sir Percival David.[78] The picture has often been repaired and repainted, and in the process the tail of the animal was lost, and legs and hindquarter badly restored. The magnificent head and powerful chest are in their original state. The nobility and nervousness of this horse are marvellously caught in a few clear and simple strokes. Among the things Sir Aurel Stein found in the refuse heap of the abandoned Tibetan fortress of Mazār Tāgh, in central Asia, was a scrap of paper. It has a Tibetan inscription and a Chinese painting of galloping horses.[79] Their style is a coarse version of Han Kan's style, with ampler use of the modulated line. This fragment is important because Mazār Tāgh was given up before the end of the eighth century. With the knowledge thus gained from various sources, a scroll in the Freer Gallery,

PAINTING

Horses Brought as Tribute, must be regarded as an excellent copy of an outstanding work by Han Kan.[80]

Scanty as the monuments are, they suffice for attaining a good idea of the aims and achievements of painting in the first two centuries of the T'ang dynasty.

There is, above all, the ideal of perfect clarity. Each form has to be clearly and definitely presented; it has to be built up of sharply delineated parts; these parts unite into a whole that is for this very reason very lucid. The means to achieve this end is a line which is fine, exact, and imbued with a rhythm that makes it flow with ease and grace. The jauntiness and harshness of the sixth century are overcome. All this would not have been achieved but for a strong emphasis on tectonics, for the single figure as well as for a composition; both are always well articulated. Along with this goes a tendency toward generalization and typification. Deities, men, animals, and trees are conceived as representatives each of their kind rather than as individuals. They are stripped of their individual appearance, which is thought of as haphazard, and only the purified generic form is presented. It is, of course, no contradiction that this era knew and appreciated portraiture. The persons depicted were certainly recognizable, and must have been so by their individual characteristics; yet a portrait like that of Amoghavajra is much more than a likeness. It is the picture of a certain type, the intense religious fanatic.

In the field of devotional painting, this trend led to the creation of the types of the Buddha, the Bodhisattvas, and other figures. These solutions were regarded as so perfect that later times did not want or dare to alter them. Under the T'ang dynasty the large configurations became empty schemata and the holy persons utterly devoid of meaning and expression. In later configurations such as the large fresco from the Monastery of Joyful Transformation in southern Shansi, which is now in the museum in Toronto, these stereotyped figures and faces stand out very strangely from those parts that were painted in the style of their time.[81] In this case Maitreya and his celestial *cortège* are depicted in a sort of petrified T'ang style; only the clustered folds and curly edges of their garments are different; they correspond strikingly to those found on contemporaneous Buddhist sculpture, i.e., statues of the first half of the fourteenth century, for the fresco itself was painted by the *tai-chao* Chu Hao-ku and his pupil Chang Po-yüan in 1320 A.D. What they contributed to the T'ang schema was, besides the change in the rendering of garments, the group of female attendants around Brahmavatī, the mother of Maitreya, at the left side. The counterpart at the right side, King Śaṅkha of Ketumatī and the persons around him, are rendered in compliance with the T'ang schema. To the same category belong the gigantic wall-paintings in the University Museum in Philadelphia and in the Nelson Gallery in Kansas City, which come from the Kuang Shēng Monastery in southern Shansi. They also date from the fourteenth century.

PAINTING

The great masters of the eighth century felt no ambition to transcend the ideals of their time. They, too, sought the perfect form; their greatness consisted in being subtle and profound where others were crude and obvious. They probably were anything but revolutionary innovators. The "garments fluttering in the wind," with whose "invention" Wu is credited, would scarcely have sufficed to secure him immortality.

What has been said about the tenacity with which later generations stuck to the decorative schema of the eighth century in religious painting holds for other fields too. Chou Fang, who was active from ca. 780-810, is known from copies of his scrolls depicting *Ladies Listening to Music,* and *Ladies Fatigued by Embroidering*.[82] He obviously did not introduce new ideas or new forms. Nor did Chou Wēn-chü who worked at the court of Li Hou-chu (923-934) and whose *chef-d'œuvre, Ming Huang and Yang Kuei-fei Listening to their Orchestra,* is known from several copies.[83]

The first to signal the coming of a new era was Kuan-hsiu (832-912) with his pictures of Lohans, saints who at the request of the Buddha postponed their death, and with it their final deliverance from re-birth, till the advent of Maitreya. Kuan-hsiu painted them as old men of repulsive ugliness.[84] They were a protest against the elegant and beautiful beings as which these saints had been represented by the artists of former times. Kuan-hsiu's Lohans look like beggars. They can scarcely be imagined as objects of devout worship; they are meant to be an appeal and a stimulus to the individual. To him, and probably to many more, individual achievement counted more than the easy and pleasant submergence in mass excitement, and the vague hope for a better future.

Of the two series of Lohans ascribed to Kuan-hsiu only that in the Kōdaiji of Kyōto has a claim to being original. These pictures were brought to Japan by the priest Shunjō in 1211 A.D. The Lohans are seated on rocks, with trees behind. The fifth, whose name is Nakula, is represented in the unsaintly act of scratching his back. This very motive, impossible a hundred years earlier in religious painting, occurs in the rows of Lohans of Cave 76 in Tun-huang, which can be dated to the tenth century.

The glory and fame of T'ang painting rests on the treatment of the human figure. This does not mean, however, that landscape as a subject matter was neglected. There were two men who became immortal as landscapists, Li Ssŭ-hsün (651-716 or 720) and Wang Wei (699-759).

Li is reported to have used very fine and exact lines and strong colours. Not one of his works has survived, and even the alleged copies of them must be viewed with suspicion.

To judge from the wall paintings of Tun-huang, the painters by the end of the seventh and the beginning of the eighth century had succeeded in representing the interiors of temple courtyards, large compounds, and landscapes with hills that receded into the distance. Yet space was still to them the nothing between solid bodies; and they still proceeded by adding one space cell to another. This can be deduced from the large compositions that flanked the main configurations from the first half of the seventh century. In those apparently large mountainous landscapes, especially when they are the setting for a story that is told in continuous narration, time and again a view is given of a valley bordered by hills that grow smaller with distance; yet the sky over these hills serves as the ground for the preceding scene.

The motives and style of these little landscapes occur again on two lutes in the Shōsōin which must be earlier than 756 A.D. And they, in turn, are identical in style and such details as costumes with a landscape in the National Museum in Peking (fig. 94).[85]

In its middle ground the rocks soar to great heights, a large mass in the centre, two smaller walls on either side. The tripartition is carried forward by two little brooks. Thus fore- and middle ground, which form a sort of stage, are well articulated. This division into three sections is enhanced by the human beings who people it, and by their actions. At the right, a company of gentlemen and ladies on horseback emerges from behind the rocks; in the centre, a caravan is resting, the horses unsaddled and some of them rolling in the grass; at the left, another caravan is leaving over a dangerous road winding around the cliff.

The most remarkable feature of this landscape is the almost incredibly exact rendition of every detail. Each object is delineated with a clear, sharp, and even contour. Every leaf of the trees and even such amorphous phenomena as clouds are exactly outlined. A vigorous colouring in blue, pink, green, and grey assists in the separation of one element from another.

This is the style one is prepared to encounter in the eighth century. It corresponds very neatly to the description of Li Ssŭ-hsün's style. What must come as a surprise to one who accepts the statements of later Chinese critics is the fact that it is also the style of Wang Wei.

There is only one work that can be connected with Wang Wei; it is an enormous scroll depicting his country seat near Wang-ch'uan. The original itself is lost, but the painting was famous and often copied. In 1617 A.D. it was engraved in stone, after a copy by Kuo Chung-shu (ca. 918-978), and rubbings of this engraving have often been published. It is clear that in this case only the general features have been preserved; but some of these features, such as a house which is represented with converging depth lines, indicate that the copy was reliable. After the tenth century such a representation would have been impossible; in the eighth century it was the most modern way to treat such a subject.

XVI. SECTION OF THE WANG CH'UAN SCROLL BY WANG WEI

XVII. SECTION OF THE WANG CH'UAN SCROLL BY WANG WEI

PAINTING

The British Museum possesses a copy of the Wang-ch'uan scroll made in 1309 A.D. by Chao Mēng-fu, according to an inscription. Attribution and date are doubtful; but it is not doubtful that Chao Mēng-fu copied after the great T'ang painters extensively. A copy by him certainly served as model for the version in London which is the work of an anonymous seventeenth century painter. The main point is that this copy of Wang Wei's famous painting uses blue and green colours, and the black contours are even heightened by thin lines in gold. This was a characteristic of Li Ssǔ-hsün's manner that is always mentioned; here it appears in a work that goes back to Wang Wei.

The Wang-ch'uan scroll is rather disappointing. It does not look like a landscape but more like an illustrated entry in a ground book. It depicts the mansion, the outhouses, parks, and orchards with sober fidelity. It, too, is but an aggregate of space cells.

TENTH CENTURY

A GLANCE at the landscapes of the tenth century suffices to show that painter and public saw and sought something new in nature. In what seems to be a mysterious way, the paintings appeal intensely to the spectator and succeed in stirring his emotions. A landscape of the eighth century may arouse one's curiosity: for the rest it leaves one unmoved.

It is certainly true to say that the attitude towards nature must have changed profoundly to bring forth such results. It would be naive to think that this alone sufficed. Since a painter has only one means for expressing himself, namely form, he must find the appropriate form for conveying this changed apprehension of nature. He did. The back wall of Cave 117 in Tun-huang, which can be dated between 980 and 1001 A.D., is covered with a vast landscape, the panorama of the Wu T'ai Shan. It carefully depicts the various monasteries and shrines of that sacred Buddhist mountain. The rendering of hills and edifices is singularly crude. Yet the painting is closed in composition because the whole is constructed with the help of a vanishing axis. The vast landscape is, in other words, conceived as a whole, and no longer as an aggregate of space cells. Space is no longer conceived as the nothing between solid bodies, but as something infinite, indivisible, and all-embracing. The elements of a landscape no longer build space, but exist in space.

A few other paintings of much higher quality prove that space was apprehended in this way before the end of the tenth century. Among them is the sixfold landscape screen of the Tōji in Kyōto. Temple tradition maintains that it was brought from China by Kōbō Daishi in 806 A.D. Some Japanese art historians think it a Japanese copy of the eleventh century after a much damaged Chinese original.[86]

However, such motives as lend themselves to comparison with Chinese paintings from the end of the eighth and beginning of the ninth century show no difference in style. This goes for men, animals, trees, and architecture; and it is certainly no unwarranted assumption that it also holds for the hills in the background (fig. 95).

The screen illustrates the visit of a young Chinese gentleman with a hermit. A house stands in a grove near a little stream in the foreground. Middle and background are occupied by softly rounded hills and by a large bay.

The men and the horse are drawn with the modulated line that was used in Mazār Tāgh at the end of the eighth century, on frescoes from Kumtura, and in numerous scrolls found in Tun-huang. The colouring is strong. The hills in the distance look as if they were powdered with snow; their tops are covered with opaque white, as the elevations of the middle ground are with green. These white and green patches, strongest along the upper edges, fade imperceptibly into the dark ground of the silk. This quick fading of colour is a new phenomenon. Another is the peculiar effect of the composition. Though the picture is intended to be narrative, in keeping with an old tradition, the eye is irresistibly drawn away from the scene in the foreground into the distance to wander there over the white-capped hills and explore the delightful inlet. It is a new sensation, that of space extending unchecked in all directions.

A group of landscapes show a remarkable similarity of technique with the screen in the Tōji. They are all winter landscapes; the hibernal effect is always achieved in the same way; thick white is laid upon the edges of knolls, slopes, hills, and mountains, and over trees and houses. These white patches always fade quickly into the artificially darkened ground. The impression is invariably sombre, for all forms emerge from a common dark ground in a pale and ghostly glow. The most striking of these landscapes is one in the Palace Museum in Peking (fig. 96).

The eye has some difficulty in connecting these shreds of white scattered over a dark ground. They reveal themselves as a rocky foreground with a group of trees that are executed with extraordinarily fine lines; then comes a body of water, suggested rather than represented; and then hills and mountains tower above one another. Form is rendered in a rather contradictory manner. The white, swiftly fading edges of hills and mountains have been mentioned. Men, trees, and huts are rendered with thin, sharp lines in black, but they cannot stand up against the white patches overlaying them. The white spatters determine the peculiar effect these landscapes produce; the eye is forced to move from one to the next, often by leaps and bounds. Yet the total effect is more homogeneous than that of any older landscape, for all elements have now a common visual denominator. It is true that this was done forcibly by the white snow that covers them all. But the final result is a unity that was neither sought nor achieved in former times.

PAINTING

The landscape in Peking does not stand alone. The British Museum possesses a scroll painting of a wintry landscape that is executed in the same style and technique. The two pictures must be contemporaneous, and from this point of view it is interesting that the scroll in London is attributed to Fan K'uan, a famous landscapist who worked from ca. 990-1030 A.D. Such an attribution does not carry much weight. It is valuable only as a possible hint at the time when such paintings were created.

It is, however, of interest that the same name is attached to a large winter landscape in Boston (fig. 97). Too little is known of the *œuvre* of Fan K'uan to prove or disprove the correctness of the ascription, and this goes for most painters of this and the following centuries. But in composition, treatment of form, and technique this painting is definitely earlier than the eleventh century. It is one of a fairly large group of pictures that adhere to the same decorative scheme, i.e., a definite pattern of form, composition, and expression under which nature was apprehended at a given time. In this case, a broad large mountain rises in the centre, dividing two small valleys.

The Boston landscape also glows in a spectral light, as if the mountains and rocks were illuminated from within. A peculiar treatment of form produces this effect: the edges are lighter than the rest. This was achieved by leaving the light silk practically untouched, and covering the interior with innumerable tiny dots in India ink. The general result comes close to that of the landscapes in white on black; it was achieved, however, by the reverse method of putting black ink on white ground.

By building up the whole picture in little dots, a unity was reached that excedes by far that of the paintings in white on black, the new technique being more flexible and allowing of subtler gradation. The Boston landscape, undoubtedly dependent on works like the one in Peking, is a true monochrome painting of the category the Chinese call *p'o mo* ("Breaking the Ink"), and we call *en lavis*.

Much has been written about this technique which plays a rôle in Far Eastern painting comparable in importance, though not in intention, to that of oil painting in Europe. Most of the explanations miss the point altogether. It has to do neither with calligraphy, which was practiced for three quarters of a millennium before the first true monochrome paintings appeared, nor with Ch'an Buddhism, which saw its heyday in the seventh and eighth century. The correct and simple answer to the problem is that the technique *en lavis* was not an end in itself, but only a means to a definite end. This end was the complete unification and merging of all picture elements. The resulting unity is something different from the unity as understood by a T'ang artist; at that time the parts and particles still retained some sort of independence; now they are completely subservient to the total effect. The breaking down of the separating lines and the abolishing of the separating colours were the obvious methods to employ in order to gain the desired effect. The winter landscapes in white on black were a first attempt to find for all phenomena a common visual denominator; with the discovery of the technique *en lavis* the goal was attained. It is patent that such an ideal could have been set up only after the classic ideal of perfect all-round clarity had lost its power. Some paintings are tinged with bluish green and very light brick red; but these two colours are so thin, and so delicately applied, that the basically monochrome character is in no way disturbed.

Later Chinese writers on art unanimously credit Wang Wei with the "invention" of monochrome painting; in this capacity he is called the founder of a Southern School, as opposed to a Northern School which used strong colours and was allegedly founded by Li Ssŭ-hsün. This sounds like a discrimination based on the typical styles of the T'ang and Sung painters. But masters who worked exclusively in monochrome were quite arbitrarily put into the Northern School. The division was first made at the beginning of the seventeenth century by Mo Shih-lung, a painter and critic; it became generally accepted when it was taken over by Tung Ch'i-ch'ang, the best known of all later writers on painting. The terms have no value whatever, and have hindered rather than helped a proper understanding of Chinese painting.

Wang Wei was certainly not the inventor of the technique *en lavis*. Yet it is a safe assumption that he, like so many of his contemporaries, painted a good many pictures in black and white, i.e., without any colours. Such pictures were called *po hua*, "white pictures." This is a very apt designation which describes the effect of such works admirably. It was used by Chang Yen-yüan in his *Li Tai Ming Hua Chi* of 847 A.D., when speaking of uncoloured frescoes. But there is no trace of evidence that Wang Wei ever substituted varying monochrome tones for colours, which is a very different thing from simply omitting them.

ELEVENTH CENTURY

EVERYONE familiar with Chinese painting must have been struck by the fact that all pictures composed after the schema described above are consistently attributed to artists of the tenth and early eleventh century, and that they represent almost exclusively winter scenes.

In the Boston landscape, rocks and trees have a compactness that differs very advantageously from the effect given by the white shreds with which they were previously represented. The first enthusiasm on discovering this new world, which had led the painter to pile mountain above mountain in fantastic shapes, is gone; he has become conscious of the immense task ahead of him.

Pointillism was not the only technique known to the painters at the end of the tenth and the beginning of the eleventh century. Other artists used broad, crumbly lines combined with washes; rocks so treated look as if fashioned of cotton wool. Yet when it came to creating a picture, these painters adhered to the decorative scheme of their time with tenacity, as may be seen in a winter landscape in the Freer Gallery (fig. 98).

In spirit and treatment of form it differs from the landscape in Boston; in composition and motive it comes very close to it. Here again are the two small valleys divided in the centre by a mountain. The meticulous care with which every detail is rendered is another trait it shares with the early landscapes. The painting was once attributed to Wang Wei, and it is possible that the rather ludicrous rocks go back to forms Wang Wei may have used.

The landscape is a charming picture that interprets nature in a spirit of gay adventure. It is important because it provides a clue to how the artist wants it to be looked at. The scene is entered at the right bottom, over a little bridge; after a little rest in the village that nestles at the foot of the towering mountain, the eye follows the road winding around the precipitous crags to where it disappears below the top. By this device it is clearly indicated that height was then considered the most impressive and most characteristic dimension. Depth is there, but it scarcely counts.

Strangely enough, it was this peculiar way of depicting rocks that became a most important feature during the eleventh century. The greatest figure in Chinese painting of that century was Kuo Hsi (ca. 1020-1090). The Palace Museum in Peking possesses a large landscape by him, dated in 1072 A.D.[87] In composition it follows the schema of the Freer landscape; an enormous mountain, dividing two valleys, ascends from the foreground. The rocks look like crumpled pillows; their contours, when there are contours, are soft, broad, and crumbling, and so are the washes of India ink. The trees are twisted and their boughs drawn with many short curly strokes. The same style is found in a scroll depicting the scenes along a wintry river, in the Museum in Toledo, Ohio (fig. 99). The utter gloom and desolation of nature on a dark day in winter is admirably felt and represented. Better known and often reproduced is a scroll in the Freer Gallery, entitled *Autumn in the Valley of the Huang-ho*.[88] It is more delicate in facture and more variegated in motive. The scroll opens with the view of a receding valley; a large mountain separates it from another valley with a town in the distance, faintly visible in the autumnal haze. A large knoll brings the eye back to the foreground, where a farm house stands under a few trees; immediately behind it is a steep mountain and another town in the misty distance. The end is the most remarkable part: a vista over rolling country to far-away hills.

Such scrolls, which are sometimes very long (the one in the Freer Gallery measures 26 cm. by 206 cm.; others are as long as 12 m.), were used from the beginning, even for landscapes. It was the ideal format for narrative painting, and it never lost this character completely. It always gave an opportunity for a broad and leisurely

111

account. It must be borne in mind that such a scroll was slowly unrolled with the right and rolled up with the left hand so as to show but a comparatively small section at a time.

The scroll in the Freer Gallery begins with a familiar motive, the mountain dividing two valleys. Yet the effect is totally different from that of older landscapes; the eye does not climb the mountain, but is drawn into the distance. This is something new, as is the observation of atmosphere and its use to bring about the effect of depth.

Looking back upon the early landscapes (fig. 96-98), it will be noticed that a form in the background was rendered with as much exactness as one near by. Space seemed to be filled with crystal clear air. Kuo Hsi was very likely not the first to observe that things lose in substance and distinctness with increasing distance. But he made systematic use of this phenomenon in his pictures, and expressly mentions it in his essay on landscape painting.

Along with the observation of atmospheric effects goes a remarkable change in problem; distance becomes of overwhelming interest to the landscapist. Depth replaces height as the direction symbolic of the boundlessness of space. The discovery of atmosphere and its qualities amounted to the possibility of making space itself visible, by the ingenious reasoning that space is filled with air, and air is perceptible in the state of mist, fog, and haze.

Pointillism, first met with in the Boston landscape (fig. 97), was used by the master who painted a magnificent mountain view in the Palace Museum in Peking.[89] The work is attributed to Kuan T'ung who lived in the first half of the tenth century. In subject matter and composition this painting comes very close to another grandiose mountain landscape in the same museum, which is ascribed to Fan K'uan,[90] and to the landscape of 1072 by Kuo Hsi. In the alleged Fan K'uan, the dots are replaced by delicate washes. What with their composition and the subtle use of atmospheric observations, the two landscapes are certainly works of the eleventh century. It is interesting to note that Kuo Hsi speaks of two distinct styles being in vogue during his time; one, he states, goes back to Li Ch'ēng (916-975), the other to Fan K'uan. The two styles can be easily discerned in the extant paintings from the eleventh century.

What became of pointillism at the end of the eleventh century can be seen in the small landscape (fig. 100) by Chao Ta-nien (active ca. 1080-ca. 1100). Only two works of this gentle artist have survived. What lends the *Cottage by the Lake* its specific character is the clear division into fore, middle and background. The artistic and objective centre of gravity is laid in the middle ground, as of old. Though only half of it is filled with form, it is heavy enough to prevail over the foreground and the background.

PAINTING

TWELFTH CENTURY

The twelfth century saw important changes in the conception of a landscape. The vast vistas of mountains, deep valleys, and rushing streams were replaced by less pretentious themes. The spectator is moved more closely to the objects. This narrowing of the section presented in a picture was anything but a simplification or impoverishment. It was made possible by a deeper and more mature understanding of nature; only now, when the interdependence and interrelation of all her elements were grasped, could the part stand for the whole. The restriction in motive holds for large paintings as well as for small ones, though small formats seem to have become more popular than before. This means that a leading motive takes the place of many motives of equal importance. At the same time, form was rendered more broadly, freely and loosely. The artist strove more consciously than ever before to make the parts merge and to attain movement from form to form.

All this is evident in an admirable fan painting of a few bare trees and rocks in the Museum of Fine Arts in Boston (fig. 101). There is the soft and crumbly line that often broadens into dark blotches, and the characteristic alienation of representation from its object. The painting is often ascribed to Fan K'uan; and though it is impossible to attribute it to a definite master, it is possible to ascribe it to one who worked in the twelfth century. In fact its style, especially the rendering of the trees, brings it very close to a famous winter landscape by Li Ti, one of the great painters of that epoch, who lived and worked from ca. 1100 to at least 1187 A.D.

As the style is different from anything painted during the eleventh century, so is the spirit in which the theme is conceived. These trees are no longer taken as more or less interesting motives, as they had been in the works attributed to Li Ch'êng and Kuo Hsi; they are rather the visible expression of that mysterious force of the soil that made them grow and survive in the relentless struggle for life. The idea of the identity of all things has found in such paintings its adequate visual expression. Small in size and insignificant in motive as these landscapes may appear, they possess a symbolic grandeur. This is a symbolism incomparably more profound than the ludicrous symbolism of homophones in later Chinese painting which does not rise above the level of a pun or rebus.

The *Bare Trees* in Boston resemble very much in style another painting there, a shivering lady by the side of a wintry lake (fig. 102). In composition this work adheres very strictly to the scheme of Li Ti's two famous landscapes. The small foreground, with tree and ascending ground pushed to one side, is a typically atectonic arrangement. Middle and background are veiled by mist. This device, suggestive of an indefinite extension of space, was for some time used by every great painter. Another characteristic trait is that the solid objects are placed in one half of the picture, the halving being done by an imaginary diagonal.

PAINTING

The picture of the lady in the winter landscape is attributed to Ma Yüan, one of the greatest painters not only of China, but of the whole world, born probably around 1150, and living into the twenties of the thirteenth century. The likely reason for this attribution is the fact that one of his most famous works, the *Scholar Gazing at the Moon,* is composed in exactly the same way.[91] There, too, a rock occupies the foreground, and an overhanging cliff with a tree is placed at the left side; middle and background are filled by a nocturnal haze in which floats the moon.

To call such landscapes romantic, as many Westerners are inclined to do, sadly misses the point. They are not intended to express the wish to flee from the sordid realities of life; they do not conjure a world of dreams. They express rather the great and mysterious power of nature to console man, to set his mind at rest, and to strengthen his soul. Laurence Binyon has described their purpose admirably: "It is not an escape from life, but to life."

All this holds, too, for the three landscapes of *Summer, Autumn,* and *Winter* in the Konchiin in Kyōto. The *Summer* is composed exactly like the *Scholar Gazing at the Moon* by Ma Yüan. A gentleman leans on a tree and looks up into the sky where a few clouds drift in the gentle breeze and two cranes wing away into the infinite (fig. 103). The serenity of nature and the bliss and delight she bestows on man were never and nowhere more intensely expressed. *Autumn* and *Winter* depict with equal power the turbulence and adversity of which nature is also capable, and show man as braving and defying them. Of such landscapes it may truly be said that *paysage, c'est un état de l'âme.* These three landscapes are often attributed to the emperor Hui Tsung. There can be no doubt that they were painted at the end of the twelfth century.

In *Autumn and Winter,* a few forms emerge from the mist that envelops the background. This is exactly what can be seen on many landscapes painted in the decades around 1200 A.D. A typical example is the fan-shaped picture in Berlin (fig. 104). It presents a favourite motive of that epoch, a man looking into the landscape, thus acting as a guide to the spectator. He sits at the bend of a road, contemplating a waterfall across a stream. The composition is characteristically acentric. Haze and mist have lifted sufficiently for water to be seen coming over a rocky ledge, and debouching in a gully. By letting form appear in the background, the problem of depth, which had been shelved for a long time, again became actual. The rocky mass at one side of the foreground assumes a new rôle; it serves as *repoussoir,* i.e., as a sort of diving board whence the eye plunges into depth. The deliberate contrast of dark and light and the diagonal arrangement facilitate this movement. In short, the spectator is forced to connect the things close by with those far away and the result is a definite sensation of space. Compared with earlier paintings where depth was also represented, it is an important innovation that the elements in the background are so treated as to lead the eye out into infinity.

This little landscape is the work of Li Kung-nien, an artist working around 1200

PAINTING

A.D. He belongs to that galaxy of painters who were born between 1150 and the end of the century. The greatest of them was Hsia Kuei. The exact dates of his birth and death are unknown, like those of his rival and contemporary Ma Yüan. Both were active from the seventies of the twelfth to the twenties of the thirteenth century. Both were members of the Academy, attained the rank of *tai-chao,* and were awarded the "Golden Girdle," the highest decoration an artist could expect.

Ma Yüan and Hsia Kuei are usually mentioned together as the greatest artists of their time. They fully deserve this praise. But, great as Ma Yüan was, Hsia Kuei was greater still. Enough had survived of their *œuvres* to venture the verdict. Ma Yüan clings more to tradition; he renders his rocks and trees in a manner which he shares with many other painters. In his famous *Rain in the Mountains,* in the Iwasaki Collection, he uses the old formulæ to discriminate between the several kinds of trees. These formulæ consist of tiny and closely packed linear patterns in the shape of characteristic leaves. The practice had its origin in the way T'ang painters represented the foliage of various trees. The smallness of these particles enables a painter to use the new formulæ without running the risk that they will stand out as a linear section in an otherwise painterly work. Their effect is rather one of a mass than of single elements. In this manner they were used in the grandiose mountain landscape attributed to Fan K'uan, in the Palace Museum in Peking, and throughout the twelfth century. When handled with understanding and sensitivity, as by Ma Yüan and his contemporary Liu Sung-nien, a group of trees looks remarkably neat (fig. 105). This is solid and reliable craftsmanship, well founded in the past.

Yet these huts, rocks and trees appear rather dry when compared with a work by Hsia Kuei (fig. 106). Here, the wind blows, the air is humid, the trees shake their leaves grown luscious in the warmth of the summer. Hsia Kuei achieves this effect of movement and life with innumerable broad little strokes of no definite shape, varying in direction and tone, but meaningless in themselves.

He used the same technique in the small landscape of the Del Drago Collection in New York (fig. 107). The quiet and peace of a summer evening when the fisherman returns to his cottage and the birds fly home is admirably represented. The composition, with its emphasis on horizontals, contributes much to this effect; yet by opposing a broadly treated and optically heavy foreground to a softer, lighter, and summarily treated background, the impression of great depth is attained. The eye glides over these halcyon waters to be lost in the space beyond the distant hills.

Paintings like this appeal at once to the Westerner because the horizon is very low and the ground in the picture seems to continue the ground upon which the spectator stands. This apprehension of space was popular with Chinese artists for some time shortly after 1200 A.D. Ma Yüan, too, was aware of it, as is shown by his landscape in Boston (fig. 108). Here the foreground with its elegant willow tree has lost in importance; the interest is shifted to a rather distant middle ground that recedes diagonally into a hazy depth.

PAINTING

It was at this time that Chinese landscapists discovered the "oversized" foreground and its power to propel the eye into depth.

The horizon is also very low in the magnificent picture of a mountain brook in the Freer Gallery (fig. 109). The motive could not be simpler: a wall of rocks, polished by the little rivulet for millions of years, a few trees upon the high ledge, and a slight haze over the brook. But here is the grandeur of nature, before which all the sorrows and ambitions of man become utterly insignificant.

The painting is inscribed Ma Yüan, but this is definitely a later addition. Half effaced is the signature of Hsia Kuei. It is more than plausible that he created this work. Its style is certainly that of the beginning of the thirteenth century. And there was no man besides Hsia Kuei then living, whose heart was great enough to see such greatness in so humble a subject.

THIRTEENTH CENTURY

The relative firmness of form and solidity of space were given up by the next generation. Hsia Kuei himself did not pay so much attention to them in his late works. Painters such as Mu-ch'i (1181-1269), Liang K'ai and others dissolved form to a degree unheard of in the immediate past and they composed their landscapes to appear as if seen by someone floating in the air. Nothing is more instructive than to compare the new rendering of an old theme, that of huts under trees by a lake, with those of former times (fig. 110). Chao Ta-nien had treated it (fig. 99), and Hsia Kuei also (fig. 109). When the two paintings are placed alongside each other, it will become clear what I meant by the increasingly broader and looser treatment of form, the fusion of elements, and the working out of a leading motive.

The picture on fig. 110 is variously ascribed to Mu-ch'i or Ma Lin, the son of Ma Yüan. What the attributions amount to is the knowledge that it is the work of a painter belonging to the generation after Hsia Kuei and Ma Yüan. This dissolution by excessive vapours, rain, and mist was a device widely employed by Mu-ch'i, Ying Yü-chien and others in their landscapes and paintings of animals. It was but a pretext for breaking up form into small, seemingly incoherent splashes and strokes of ink. It would prove hard to find an objective reason why any such blotch or stroke stood at its place or had its particular tone. Form appears as torn and shredded, and the eye is meant to see that a painting is no longer the result of long and careful observation, but of sudden inspiration. In fact this stress laid upon instantaneous enlightenment, as though the artist had been struck by his motive with irresistible force and had to work rapidly to catch up with it, is highly characteristic of these painters. It gives their works a curious resemblance, independent of motive; the

PAINTING

Magpie by Mu-ch'i, the *Li Po* by Liang K'ai and the *Mountain Village* by Ying Yü-chien treat their subject matters in the same manner.

This last phase in the evolution is often presented as a special development restricted to members of the Ch'an sect. It is true that the flash of inspiration, after long meditation, played a great rôle in the teaching of that sect; it is also true that Mu-ch'i was a Ch'an priest, like Wu-chun, his teacher (d.1249 A.D.), and Ying Yü-chien. It is also true that Liang K'ai, a *tai-chao* in the Academy and decorated with the Golden Girdle, gave up his official position and evidently became deeply interested in Ch'an Buddhism. Yet there was no such thing as a special "Ch'an style"; there was only the last phase of the baroque style in Chinese painting. Its roots go back to late works of Hsia Kuei's, like the *Autumnal Storm* in the Kawasaki Collection in Kobe.[92] It was shared by many painters, some of whom were Ch'an monks and some of whom had nothing to do with Buddhism. It is the style of a generation rather than a religious sect. It is more than probable that this style found a friendlier reception in the monastery than in the Academy, to which this radical destruction of form must have appeared revolutionary.

As is so often the case, a style that was decried as revolutionary by one generation, or part of it, quietly became the generally accepted style of the next.

FOURTEENTH CENTURY

A WORLD soaked in humidity, which in the shape of clouds, mist, and fog occupies the better parts of a picture, is still the ideal landscape for Kao K'o-kung (1248-1310).[93] Like Mu-ch'i in his views of lakes and streams, he uses broad watery washes to represent the foliage of trees;[94] he usually represents them in clumps, and then a single broad wash suffices to depict them. In some of his large paintings he introduces a new manner; a mountain side is built up of many small, short and broad horizontal strokes. A small landscape which is ascribed to him and certainly shows his characteristic style is in the Del Drago Collection (fig. 111). Its subject matter is quite familiar: a few huts under trees, near a body of water, and mountains in the background. There is still a great deal of mist, but it is an innovation that it has gathered in rather definite shapes. New, too, is the treatment of the mountains in the distance, in the same deep and heavy tones of ink as the objects near by. Mountains, clouds, and groups of trees form large coherent masses which are little differentiated. All the solid parts are rendered with the typical horizontal strokes.

The same attitude toward form and the same mannerism can be found in the admirable view over hills and mountains in the Freer Gallery (fig. 112). It is incomparably more delicate in feeling and more subtle in execution. The peculiar technique of rendering trees and mountains by innumerable little horizontal strokes is said to

PAINTING

have been a revival of a technique first used by Mi Fei (1051-1107) and his son Mi Yu-jēn (1086-1165). A great many paintings, some of them with long, dated inscriptions, claim to be the works of these two artists. All of them are done in the extremely mature, diffuse style that is characteristic of the end of the thirteenth century. That a contemporary of Kuo Hsi and Chao Ta-nien should have painted them is as likely as if a contemporary of Jan van Eyck should have painted in the manner of Frans Hals.

Kao's style is the direct descendant of the style that reigned about the middle of the thirteenth century. This is true also for that of a painter like Yin-t'o-lo who, despite the transliteration of the Indian name Indra, was a native Chinese; he painted Buddhist subjects from before 1274 until after 1288 A.D. Even a member of the younger generation, such as Wu Chēn (1280-1354), was deeply indebted to Mu-ch'i and his fellow artists. His magnificent *Bamboos* in Boston uphold in form and spirit the best tradition of the thirteenth century (fig. 113).

It was different, however, when it came to landscapes. Wu Chēn's mountains, trees, and villages no longer rise from a sea of mist; the single object regains importance and asserts itself with greater emphasis than in the last one hundred and fifty years.

This attitude is carried much farther in the early paintings of Huang Kung-wang (1269-1354). He left a few pictures of hills and plains with their coat of trees, bushes, and scrubs.[95] There is no leading motive; everything is of equal interest to him. No part is hidden by haze or fog; the whole landscape is bathed in a clear light.

For his trees Huang Kung-wang uses a formula which is plainly derived from paintings like those of Kao K'o-kung's: a cluster of small broad horizontal strokes. Yet in such works Huang Kung-wang had discovered aspects of nature that were formerly ignored. It was not breath-taking beauty he looked for, but simple, soothing, unaffected plainness. This rather humble apprehension of nature prevails also in the *œuvre* of Wang Mēng (1308-1385).[96]

Due to the impartiality with which everything is depicted, such landscapes often lack clarity. In his later works, Huang Kung-wang tries to avoid this by reducing a landscape to its essentials. He does so by giving only a few large forms. The result is more lucid, but at the same time curiously weak (fig. 114). A web of dry lines is cast over the surface of the picture; there is little depth and no atmosphere in it.

It was this peculiar style which deeply impressed Ni Tsan (1301-1474). A landscape in the Del Drago Collection deals with the old subject matter of cottages by a lake (fig. 115). Such an anæmic painting expressed, as he himself said, the overflowing joy of his heart. On another occasion he wrote that what he calls painting does not exceed the joy of careless sketching with a brush; yet he had to confess that these children of his joy often met with fierce disapproval: "People went away insulting, scolding, and cursing in every possible way."[97]

PAINTING

Ni Tsan also asserted that he did not wish to represent the likeness of things. These were typically Sung ideas; they were already expressed by Su Tung-p'o (1036-1101).[98] This famous poet, statesman, and calligraphist was deeply interested in painting. He coined the term "gentleman painter" for one who did not so much care for the outward appearance of things as for the expression of their "essence." Cognition of this "essence" is not the result of study, but of sudden inspiration. But even "essence" had to be interpreted by form; these forms expressing "essence" were in fact but formulæ which by common agreement were accepted in this rôle.

It is usually ignored that Su Tung-p'o wrote *pro domo*. He defended and explained the attitude of a small group of talented scholars who considered themselves different from and superior to the "professionals." The professionals of his time were the members of the Imperial Academy. They, too, were gentlemen; but their status forced them to paint, whether they felt like it or not. There had been no such distinction in the T'ang epoch; Chang Yen-yüan could write in his *Li Tai Ming Hua Chi* that "from old, painters were gentlemen and literati, famous among their contemporaries, and influencing the future; the lowly cannot do this."

Under the Yüan dynasty (1271-1368), a period of foreign rule, patriotism came to bear on the question. Huang Kung-wang, after having been a clerk for some years, held no office; Ts'ao Chih-po (1272-1355), a forerunner of Ni Tsan, and Wu Chēn lived as hermits, Ni Tsan as a private scholar with independent means. All of them declined to serve under the usurpers. Their contempt for the professionals, i.e., those who worked at the court, was not only a matter of art, but also one of politics. To the "gentlemen painters" the professionals were renegades and hateful collaborationists.

The first of the court painters was Chao Mēng-fu, Duke of Wei (1254-1322), equally famous as statesman, poet, calligraphist, and painter. As a painter, he was also the exponent of a neo-classicism in which many artists saw salvation from the utter destruction of form wrought by a baroque style. Chao and his followers turned deliberately to the linear art of the great T'ang masters. Chao himself said of his pictures that they came close to the models of old, and considered that as the decisive criterion of their quality.

As a matter of fact, the T'ang style with its ideal of perfect clarity, its sharp contours and bright colours has never completely died. At long intervals appeared artists who, by inclination or disposition, felt attracted by an art that interpreted the world in terms of exact forms. Li Lung-mien (1049-1106) was one, Chao Po-chü another. The latter worked under Kao Tsung (1127-1162), and was in fact a favourite painter of that emperor. His long scroll in the Museum of Fine Arts in Boston, entitled *The First Han Emperor Entering the Capital of Ch'in*

PAINTING

is a magnificent work of narrative character.[99] Its style is deliberately antiquated. As always, however, the achievements of the intervening time left their indelible mark; space is here apprehended as infinite, and though the rendering of rocks and palaces clings to the decorative schema of the seventh and eighth century, the trees are plainly done by a Sung artist.

It was not different with Chao Mēng-fu. Though he left a few paintings of horses that follow very closely those ascribed to Li Lung-mien who, in turn, emulated Han Kan, such works are scarcely more than free copies, or, at best, paraphrases of old paintings. There is no originality whatsoever in them. But when he is not dependent on ancient painting, Chao reveals himself a master. His *Departure of Wēn-chi* of 1301 A.D., in the Del Drago Collection, is the work of a truly great artist (fig. 117). Its most striking feature is the contrast between the large landscape in monochrome, and the small figures before a tent which were painted with clear lines and strong colours. These tiny figures are placed in the right corner at the bottom, i.e., according to the Chinese way of looking at a picture, at the very entrance. They are the actors of a human tragedy. Wēn-chi, captured in 195 A.D. by raiding Huns, and finally ransomed by her father, is about to leave her barbarian husband and the sons she had borne him. The figures in the painting are lined up in a row. What makes them great and unforgettable is the way in which the grief of their faces increases as the eye wanders along them: from the distressed maids to the husband who is deeply moved as he offers the cup of leave, on to the boy who implores his mother to stay: another son, a babe in arms, is presented to Wēn-chi who seems at the point of breaking down; behind her a maid cries openly into her sleeve (fig. 116).

The scene takes place at the foot of some barren hills. There is a suggestion of the endless steppe behind these hills. Only a great artist could thus oppose the indifference of Nature to human grief.

Scenes from the life of horsemen and hunters were close to the hearts of the new rulers of China. Many pictures, large or small, show life in the grasslands. They are usually executed with thin, fine and even lines, dark brown, a bright blue, and light red. A cluster of subdued green dots at the feet of animal and man is often the sole indication of the ground. This device, usually coupled with an acentric composition, most forcefully evokes the immensity of the steppe. Such paintings were possible only after the great masters of the twelfth century had discovered the charm and suggestiveness of a veiled background.

Chao Mēng-fu became so famous during his life for his paintings of horses that practically every mediocre picture of horses is ascribed to him. There must have been many artists who treated the same subject matter. One who reached him in quality was Jēn Jēn-fa. His *Feeding of the Horses in Moonlight* in the Victoria and Albert Museum in London is his best known work of that genre. But Jēn Jēn-fa excelled also in scenes depicting the ideal life of scholars: inspecting paintings and calligraphy, reciting poetry, listening to music, drinking, or relaxing out in the country near a murmuring brook. They are delightful works: the figures are drawn with unsurpassable elegance, trees and rocks with an unremitting love for detail. Like Chao, he relied on a fine line and strong colours. This is, of course, the characteristic neo-classic style. It is also found in the excellent landscape with two horsemen in Boston (fig. 118). A work like this shows better than words that a new objectivity had sprung up, and a new respect for each and every thing.

To sum up: in the fourteenth century, one has to reckon with three distinct styles. There was first the neo-classic style, which enjoyed official recognition as the leading form of visual expression. Secondly, there was the style of Kao K'o-kung and the early Huang Kung-wang; it sprang from the mature baroque style of the middle of the thirteenth century, but developed into something new when Huang saw nature with impartial interest. Tonality disappeared in this style; a picture is built up of innumerable elements, all of them presented with crumbly lines. The *œuvre* of Wang Mēng belongs to this category. Thirdly, there is the style that was created by the late Huang and Ts'ao Chih-po, and consummated by Ni Tsan. It also is a linear style, though the line is not strong, even, and continuous, but intermittent, brittle, and frail. This is a pure and unadulterated manneristic style, working with cut-and-dried formulæ. It was and remained the style of the scholars who fancied themselves artists.

FIFTEENTH CENTURY

WHEN the native Ming dynasty came to power in 1368 A.D., the political antagonism between the independent gentlemen painters and the court painters became meaningless; the artistic antagonism however stayed on. As time went on, it became increasingly the antagonism between the arrogant dilettante and the genuine artist. There is no doubt that a strong national feeling tinged every field of Chinese life at the beginning of the Ming epoch. The Ming rulers stressed the fact that they were true Chinese, and that they took up where the Chinese Sung had been forced out by the foreign Mongols. This general spirit of national renaissance is well reflected in the kind of painting that was favoured and aided in official quarters. The new programme was announced as early as toward the end of the fourteenth century, when Wang Li, physician, poet, and painter wrote: "There are many fields of painting, but I love landscape painting most. Of painters there are many; but I appreciate Ma Yüan, Ma Kuei (the less gifted brother of Ma Yüan), Ma Lin and Hsia Kuei most."[100] This must have been an opinion held by many; it was certainly the guiding principle of the reorganized Academy. For more than a hundred and fifty years artists strove to paint pictures in the vein of the great Sung masters.

PAINTING

The new interest in Ma Yüan and Hsia Kuei led to extensive study and copying of their works. One of the most interesting and revealing of such copies is the long scroll in the Freer Gallery. Not so long ago this scroll was considered to be an original by Ma Yüan. In fact it is a more or less free replica of the wonderful scroll by Hsia Kuei in the National Museum in Peking. Another though not complete copy is in the Metropolitan Museum in New York. It was made at about the same time as that in Washington and is done in the same characteristic style of which I shall presently speak, but is correctly attributed to Hsia Kuei. This ignorance about the authorship is quite telling; after two hundred years the two great masters had merged into the great ideal Sung landscapist who usually passed by the name of Ma Yüan.

The scroll in the Freer Gallery has three dated inscriptions; one, in minute script, contains the date 1192 A.D., and this is very likely the year when the original was painted. A long inscription in thin characters tells that Yung-lo had bought the picture in 1380, though he showed it only 27 years later. The writer, Chin Yu-tzŭ (1368-1431), a well-known scholar and collector, saw it in 1421. Since there is no reason to doubt the authenticity of the inscription or the veracity of its content, the scroll was probably painted about 1380 A.D. The third inscription, of 1428, is unimportant. As far as the general features go, the copy follows the original rather faithfully; but here and there new elements were introduced, such as mountains in the background where the original has none; sometimes the copyist compressed a scene where Hsia Kuei had presented wide open spaces, as at the very beginning of the scroll. Most striking is the difference in the rendering of trees and rocks; they are coarser and cruder in rendering, and therefore more isolated within the whole; they stand out more harshly than they ever did in a painting of around 1200 A.D.

This was not an individual peculiarity of the copyist, but a distinctive characteristic of his generation. The same treatment is found in a great many large landscapes, as in the magnificent painting in the Freer Gallery (fig. 119). It is typical of such landscapes that the steep mountains of the background are as "heavy" as any form in the foreground. The representation of rocks is especially characteristic; they have broad surfaces of which the nearer one stands in almost pure white before a black one; the edges of such rocks are left white, and indicated by a few coarse oblique strokes. The distribution of dark units, independent of the distance from the spectator, and the somewhat schematic application of empty patches suggesting atmosphere are more traits specific of this style.

Another and rather amusing difference from Sung landscapes may be pointed out. When a Ma Yüan, a Hsia Kuei or a Liu Sung-nien painted a house, a bridge, or a fence, it was always done with a few broad swift strokes that made the thing look rather ramshackle; the painters of the fifteenth century invariably represented these objects very neatly as if the carpenter had just left. The houses and pavilions

PAINTING

are usually well-kept and sometimes luxurious edifices. There is an air of well-to-do respectability in these works that is absent in the paintings of the Sung artists. It will be noticed that the attitude toward nature has again changed. It is neither her greatness nor her bounty the artist tries to express. He stresses those aspects that might appeal to the scholarly gentleman.

The same atmosphere of leisure in comfort occurs in a charming little album leaf in the Del Drago Collection (fig. 120). It permeates also the only certain painting of Chou Wēn-ching, dated in 1463 A.D. It represents a gentleman sitting in a sumptuous pavilion, looking out over a lotus pond in the mountains. Chou Wēn-ching is reported to have despised the crude style of his contemporaries, and essayed to come as close as possible to the Sung models. In fact there is a delicacy and subtlety of tone in his picture that differs very advantageously from the coarse facture of most fifteenth century landscapes. A magnificent painting in the Freer Gallery comes very close in spirit and style to his picture of 1463 (fig. 121). Legendary or historical scenes were now often immersed in a vast landscape, as here, where King Wēn of Chou visits the sage Chiang Tzŭ-ya.

Chou Wēn-ching was called to the court at about 1426 A.D., together with another painter, Tai Chin, one of the great masters of his century. By 1436, envious colleagues had succeeded in making Tai Chin's position untenable. He returned home and lived henceforth by his art; he died in poverty.

Tai Chin was too independent to stick to a single manner throughout his life, which seems to have lasted quite long. An early work of his, a view along a winding river with a town at the foot of an overhanging mountain, in the Preetorius Collection in Munich, shows him still dependent on Wang Mēng. The Palace Museum in Peking possesses a large landscape that comes as close to a painting done about 1200 A.D. as was possible for an artist of the fifteenth century. By 1440-1446 he had developed a loose and nervous style of his own, as dated pictures prove. And there is finally a scroll depicting a *Storm along the River,* in the Freer Gallery (fig. 123), where he employs broad soft washes, as did the painters of a younger generation, like Chang Lu (ca. 1464-1538) and Wu Wei (1458-1508).

Of Chang Lu it is reported that he followed Wu Wei in his figures and Tai Chin in his landscapes. In a very few works he treats his subjects in a rather objective way, but most of his paintings were done in an extremely broad manner. The *Scholar Wandering along a Mountain Stream,* in the Del Drago Collection, is a typical example of it (fig. 124). The patches of thin watery ink were used by many painters of this generation, especially by the members of the Chē School, so-called after the province of Chēkiang where most of them were born and lived; they held "finish in utter disdain." Lü Chi and Lin Liang, both active ca. 1488-1505 and famous as painters of birds, treated these animals exactly as Wu Wei and Chang Lu treated their figures and landscapes. The nervous, even irritated technique was meant to suggest that such pictures were painted rapidly in a state of high excitement, with the brush flying over silk or paper to catch up with the fleeting impressions of an eye that sees large forms and disregards details. The same attitude and a similar style existed in the first half of the thirteenth century; yet, for once, this broad manner of Tai Chin's and Chang Lu's was not fashioned after an earlier style. The change from the early to the late style of Tai Chin was a natural and logical evolution.

It seems that the revived and simplified pseudo-Sung style lived on throughout the second half of the fifteenth century. An eminently characteristic work of this kind is the landscape illustrated in fig. 125. Such paintings are commonly attributed to the Chē School, if they are not presented as Sung paintings. They are mostly of considerable size. They possess a certain brutal force and serve well as pieces of decoration. They have nothing to do with Tai Chin and his followers; they are the vulgar descendants of paintings like that illustrated in fig. 119. They have still less to do with Hsia Kuei and Ma Yüan, for whose works they often pass in public and private collections all over the world. They are exactly three hundred years younger than they pretend to be.

A few words must be said about portrait painting. The upper classes needed portraits to display in funeral processions and to hang in ancestral halls. They were sometimes made during the lifetime of an individual, but more often after his death. Strict likeness was an implicit postulate; artistic merit did not matter very much, and in most cases free use was made of this license. It is, therefore, not surprising that but a few portraits of quality are known.

Ch'ēn Chien-ju, who was called the first painter of the Yüan dynasty by Hsia Wēn-yen in 1365 A.D., painted the Korean statesman Li Ch'i-hsien in 1319 A.D.[101] It is a delicate work, in the tradition of thirteenth century portraits. To the fifteenth century can be ascribed the pictures of a gentleman, I Chai-ts'ao by name, and his wife, by their grandnephew Tsu Tē, in the Del Drago Collection.[102] One picture bears a date that probably corresponds to the year 1441 A.D. More striking still is the portrait of an old lady in the same collection (fig. 126). In these three paintings the heads are seen full face, and not in three-quarter view as formerly; from the beginning of the fourteenth century down to our day, there exist enough dated or datable portraits to show that the sitter was always presented in a strictly frontal pose.

But all this is irrelevant beside the incredible insight into human nature and the ability to express it in adequate forms. The head of the old lady is more than a mere likeness; a long life, with its joys and griefs, its triumphs and disappointments, has shaped this face. This was a woman of strong will and uncommon intelligence. Hers are eyes that are not deceived by appearances. Her thin mouth is slightly contemptuous of this world and its pretensions. It is quite in character that this lady should have turned to Buddhism and devoted herself to Kuan-yin, the Bodhisattva of Mercy, whose embossed image she wears in her headdress.

As a whole, portraits of the sixteenth century show little of the strength that was apparently quite common in the fifteenth. The ancestor portraits that are usually seen in Western museums and private collections are mostly of very recent date. With their garish colours and lifeless draughtsmanship they are exceptionally devoid of artistic merit.

SIXTEENTH TO EIGHTEENTH CENTURY

THE neo-classic style which saw its heyday in the fourteenth century was pushed in the background during the fifteenth century, as can be well understood. Yet an inveterate adherent of it like Shih Jui was called to the court in 1426 A.D., with Tai Chin and Chou Wēn-ching. Shih Jui painted landscapes with minute details, executed in extremely fine lines and gorgeous colours. His art is directly descended from the court art of the Yüan. Its ideal of clarity, at least, was kept alive by Chou Ch'ēn, who must have lived from ca. 1450 until ca. 1535 A.D. Compared with his fellow artists Wu Wei and Chang Lu and their reckless handling of form, he appears a timid soul. By nature, he was interested in the solid and lasting, not in the ephemeral aspects of nature. He found an adequate means of expression by putting the monochrome Sung manner at the service of a very detailed representation. His pictures are often hard and dry. But his rocks have a stony character, differing very much from the soft, crumbly things Tai Chin had introduced. His style is a curious and quite successful blend of two apparently incompatible tendencies. His influence reached beyond China. Kano Motonobu (1479-1559), the great Japanese painter and founder of the Kano School, was as profoundly indebted to him as Sesshū (1420-1506) was to the *fauves* of the last decades in the fifteenth century.

Chou Ch'ēn himself painted occasionally landscapes in the vein and manner of the Yüan academicians, i.e., with extremely fine lines and a few strong colours. He was not the only artist of his time who tried to revive the delicate and sumptuous style of the fourteenth century. Lü Chi, the painter of birds and flowers, did so, too, and quite successfully. I mentioned him already as having treated his subjects in the rather flashy manner of Chang Lu and Wu Wei. But along with these monochrome pictures he produced others in rich colours; in them he showed himself so dependent on the works of Wang Yüan, a pupil of Chao Mēng-fu, and the most famous painter of flowers and birds in the fourteenth century, that it is often difficult to tell their pictures apart.

Such paintings were extraordinarily decorative, and this was a quality that was then and later highly appreciated by all except the uncompromising scholars. No wonder that many artists perpetuated the kind and the style. The *Peacocks and Peonies* in the Del Drago Collection is a typical specimen of this group. It is an excellent work, admirably composed, well-drawn and delicately coloured; it was done by Lu Chao-yang in 1552 A.D. (colour plate, frontispiece). A painting with *Pheasants and Peonies* of 1662 A.D. by Wang Shih, formerly in the Eumorfopoulos Collection, does not show a marked difference in style; and Yün Shou-p'ing (1633-1690), the best-known painter of flowers in the seventeenth century, has left many works in the same manner, besides exquisite sketches of blossoms that were inspired by Shēn Chou, and landscapes emulating Huang Kung-wang and Ni Tsan.

With Chou Ch'ēn, Lü Chi, and Chou Ch'ēn's pupil T'ang Yin (1470-1524), a new phenomenon appears in the history of Chinese painting: the artist who masters a variety of styles. There was no inner necessity to use the one or the other style, but only the wish of his patrons. T'ang Yin's *œuvre* is large, but very uneven in quality. It comprises pictures in gaudy colours of girls with vacuous expressions; large landscapes in the hard deliberate manner of Chou Ch'ēn, whose pictures, by the way, T'ang Yin signed with his own name and sold as his own when he had become well known; and landscapes and pictures of bamboo in the splashy style of his time. One of his best works is in the Art Institute of Chicago, a short scroll depicting a scholar and a priest drinking tea on a hot day near a brook (fig. 122). It is a delicate work, masterful in composition and drawing. In the treatment of rocks and trees it is obviously influenced by the pictures of Shēn Chou (1427-1509), the only gentleman painter of the fifteenth century worth mentioning.

Shēn Chou was undoubtedly a good artist, and he might have become an excellent one, had he felt himself more obliged to his talent than to his class. He is responsible for the idolization of Huang Kung-wang and Ni Tsan. He set an example of disastrous consequence when expressing his admiration by paintings which can scarcely be told from original Ni Tsans. By doing so, he elevated the style of Ni Tsan and of the late Huang Kung-wang to the rank of a *style de corps* for all class-conscious scholars in the centuries to come. When he relied on himself, he created pictures of a charming lightness. It is interesting to note that such paintings come very close in spirit and style to the works of Tai Chin and Wu Wei.

Shēn Chou was reputedly the founder of the Wu School, so called after Wu-hsien, part of modern Su-chou. The school was the rival of the Chē School. Artists were allotted to one or the other, not by virtue of their style, but by their status as professional or amateur.

The loose, broad manner, a sort of slapdash reaction to sudden inspiration, may indeed be considered the prevalent style at the end of the fifteenth and the beginning of the sixteenth century. It continued to be the normal means of representation for many artists. It lost, however, much of its suggestive power. Verve can be found in many works, but it is seldom convincing, and "much ado about nothing" would be quite an appropriate title for many pictures, regardless of subject matter.

The gentlemen painters travelled along the same road. Shēn Chou's pupil, Wēn Chēng-ming (1470-1559), did not keep exclusively to the desiccated Huang Kung-wang—Ni Tsan formula; he left paintings in the broad, watery manner reminiscent of Kao K'o-kung, others in the manner of Wang Mēng, and some in an exact linear style. A few of his pictures are not bad; but the chief interest of all of them lies in the affinity with one or another master of the past. This eclecticism is symptomatic not only of Wēn Chēng-ming, but of all the artists of his and later times, dilettantes and professionals alike.

On the whole, the formula grew worse as time went on. Too many scholars suffered from the delusion that a man with a humanistic education had acquired with it not only the obligation but also the gift to paint. They did so with a complacency matched only by their lack of talent. Tung Ch'i-ch'ang (1555-1636), the *pontifex maximus* of the group, who so eloquently described the lofty aims of this noble art, was an execrable dilettante. Wang Shih-min (1592-1680), a friend of Tung's, and Wang Chien (1598-1677) fought for the same ideals with no better results. The latter two are usually named together with Wang Hui (1632-1717) and Wang Yüan-ch'i (1642-1715) as the Four Wang. Wang Hui was praised in the most exuberant terms by his elders and contemporaries. In fact he was a mediocre artist. Wang Yüan-ch'i was only a trifle better.

There were, of course, a few exceptions. Ko Chēng-ch'i was one; he left a landscape, dated 1634, with space and air in it; he had in his handling of form an ease and freedom that is born of mastership and not of a naive disdain for technique. A little fan-painting with a man under a tree looking out over a river comes very close to Ko's work in spirit and style (fig. 127). It has the same lightness of touch and the same lyrical quality. Here, after a long interval, the fullness of nature was again felt and expressed, and man was part of it.

Neo-classicism was fully reinstated by one of the greatest painters of the sixteenth century, Ch'iu Ying. He was, like T'ang Yin, a pupil of Chou Ch'ēn, who had discovered his talent when he was a little boy. By 1552 Ch'iu Ying did not paint any more; he was either dead or unable to work. It is universally reported that he died very young.

Ch'iu Ying copied the works of T'ang, or what passed for them, and Sung and Yüan masters extensively. Though the meticulous linearism of T'ang and Yüan painters must have appealed most strongly to his own nature, he sometimes used the broad monochrome manner of his time, as if to show that he was as good at it as anyone else. One picture of this kind, in the P'ang Collection in Shanghai, represents a scholar with his servant under a tree; it is much better composed and drawn than the works of his contemporaries.

But what made Ch'iu Ying famous, and indeed known all over the world, were his paintings which show cultivated gentlemen and handsome women moving in an enchanted world of beauty and luxury. These pictures are executed in minute detail with an incredible clarity of design and a perfect harmony of colours. There is an atmosphere of well-bred felicity and innate grace about his figures that make them equal, if not superior to the work of Jēn Jēn-fa. An excellent example of this charming art is the landscape in the Wells Collection in Munich (fig. 128). His paintings of fairies and girls make the ladies of T'ang Yin appear stiff and dull. So well-beloved were his interpretations of female beauty that they were put a hundred years later upon the porcelain vases and dishes of the K'ang Hsi period (1662-1722). Lēng Mei, the painter of fragile girls at the court of K'ang Hsi, is unthinkable without Ch'iu Ying (fig. 129). And when as late as in 1811 A.D. a certain Ch'ēn Tao wanted to depict a dreamland of peace and happiness, he did so in the style of this master of the sixteenth century.

Ch'iu Ying got his firm hold on the Chinese because he gave form and expression to their ideas about the pursuit of happiness. They were extraordinarily humane: to stroll along a gentle brook; to look at lofty mountains and the clouds sailing around their peaks; to gaze at placid hills beyond a peaceful lake; to sit under trees, on terraces, or in beautiful rooms, drinking, discussing literature, and painting "with charming friends and slender concubines." For a thousand years, the poets had sung of these pleasures. Ch'iu Ying's brush brought them to life, and his genius imbued them with a delicate grace and a lyrical beauty that transcend the keenest fantasy of common man.

NOTES

I. THE NEOLITHIC AGE

J. G. Andersson: Researches into the Prehistory of the Chinese. *Bulletin of the Museum of Far Eastern Antiquities BMFEA* xv (1943). L. Bachhofer: Der Zug nach dem Osten. *Sinica-Sonderausgabe*, 1935, pp. 101 ff., China-Institut der Universität Frankfurt a.M. A book of mine on the late neolithic and early bronze age in China is in preparation (Harvard-Yenching Institute).

II. THE BRONZES

Cf. Max Loehr: Beiträge zur Chronologie der älteren chinesischen Bronzen, *Ostasiatische Zeitschrift* N.F. xii, 1936, pp. 27ff. L. Bachhofer: The Evolution of Shang and Early Chou Bronzes, *The Art Bulletin*, xxvi, June 1944, pp. 107 ff.

B 117 (p. 39), C 183 (p. 45) refer to B. Karlgren: Yin and Chou in Chinese Bronzes. *BMFEA* viii, 1936.

For Early Chou chronology, cf. Ch'ēn Mēngchia: *Hsi Chou Nien Tai K'ao* (Examination of Western Chou Dynastic Chronology), Chungking, 1944.

For Li Yü, Huai and Chin Ts'un, cf. L. Bachhofer: Bronze Figures of the Late Chou Period, *The Art Bulletin*, xxiii, pp. 317 ff., December 1941. For mirrors, cf. B. Karlgren: Huai or Han, *BMFEA*, xiii, 1941.

1. Cf. O. Karlbeck: Anyang Moulds, *BMFEA*, vii.
2. For the bird's head in southern Russia, cf. C. Borovka: *Scythian Art*, New York, 1928, Pl. viii-xi. The specimens date from the sixth century B.C., as do the two *hu*.
3. *BMFEA*, ix, Pl. 64/3.
4. M. Loehr: Das Rolltier in China. *Ostasiatische Zeitschrift*, N.F. 14, 1938, pp. 137 ff.
5. J. G. Andersson: The Goldsmith in Ancient China. *BMFEA*, vii, Pl. 2-3.
6. Andersson, l. c. p.27. The date 314 B.C., correcting Kuo Mo-jo's 279 B.C., is given by Professor Ch'ēn Mēng-chia.
7. Cf. Y. Harada: *Lo-lang. Report on the Excavation of Wang Hsü's Tomb*, Tōkyō, 1930.
8. B. Karlgren: Huai and Ordos. *BMFEA*, x, Pl. 40/3.
9. S. Umehara: *Okeru Shina Kokyō* (Chinese Mirrors in European and American Collections), Tōkyō, 1931, p.34, and plate.
10. Cf. the learned discussion by W. P. Yetts: *The Cull Chinese Bronzes*, London, 1939, pp.116 ff.

III. SCULPTURE

Cf. O. Sirén: *La Sculpture Chinoise*, Paris, 1926. O. Sirén: *Histoire des Arts Anciens de la Chine*, Paris, 1929-1930. *International Exhibition of Chinese Art. Catalogue and Illustrated Supplement*, London, 1935-1936 (*Cat. London Exh.*) L. Bachhofer: Die Anfänge der buddhistischen Plastik in China, *Ostas. Zeitschr.*, N.F. 10, pp. 1 ff.; 107 ff. L. Bachhofer: Zur Geschichte der chinesischen Plastik vom viii.-xiv. Jahrhundert. *ibid.*, N.F. 14, pp.65 ff.; pp.113 ff.

11. Cf. *Studies in Chinese Art and some Indian Influences*. P. Pelliot: The Royal Tombs of An-yang, fig. 16-19.
12. Illustrated in *Ostas. Zeitschr.*, N.F.8, T.1/2. *Cat. London Exh.* no. 268.
13. Sirén: *Histoire*, I, Pl.102. *Cat. London Exh.* no.136.
14. *Cat. London Exh.* no. 165.
15. S. Umehara: *L'Etude sur le Miroir Antérieur à la Dynastie des "Han"*, Kyōto, 1935, Pl. v/2-3.

NOTES

16. *Cat. London Exh.* no. 217.
17. *ibid.*, no. 394.
18. Cf. W. C. White: *Tomb Tile Pictures of Ancient China*, Toronto, 1939, fig.25.
19. Sirén, *Histoire*, II, Pl. 4-5.
20. Cf. L. Ashton: *Introduction to the Study of Chinese Sculpture*, London, 1924, Pl. IV/1-2.
21. Sirén, *Histoire*, II, Pl. 9.
22. Cf. C. G. Seligman and H. C. Beck: Far Eastern Glass: Some Western Origins, *BMFEA*, X.
23. O. Sirén: Indian and Other Influences in Chinese Sculpture, fig.2, in *Studies in Chinese Art*.
24. *ibid.*, fig. 12.
25. *ibid.*, fig. 19 ff.
26. Cf. S. Umehara: *Selected Ancient Mirrors found at Shao-hing Tombs.* Kyōto, 1939, Pl.2, dated 220 A.D.; Pl.3, dated 256 A.D.; Pl.5, dated 277 A.D.
27. Admirably described in Hu Shih: The Indianization of China: in *Independence, Convergence and Borrowing*, Cambridge, Mass., 1937.
28. Sirén, *Sculpture*, Pl.16/a.
29. Bachhofer, Anfänge, Abb.15; Sirén, Indian Influences, fig. 25.
30. Sir Aurel Stein: *Ancient Khotan*, Oxford, 1907, p.371.
31. A. Priest: *Chinese Sculpture in the Metropolitan Museum*, New York, 1944, p.28.
32. Sirén, Influences, fig. 26.
33. Priest, *Sculpture*, p.29, Pl. 29-32.
34. Sirén, *Sculpture*, Pl. 472.
35. *Cat. London Exh.*, no. 2360. Height: 5.78 m.
36. Sirén, *Sculpture*, Pl. 319.
37. Priest, *Sculpture*, Pl. 85.
38. Cf. W. P. Yetts: *The G. Eumorfopoulos Collection, III: Buddhist Sculpture*, London 1932, pp.31 ff.
39. O. Sirén, *Kinas Konst under tre Årtusenden*, Stockholm, 1942, fig. 57.
40. Sirén, *Sculpture*, Pl. 403/b.
41. *ibid.*, Pl.426.
42. *Cat. London Exh.*, no.2498.
43. Sirén, *Sculpture*, Pl.407, 571/a.
44. *ibid.*, Pl.555-558.
45. *ibid.*, Pl.560/b.
46. Tokiwa-Sekino: *Buddhist Monuments*, Tōkyō, 1925-30, II, Pl.131.
47. Sirén, *Sculpture*, Pl. 580/b-581.
48. *ibid.*, Pl.584.
49. *ibid.*, Pl.582/a.
50. Sirén, *Histoire*, III, Pl.114/a.
51. *ibid.*, Pl.119/b.
52. W. Meister: Eine datierte taoistische Bronzeplastik. *Ostas. Zeitschr.*, N.F. 11, pp.93 ff.
53. Sirén, *Sculpture*, Pl.608. Tokiwa-Sekino, *Monuments*, V, Pl.86.
54. Sirén: *Studien zur chinesischen Plastik der Post-T'angzeit*, Berlin, 1927, T. 11. Abb.30.

IV. PAINTING

O. Sirén: *Histoire de la Peinture Chinoise*, 2 vols., Paris, 1934. O. Sirén: *A History of Later Chinese Paintings*, 2 vols., London, 1938. Here quoted as Early and Late Chinese Painting. L. Bachhofer: Die Raumdarstellung in der chinesischen Malerei des ersten Jahrtausends n.Chr. *Münchner Jahrbuch der Bildenden Kunst*, VIII, 1931, pp.193 ff. L. Bachhofer: Chinesische Landschaftsmalerei vom X. bis XIII. Jahrhundert. *Sinica*, X, pp.1 ff., pp.47 ff.

55. Sirén, *Histoire*, I, Pl.84/b.
56. O. Janse: Le Style du Houai et ses Affinités. *Revue des Arts Asiatiques*, 1934, Pl.57.
57. Sirén: *Early Ch. Painting*, I. Pl.4-7.
58. W. Fairbank: The Offering Shrines of "Wu Liang Tz'ŭ," *Harvard Journal of Asiatic Studies*, VI, 1941, pp.1 ff.
59. W. F. Edgerton: Two Notes on the Flying Gallop. *Journal of the American Oriental Society*, vol.56, pp.178 ff.
60. O. Fischer: *Die chinesische Malerei der Han-Dynastie*, Berlin, 1931, T.18.
61. A. Koizumi: *The Tomb of the Painted Basket*. Keijō, 1934, Pl.41-50.
62. Fischer, l.c. T.32-53.

NOTES

63. This date is given by S. Kanahara: *Studies in the Theory of Painting in Ancient China*, Tōkyō, 1924 p.6 f.

64. A. Waley: *An Introduction to the Study of Chinese Painting*, London, 1923, pp. 50 ff.

65. *ibid.*, pp.59 ff.

66. P. Pelliot: *Les Grottes de Touen-houang*, Paris, 1914-1924. For the dates cf. Bachhofer, *Raumdarstellung*, pp. 206 ff.

67. A. Soper: Early Chinese Landscape Painting, *The Art Bulletin*, XXIII, 1941, p.159, note 40.

68. For the stories cf. Chavannes: *Mission archéologique*, Paris, 1909-13, text p. 153 [Yüan Ku]; pp.65 ff. [Kuo Chü]; Ssǔ-ma Ch'ien: *Shih Chih* (transl. Chavannes I, pp.70,72 [Shun]).

69. O. Sirén: *The Chinese on the Art of Painting*, Peking, 1936, pp.14 ff.

70. Roman and very likely late Hellenistic painting knew the same system of perspective, based on a vanishing line; cf. the fresco of a villa in the house of Lucretius Fronto in Pompeii (H. Koch: *Römische Kunst*, Breslau, 1925, Abb.2). The evolution of this system in China can be traced step by step on the walls of Tun-huang.

71. Sirén: *Early Ch. Painting*, I, Pl.31-36.

72. *ibid.*, Pl.39-42.

73. *ibid.*, Pl.65-66.

74. *Cat. London Exh.* no. 788,791.

75. Sirén, *Early Ch. Painting*, I, Pl.70.

76. *ibid.*, Pl.71-72.

77. *ibid.*, Pl.46-50.

78. *ibid.*, Pl.61-62.

79. *Cat. London Exh.* no.790. Cf. L. Bachhofer: Zwei chinesische Pferdebilder des 8. Jahrhunderts, *Pantheon*, 1934, pp. 343 ff.

80. Sirén: *Early Ch. Painting*, I. Pl.60.

81. W. C. White: *Chinese Temple Frescoes*, Toronto, 1940.

82. Yau Chang-foo and Louise W. Hackney: *A Study of Chinese Painting in the Collection of Ada Small Moore*, London-New York, 1940, no.XXI.

83. Cf. W. Speiser: Eine Komposition des Dschou Wen-gü, *Sinica* XIII, pp.39 ff. G. Rowland: A Chinese Scroll of the Ming Dynasty, *Worcester Art Museum Annual*, 1936-37, pp.63 ff.

84. Cf. my notes on Lohans, in *Sinica*, X, pp.145 ff, 190 f.

85. Cf. L. Bachhofer: Chinese Landscape Painting in the VIIIth Century, *Burlington Magazine*, Nov. 1935.

86. Cf. Kenji Toda: *Japanese Scroll Painting*, Chicago, 1935, p.14.

87. Sirén, *Early Ch. Painting*, II, Pl.2.

88. *ibid.*, Pl.3.

89. *ibid.*, I, Pl.89/bis.

90. *Cat. London Exh.* no. 900.

91. Sirén: *Early Ch. Painting*, II, Pl.55.

92. *ibid.*, Pl. 67.

93. *ibid.*, Pl. 114.

94. *ibid.*, Pl. 83.

95. Sirén: *Later Ch. Painting*, Pl.2/a.

96. *ibid.*, Pl.4.

97. Sirén: *Chinese on the Art*, p.110.

98. Cf. Tēng Ku: Su Tung-p'o als Kunstkritiker, *Ostas. Zeitschr.*, VIII (1932), pp.104 ff. Tēng Ku: Chinesische Maltheorie in der T'ang- und Sungzeit, *ibid.*, X, pp.157 ff., pp.236 ff.; XI, pp.28 ff. These papers are indispensable for a proper understanding of the question.

99. Sirén: *Early Ch. Painting*, II, Pl.40-42.

100. V. Contag: Tung Ch'i-ch'ang's *Hua Shih Sui Pi* und das *Hua Shuo* des Mo Shih-lung. *Ostas. Zeitschr.*, 1933, p.94.

101. Cf. *Bijutsu Kenkyū*, I, Pl.7-8.

102. L. Bachhofer: The Del Drago Collection of Chinese Paintings, *Art News*, May, 1937.

INDEX

Academy 83, 115, 117, 119, 121
acentric 114
Achæmenian 62
Afghanistan 66
akinakes 46
allegory 59
alloy 46
altarpieces 67, 68, 72
amateur 126
Amitābha 71, 72, 98, 99
Amoghavajra 78, 101, 103
ancestors 28, 29, 55
"Ancient Bamboo Books" 35
Andersson, J. G. 17, 18, 129
Anhui 42
Aniko 84
animal décor 28, 54
An-yang 29, 55
antithetical 99
apotropæic 28, 37, 55
archaic 63, 66, 73, 82
Art Institute of Chicago 34, 41, 43, 49, 58, 75, 82, 85, 126
Ashton, L. 130
Assyrian 62
Astāna 101
atectonic 113
ātman 78
atmosphere 112
Avalokiteśvara 69, 77, 81

baroque 39, 42, 59, 63, 73, 79, 83, 84, 85, 117, 121
base line 87, 90, 91, 92
base plane 92, 94
Battle-axe folk 19
bear 60, 87, 89
Beck, H. C. 130
bell 44, 46
belt hooks 49, 58, 61, 62
Benares 95
Berlin 30, 84, 102, 114
Bessarabia 21
bhūta-tathātā 71
Bidwell Collection 58
Binyon, L. 114
black pigment 32
black pottery 24 ff.

Bodhisattva 68-70, 72-76, 79, 82, 98, 100, 103, 125
Bœotia 90
bone 17, 24, 50
Borovka, G. 129
Boston 38, 69 f., 72, 76, 80, 109-111, 115, 118, 121
Brahmanism 78
Brahmavatī 103
braid 44, 46, 87
British Museum 71, 93, 107, 109
Buddha 64-66, 68, 71, 73-75, 80 f., 100, 103 f.
Buddhism, Buddhist 63 f., 78, 98, 101 f., 117 f., 125
buffalo 56 f., 61, 87

C, "recumbent C", 33
calligraphy 100, 109
Camondo 55 f., 58
carinated 22, 31
Caucasian 87
cave temples 66, 95 f.
Central Asia 58, 61, 65 f., 74, 95 f., 101 f.
Chai Yung 64
Ch'an 109, 117
Ch'ang-an 77
Chang Hsüan 100
Chang Lu 123 ff.
Chang Po-yüan 103
Chang Yen-yüan 110, 119
Chao Mēng-fu 107, 119 ff., 125
Chao Po-chü 119
Chao Ta-nien 112, 116, 118
Chavannes, E. 131
Chē School 123 f., 126
Chēkiang 71, 123
Ch'ēn Chien-ju 124
Ch'ēn Mēng-chia 129
Ch'ēn Tao 128
Ch'ēng 35 f., 40, 53, 93
Ch'ēng-tzŭ Yai 24
Ch'i Chia 22
chia 33, 37, 56
Chia-hsiang 62, 90 f., 93
Chiang Tzŭ-ya 123
Chicago 35, 44 f., 76
Ch'ien Lung 94
chih 36, 38

Chih-k'ai 71
Chili 42, 69, 71, 80
chimæra, winged 62
Ch'in 52, 54
Chin Ts'un 41, 47, 49, 51, 53 f., 58-61
Ch'in Tzŭ 80
Ch'in Wang Chai 22 f.
Chin Yu-tzŭ 122
Ching Lu 64
Ch'ing-lung 77
Ch'ing Tai 17
Ching Ts'un 22 f.
chio 37
Chios 90
Ch'iu Ying 127 f.
Chou 34 ff., 39, 53 f., 91
Chou Ch'ēn 125 ff.
Chou Fang 104
Chou Wēn-ching 123, 125
Chou Wēn-chü 104
Ch'u 52
Chu Chia Chai 22
Chu Hao-ku 103
Chu Wei 93
chüeh 33, 37
Ch'ü-fu 61
cicada 27, 32, 37, 40
cire perdue 29
classic 64, 73, 82, 110
coiling method 18
"compound eye beads" 61
configuration 99, 103, 105
"confronted dragons" 38
Confucius 54
Contag, V. 131
continuity 53
continuous narration 95, 105
contrapposto 74, 79
converging depth lines 99, 105
copper 22, 46
copy 93 f., 100-105, 107, 120, 122
corded ware 19, 21
cross-hatching 23 f.
Cucuteni 23

David, Sir Percival 102
Del Drago Collection 115, 117 f., 120, 123 f., 126
demons 55
dhotī 69 f., 73 f., 79, 82
Dhyāni Bodhisattvas 77
diagonal recession 59
dies 40, 42, 51
dilettantes 121, 127
division of labour 89
dog 87

dragon 32, 37-42, 44 ff., 48, 51, 57
dried lacquer 72
duodenary cycle 52

E-un Sōzu 77
Earth, God of 55
East Prussia 61
eclecticism 127
Edgerton, W. F. 130
Egyptian 86
elephant 55 ff.
elevation 87, 91 f., 96
engraving 63, 90, 101, 105
en lavis 109 f.
Eumorfopoulos Collection 126
Europe 18-22, 27, 61
Eyck, Jan van 118
eye 27, 29 f., 34

Fairbank, W. 130
fan 113 f., 127
Fan K'uan 109, 112 f., 115
fang-i 35, 37
Fang Shan 80
fecundity 37, 55
Fei Lai Fēng 84
Fēng Chih-pao 84
Fēng Hsiao-chung 83
Fēng Li 84
fertility 37, 55
Field Museum, Chicago 75
filial piety 93, 96
Fischer, O. 130
fish 30, 87
flanges 32, 34 ff.
floral décor 31
fluting 39
"flying gallop" 88, 91
Fogg Museum, Cambridge, Mass. 49, 59, 100
France 61
Freer Gallery, Washington, D.C. 26, 29, 31, 34, 38, 44, 51, 56, 64, 71 f., 80, 87, 91, 103, 112, 116 f., 122 f.
frescoes 98, 100, 103, 108, 110 f.
frog 30, 55, 87
fu 41 f.
Fu-ch'ai 45
funerary chamber 86

G, "interlocked G's" 38 f.
Gandhāra 65 ff.
Ganges 95
garbhadhātu 77
Gardner Museum, Boston 60
generalization 103
"gentleman painter" 119, 121, 126 f.

134

geometric 22, 28, 40, 46 f., 51 f.
glass 61
gold 43, 46, 49, 51, 88
Golden Girdle 115, 117
granulation 43 f., 46, 51
Greek 22, 31, 62, 73
guardians 61

Hackney, L. W. 131
Hallstadt 87
Hals, Frans 118
Han 49 f., 54, 59, 89, 97
Han Kan 102 f., 120
Hang-chou 84
Harada, Y. 129
Heaven 55
Hellenistic 62, 131
highlights 96
hill censer 59
Hinduism 78
Hindukush 64
historical scenes 123
Ho Ch'ü-ping 60
Ho Ch'ung 64
Holmes Collection 55, 59
Honan 17 ff., 22, 24, 27, 40, 61, 69, 71, 80
Hōryūji 100
Hosokawa Collection 51, 87
Hou Chia-chuang 24, 55, 86
Hou Kang 24
Hsi Wang-mu 90
Hsia 26
Hsia Kuei 115 ff., 122 f., 124
Hsia Wên-yen 124
Hsiao T'ang Shan 90-93
Hsiao-t'un 29
hsien 37
Hsin Ch'êng 40-43, 46, 53 f.
Hsin Tien 22, 27
Hsiung-nu 60, 62
Hsü Shên 92
Hsüan-tsang 74
Hsüan Wang 39
Hsün Hsü 64
hu 39 ff., 43, 45 ff., 49, 53
Hu Shih 130
Huai 45 ff., 50 f., 53 f., 57
Huang Kung-wang 118 f., 121, 126 f.
Hui Tsung 100, 114
Huns 61, 120
hunting scenes 87
hypertrophy 39

I Chai-ts'ao 124
I Wang 39
iconoclastic 78

Imperial Academy, Tōkyō 88
impressionistic 86
India 18, 64, 66 f., 70, 74, 78, 96
inlay 46 f., 51, 58, 87 f., 91
inscriptions 28 f., 35 f., 52 f., 59, 71, 89, 101 f., 107, 118, 122
inverse décor 46
Iranian 62 f., 89, 102
iron 80, 84 f.
Islam 64
ivory 50
Iwasaki Collection 115

jade 27, 50
Janse, O. 130
Japan 74, 77, 88, 99, 101 f., 104, 107, 125
Java 74
Jehol 19
Jên 80
Jên Jên-fa 120, 128
Kanahara, S. 131
K'ang Hsi 128
Kano Motonobu 125
Kansas City 32, 39, 70, 97
Kansu 18-23, 27
Kao I 62, 92
Kao K'o-kung 117 f., 121, 127
Kao Tsung 119
kaolin 26
Karlbeck, O. 129
Karlgren, B. 52, 129
Kāśyapa 100
Kawasaki Collection 117
Khotan 65
Kiangsu 64
Kinnarī Cave 102
Ko Chêng-ch'i 127
Kōbō Daishi 107
Koch, H. 131
Kōdaiji 104
Koizumi, A. 130
Konchiin 114
Kondō of Hōryūji 98, 100
Korea 50, 53, 88 ff., 93, 124
ku 33, 37
Ku K'ai-chi 93 f.
Ku Têng, *see* Têng Ku
Kuan-hsiu 104
Kuan T'ung 112
Kuan-yin 69 f., 81 ff., 85, 125
kuang 37
Kuang Shêng monastery 103
Kublai Khan 84
Kuchā 66 f., 74, 96, 98, 101 f.
kuei 33 f., 36, 38 f.
Kumtura 102, 108

Kung Wang 37, 39
Kuo Chü 97
Kuo Chung-shu 105
Kuo Hsi 111 ff., 118
Kuo Mo-jo 129
Kushāna 63 f., 66 f.
Kusinārā 102

lacquer 50, 86, 89 f., 93
landscape 88, 94-97, 104 f., 107, 111, 113, 116 ff., 121-126
Lange, J. 56
La Tène 61
law of frontality 56, 58, 66
lei 33, 37
Lēng Mei 128
Leningrad 51
leopard 40
li 18, 24, 33, 37
Li Chēn 101
Li Ch'ēng 112 f.
Li Ch'i-hsien 124
Li Hou-chu 104
Li Kung-nien 114
Li Lung-mien 119 f.
Li Po 117
Li Ssŭ-hsün 104 f., 107, 110
Li Tai Ming Hua Chi 110, 119
Li Ti 113
Li Ti-mao 90
li-ting 33
Li Yü 41-46, 50, 53 f., 57 f., 86 f.
Liang K'ai 116 f.
libation 87
Ling-kuang 91
lion 62, 77, 84
Liu Hsiu 93
Liu Liang 123
Liu Sung-nien 115, 122
Liu Yüan 84
Lo Han T'ang 19
Lo-lang 50, 89 f.
Lo Shēn 95
Lo-yang 89, 93, 96
Loehr, M. 46, 129
Lohan 81, 104
Lokapāla 80, 100
Loo Collection 38 f., 47, 88
Louvre 30, 43, 55, 68, 87
lozenge 26, 29, 48, 51
Lu 61
Lu Chao-yang 126
Lü Chi 123, 125 f.
Lucretius Fronto 131
Lung-mēn 66
Lung Shan 24, 26 f.

Ma Ch'ang 22, 27
Ma Chia Yao 19
Ma Kuei 121
Ma Lin 116, 121
Ma Yüan 114 ff., 121 f., 124
macrocosm 78
magic 52, 57, 78
Mahāyāna 78
Maitreya 65, 67, 103 f.
malachite 46, 48
Manchuria 19
maṇḍala 77 f.
mandorla 64 f., 68
manneristic 63, 91, 93, 121
mat impressions 22
Mazār Tāgh 102, 108
meander 22, 26 ff., 30-34
Mediterranean 64
Meister, W. 130
Mēng Tien 86
Mēng-fu 90
Metropolitan Museum, New York 34, 65, 68, 72, 75, 79, 83, 85, 122
Meyer Collection 69
Mi Fei 118
Mi Yu-jēn 118
microcosm 78
Ming 121
Minoan 91
Minussinsk 27, 62
mirror 46, 50-53, 57, 63, 87, 88, 90
missionaries 63 f.
Mo Shih-lung 110
modulated line 100, 102
Mongols 121
monochrome 94, 109 f., 125, 127
monoculi 30, 32
mortices 29
Mou Tzŭ 65
moulds 29
Mu Wang 39
Mu-ch'i 116 ff.
Munich 68
Munthe Collection 81
Museum of Far Eastern Antiquities, Stockholm 48
Museum of Fine Arts, Boston 89, 96, 100, 113, 119

Nakula 81, 104
Nan Hsiang-t'ang 69 ff., 79, 99
Nan K'ou pass 83 f.
Nan Wu-yang 90 f.
Nara 98
National Museum, Peking 105, 122
Near East 61

"negative ornament" 19, 22, 45
Nelson Gallery, Kansas City 35, 60, 96, 103
neo-classicism 78 ff., 119, 121, 125, 127
Nepal 74, 84
New York 67, 76, 80, 83
Ni Tsan 118 f., 121, 126 f.
Niya 65
nomads 61 f.
"Northern School" 110
"Northern Wei style" 67
Northwestern India 65 f.

Oeder Collection 57
Ohta Collection 47
optic 63
Ordos 27, 62, 87
orthogonal 99
oversized foreground 116
owl 55

Painted Basket 97
Palace Museum, Peking 108, 111 f., 115, 123
palmettes 31
p'an 58
Pan Shan 20 ff.
P'ang Collection 127
Pao Chi 34 f.
parallel perspective 92, 94
Parinirvāna 102
Parthian 63
plan 96, 98
plasticity 96
Peking 109
Pelliot, P. 95, 129, 131
persecution 65
Persia 62
perspective 99, 101
Petreny 21
Philadelphia 75 f., 80
Pi-hsia Yüan-chün 85
Piao bells 45
pillars 90
Pillsbury Collection 56
plan 87, 92
plaques 61
po 46
po hua 110
p'o mo 109
pointillism 110, 112
Pompeii 131
porcelain 128
portrait 101, 103, 124
p'ou 30, 32 f., 37
Preetorius Collection 123
Priest, A. 130
professionals 119, 126 f.

protective décor 55
pseudo-Sung 124

ram 87
Ratnapāni 77
red ochre 19, 27
red pigment 32
red ware 24 f.
rein holder 28
repoussoir 114
rhythm 27, 36, 67, 72, 103
"ring foot" 46
rocaille 88
Rockefeller Collection 76
Roman 73
romantic 114
rope 42
Rowland, G. 131
Royal Tombs 86
rubbings 101, 105
Ruru Jātaka 95 f.

Sāla grove 102
Samantabhadra 77
sanctuaries 61
Śankha of Ketumatī 103
Sarmatians 62
scale pattern 34
Schelling, F. W. von 71
scholars 121
screen 101, 107 f.
Scythian 46, 62, 87, 91
Seligman, C. G. 130
serpent 31 f., 43, 57
Sesshū 125
Shang 24, 26, 28, 31, 35 f., 38, 46, 50, 53-56, 86
Shang-fang 89
Shansi 27, 42, 69, 76, 80, 82, 103
Shantung 24, 27, 42, 61 f., 90, 93
Shao Lin 80
sheep 43, 57
Shēn Chou 126 f.
Shēng-mu 85
Shensi 69, 72
Shih Huang Ti 59, 62, 91
Shih Jui 125
Shōmu 101
Shōsōin 101, 105
Shun 97
Shunjō 104
Shuo Wēn 92
Siberia 27, 51, 61
silver 49, 51, 59, 88
simplification 78, 83
Sirén, O. 129 ff.

socketed celt 27
Soper, A. 131
South Russia 27
Southern Asia 63
Southern School 110
space 87, 89, 91, 93-96, 105, 107, 112, 120
space cell 94-97, 105, 107
Speiser, W. 131
Spencer-Churchill Collection 59
spikes 35
spiral 18, 20, 44, 47 f., 51, 57
spirits 55
Spring and Autumn 54
Ssŭch'uan 62, 89 f., 92
Stein, Sir Aurel 101 f., 130
stelae 66, 75, 82, 99
stereotyped figures 103
Stockholm 29 f.
Stoclet Collection 57
stylization 86
Su Tung-p'o 119
Su-chou 126
Sumatra 74
Sumerians 31
Sun Tsung 90
sundial 52
Sung 64, 83 ff., 94, 100, 110, 120-125, 127
śunyatā 78
swathe 23 f.
sword 46, 87
symbol, symbolic 37, 59, 86 f., 113
symmetry 31, 56, 65, 68, 99

T, "interlocked T's" 26, 28 ff., 48, 50f.
Ta Lai Tien 24
tactile, tactic 63, 68, 96
tai-chao 83, 103, 115, 117
Tai Chin 123-126
T'ai I 84
T'ai Shan 85
T'ai Tsung 75
T'ang 93, 103 f., 107, 109 f., 115, 119, 127
T'ang Yin 126 ff.
Tantrism 77 f., 101
T'ao-ho 18, 28
t'ao-t'ieh 29, 31-37
Taoist 53, 75, 84 f., 88
tathāgata-garbha 78
Tēng-fēng 61
Tēng Ku 131
theopanism 78
theriomorphous décor 27 f., 30, 38, 44, 86
third dimension 87, 89, 92 f.
Tibet 84, 102
T'ien-lung Shan 76 f., 79
T'ien-t'ai 71

T'ien Tsun 75
tiger 31, 40, 55 f., 84, 87 ff.
ting 18, 24, 29 f., 32 f., 35-39, 42-45, 57, 92
TLV mirror 52
Toda, K. 131
Tōdaiji 101
Tōji 77, 79, 101, 107 f.
Tokiwa-Sekino 130
Toledo, Ohio 111
tomb figures 75
tombs 61 f., 75, 86, 89 f., 92 f.
Tomsk 51
Tonking 65
Tonying Collection 81
Toronto 29, 46, 68, 72, 82 ff., 103
tortoise shell 90
trellis pattern 24
triangle 28, 31, 43, 48
triangular blade 42
tribhaṅga 74
Ts'ao Chi 94
Ts'ao Chih-po 119, 121
Tsu Tē 124
tsun 31, 33, 36 f.
Tsung Ping 97
Tuan Fang Collection 65
Tun-huang 66, 74, 99, 108
   Cave 54   100
   Cave 76   104
   Cave 77   98
   Cave 110   95 f.
   Cave 117   107
   Cave 118/A   98, 100
   Cave 120/N   97 f.
   Cave 135   96
   Cave 138/A   99 f.
   Cave 146   98
Tung Ch'i-ch'ang 110, 127
Turfan 66, 101
Turkistan 18
turntable 17
turquoise 46
turtle 55, 87
type 82, 103

Umehara, S. 129 f
University Museum, Philadelphia 48, 67, 69, 74 f., 79, 103
Ural 19
ushnisha 64 f.

Vajrabodhi 78
vajradhātu 77
Vajrapāṇi
vanishing axis 99, 107, 131
vanishing point 99

Vase Painters 19, 21, 23, 27 f.
vertical ribs 35
Victoria and Albert Museum, London 36, 120
vīja 78
Viśvapāni 77
volute 22, 43 f., 50, 52, 88
Vosges 19
Vyāghrī Jātaka 96

Waley, A. 131
wall painting 95, 103 f.
Wang, the Four 127
Wang Chien 127
Wang Hui 127
Wang Hsü 90
Wang Li 121
Wang Mang 53
Wang Mēng 118, 121, 123, 127
Wang Shih 126
Wang Shih-min 127
Wang Wei 104, 106 f., 110 f.
Wang Wēn-k'ao 91
Wang Yüan 125
Wang Yüan-ch'i 127
Wang-ch'uan 105, 107
Wannieck Collection 79
Warring States 54
wax 29
Wei K'ai 90
Wei river 60
Wells Collection 128
Wēn Chēng-ming 127
Wēn Wang 123
Wēn-chi 120
Wēn-shu 84
Western Asia 61-64

Western Paradise 71, 98 f.
wheel, potter's 24
white pottery 24, 26, 29, 31 f.
White, W. C. 130 f.
Winthrop bequest 59
wood 50, 81
Wu, state of 45
Wu tombs 62, 90-93
Wu Chēn 118 f.
Wu School 126
Wu T'ai Shan 107
Wu Tao-tzŭ 101 f., 104
Wu Wang 35
Wu Wei 123, 125 f.
Wu-chun 117
Wu-hsien 126

Ya-chou 62, 92
Yang Shao 17 f., 24 f.
Yau Chang-foo 131
Yen Li-pēn 100
Yetts, W. P. 129 f.
Yin-t'o-lo 118
Ying 80
Ying Yü-chien 116 f.
yu 34-38
Yüan 83, 119, 124 f., 127
Yüan Ku 97
Yüan-shih 96
Yün Shou-p'ing 126
Yün-kang 66
Yung-lo 122

zigzag lozenge 50 f.
zigzag pattern 22 ff., 26 f., 29, 48
zoömorphic décor 27, 30, 51 f.

PLATES

1

2

3

4

5

6

7

8

9

10

12

11

13

14

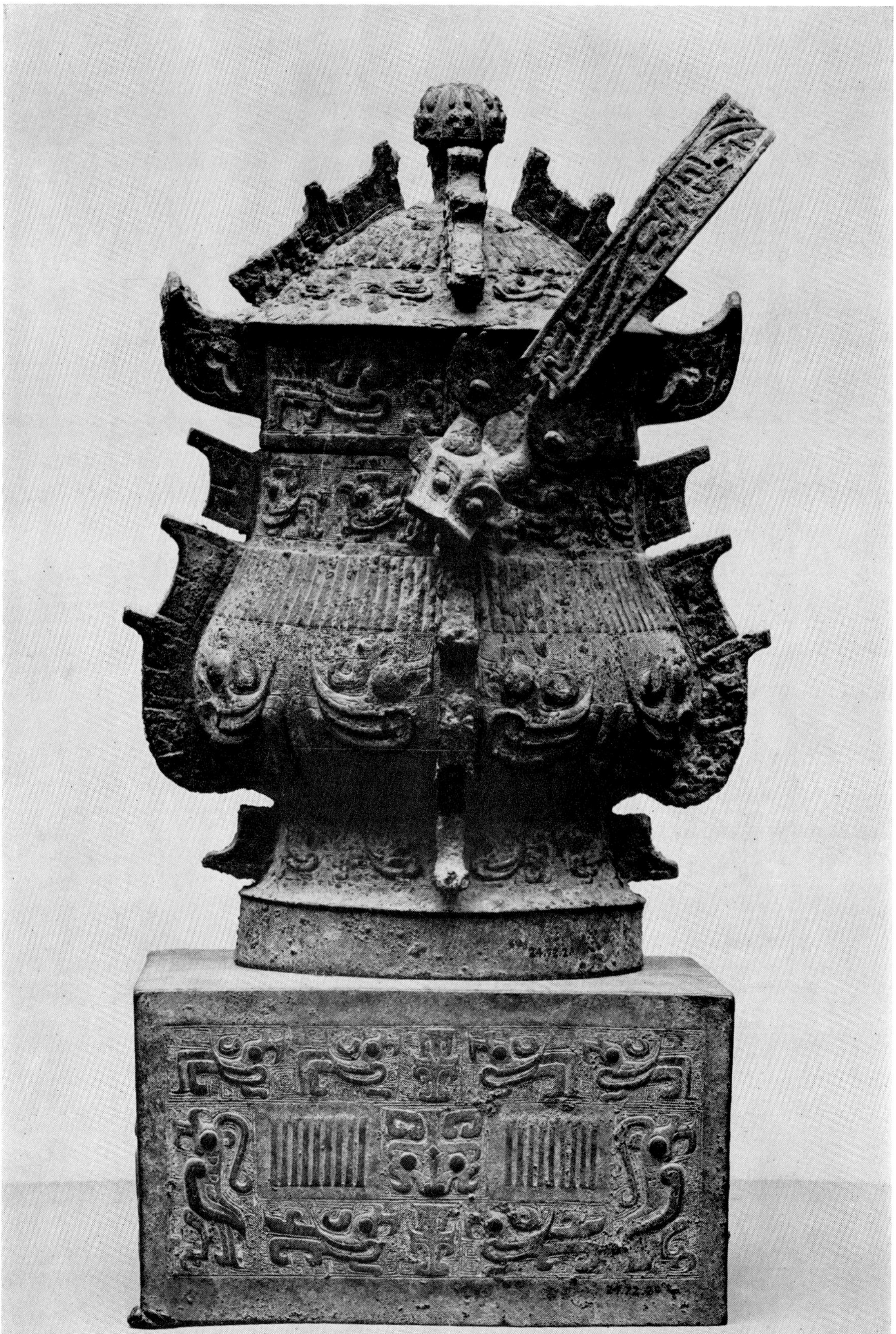

16

17

18

19

20

21

22

23

24

25

26

27

28

29

30

31

32

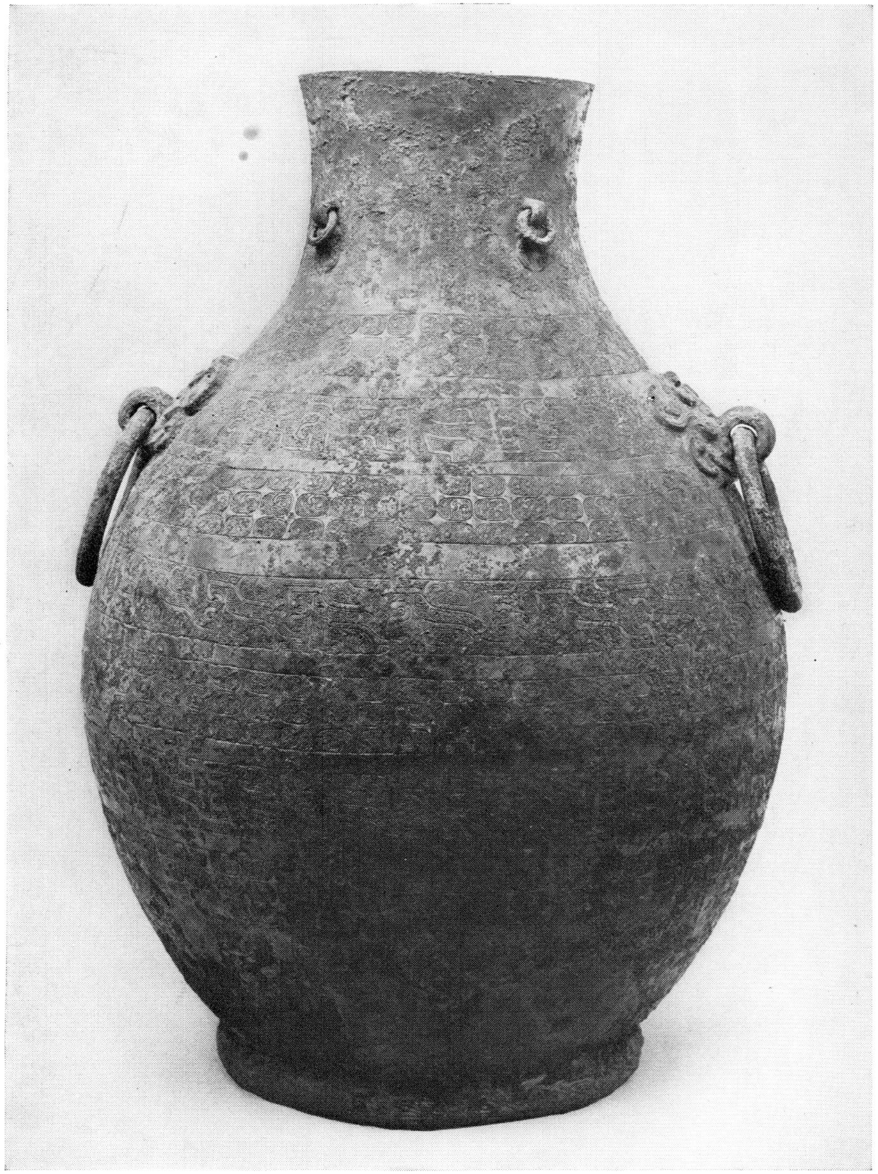
33

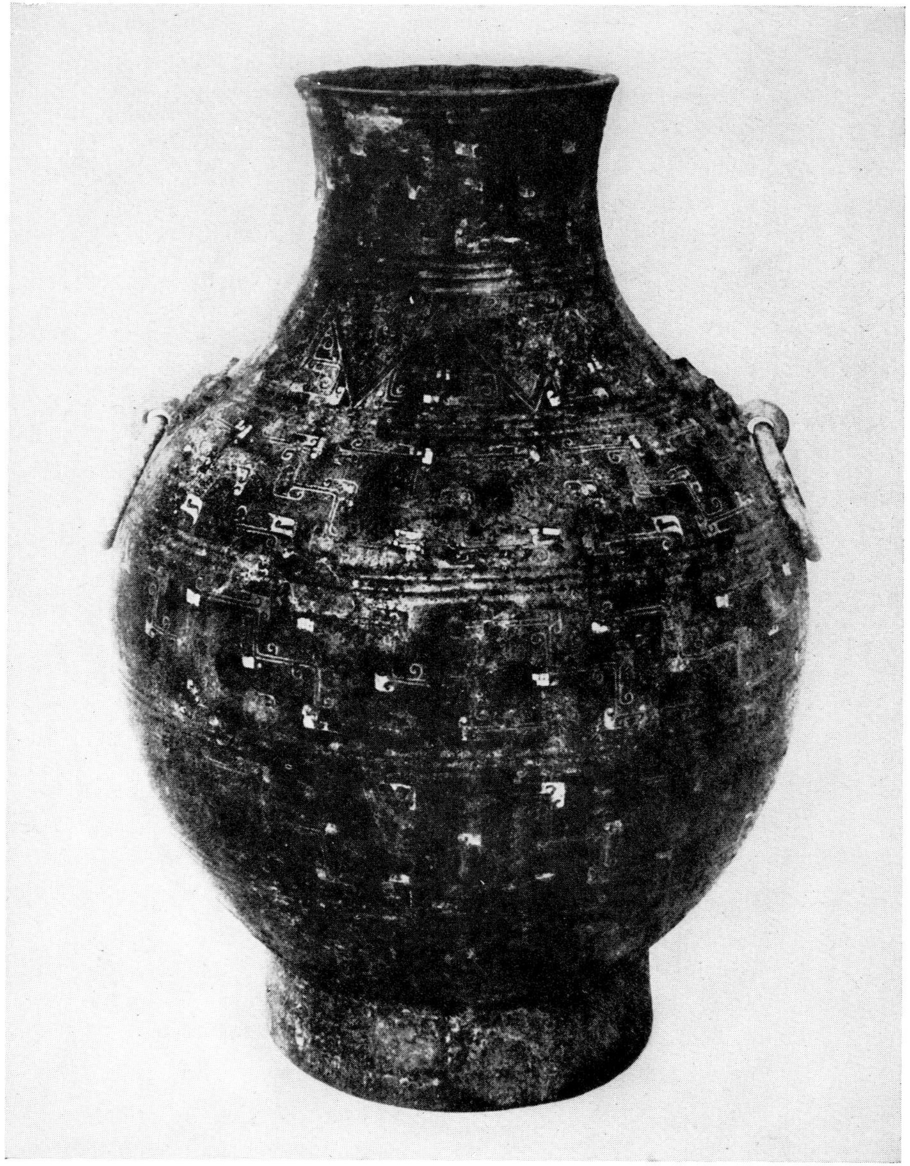
34

35

36

37

38

39

40

41

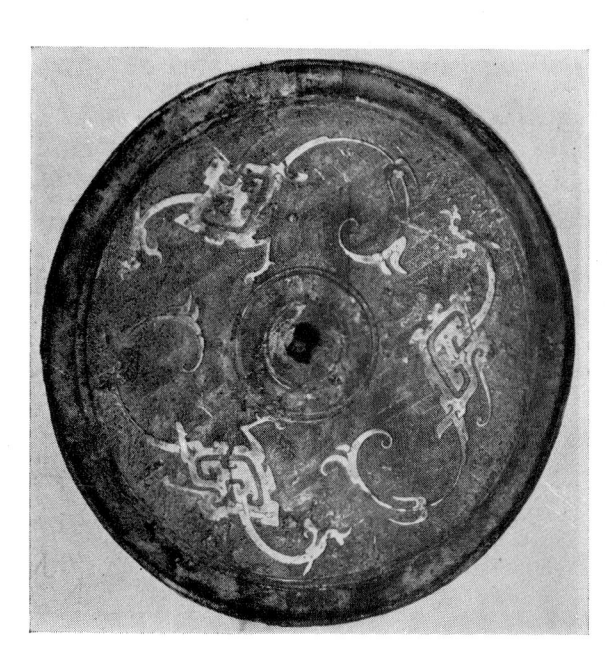

42

43

44

45

46

47

48

49

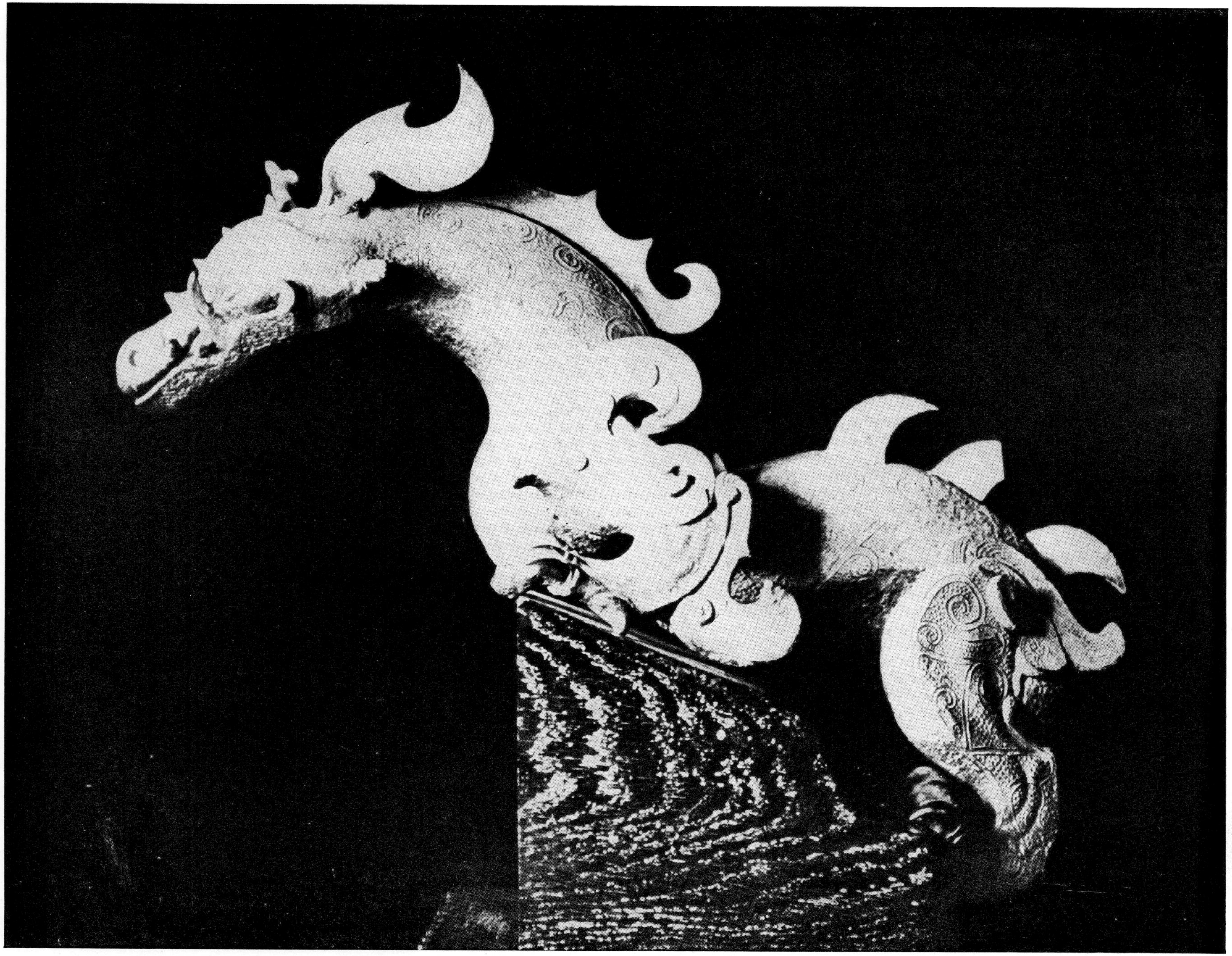

50

51

52

53

54

55

56

57

58

59

60

61

62

63

64

65

66a

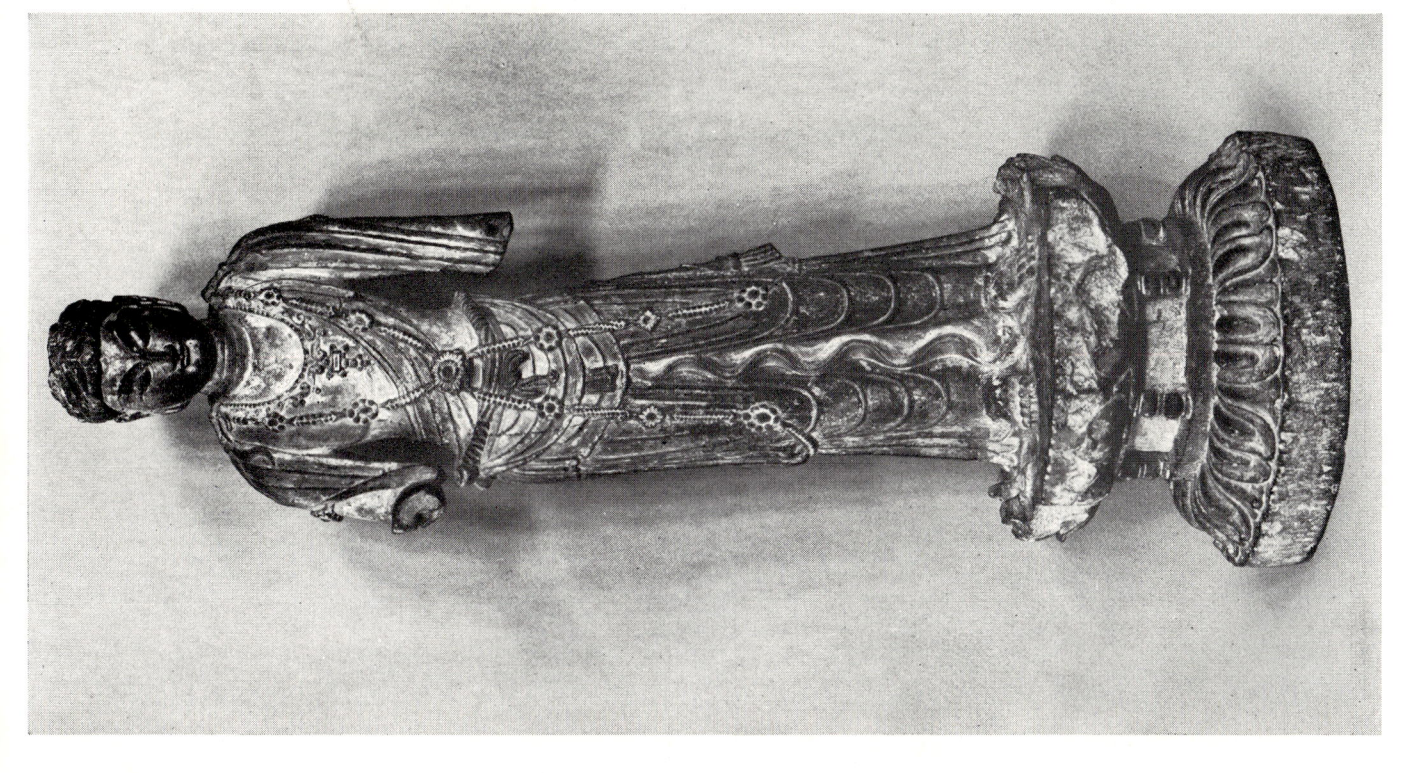

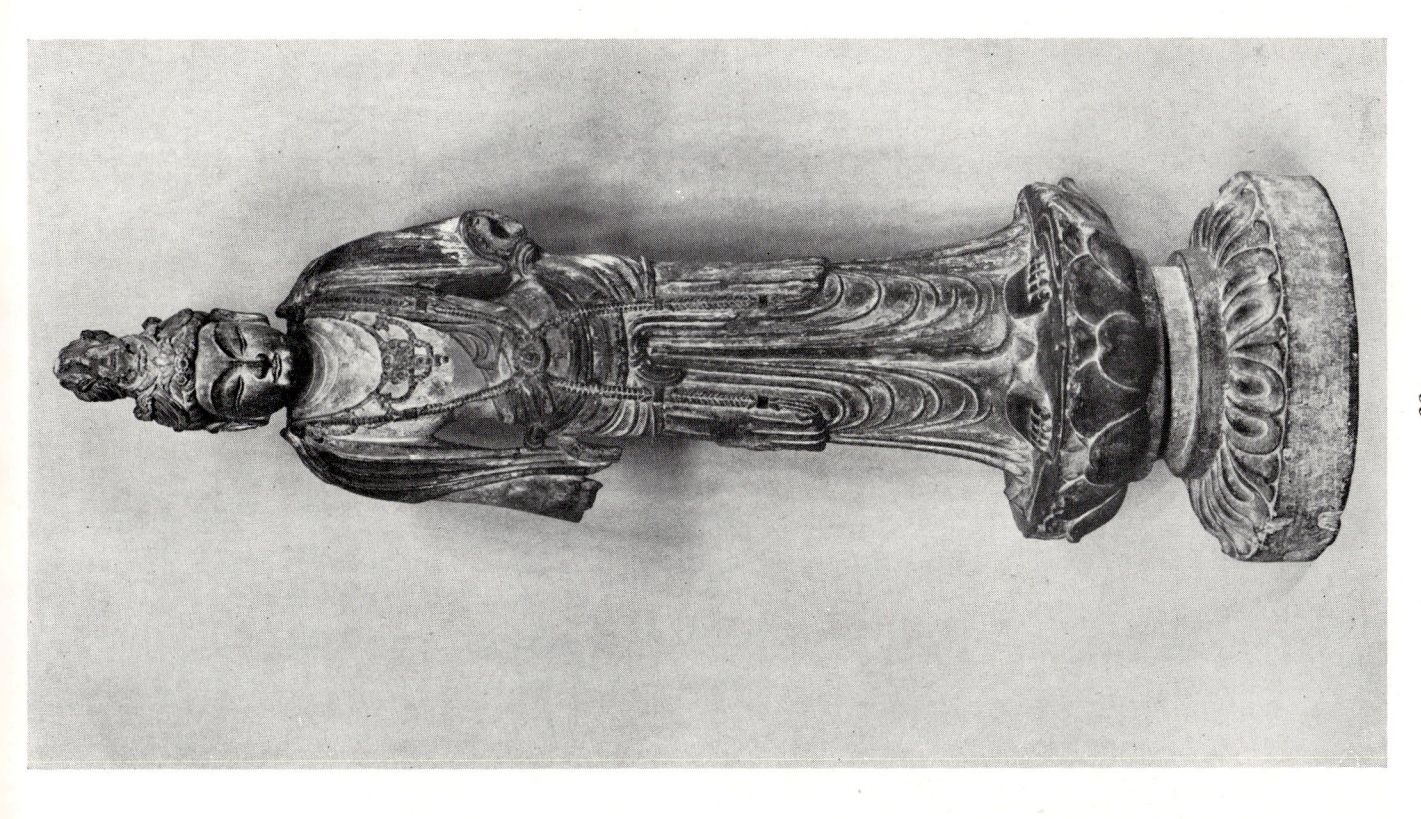

66b

67

68

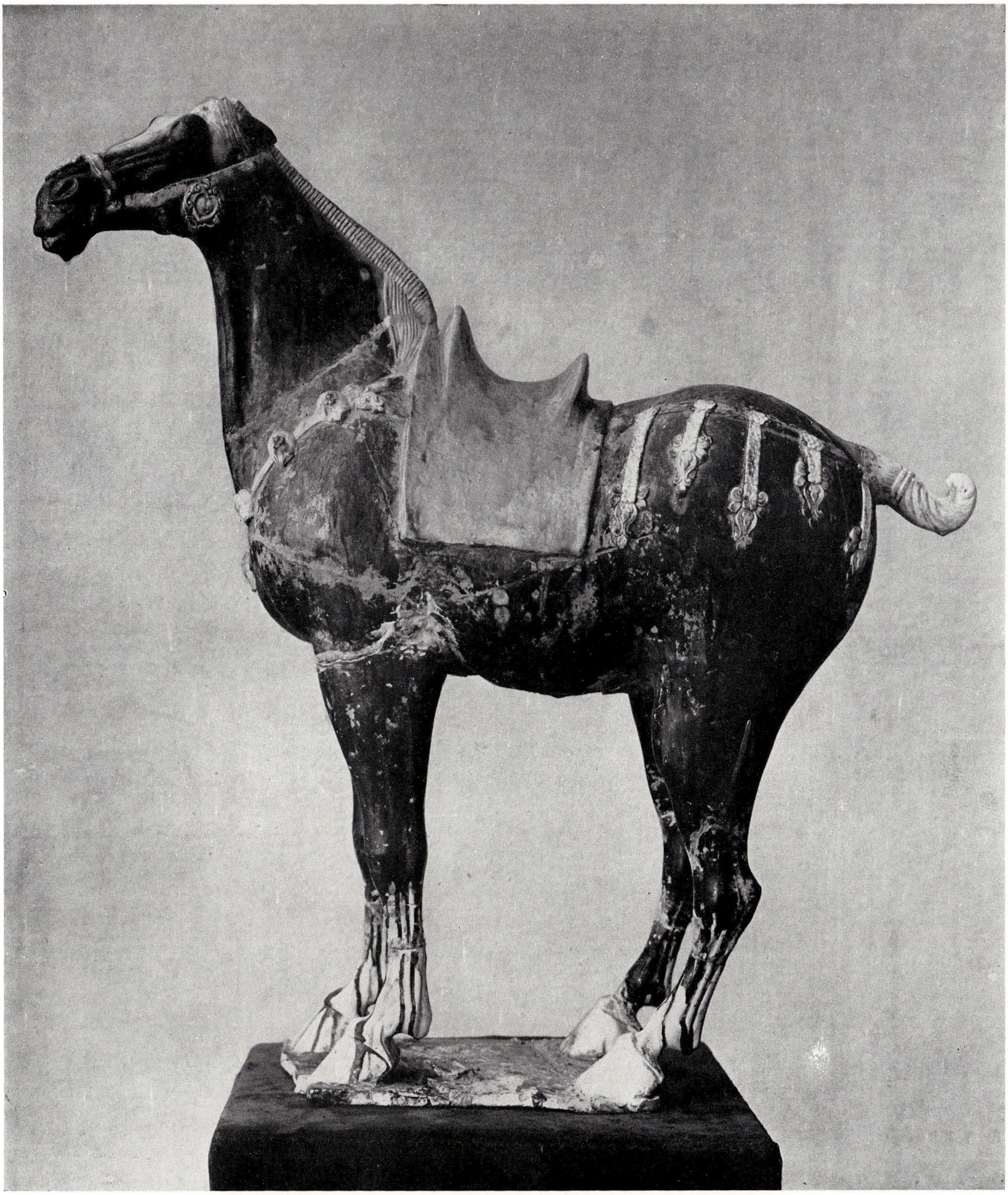

69

70

71

72

73

75

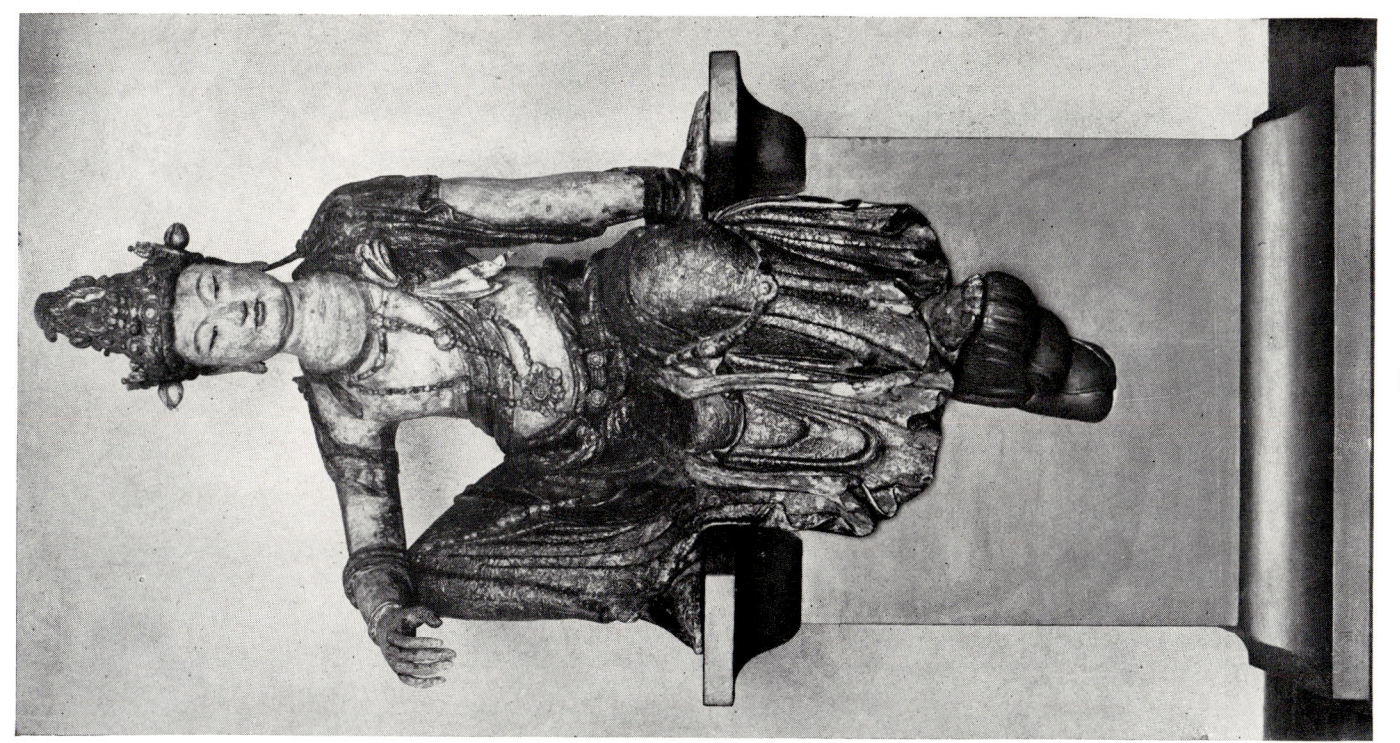

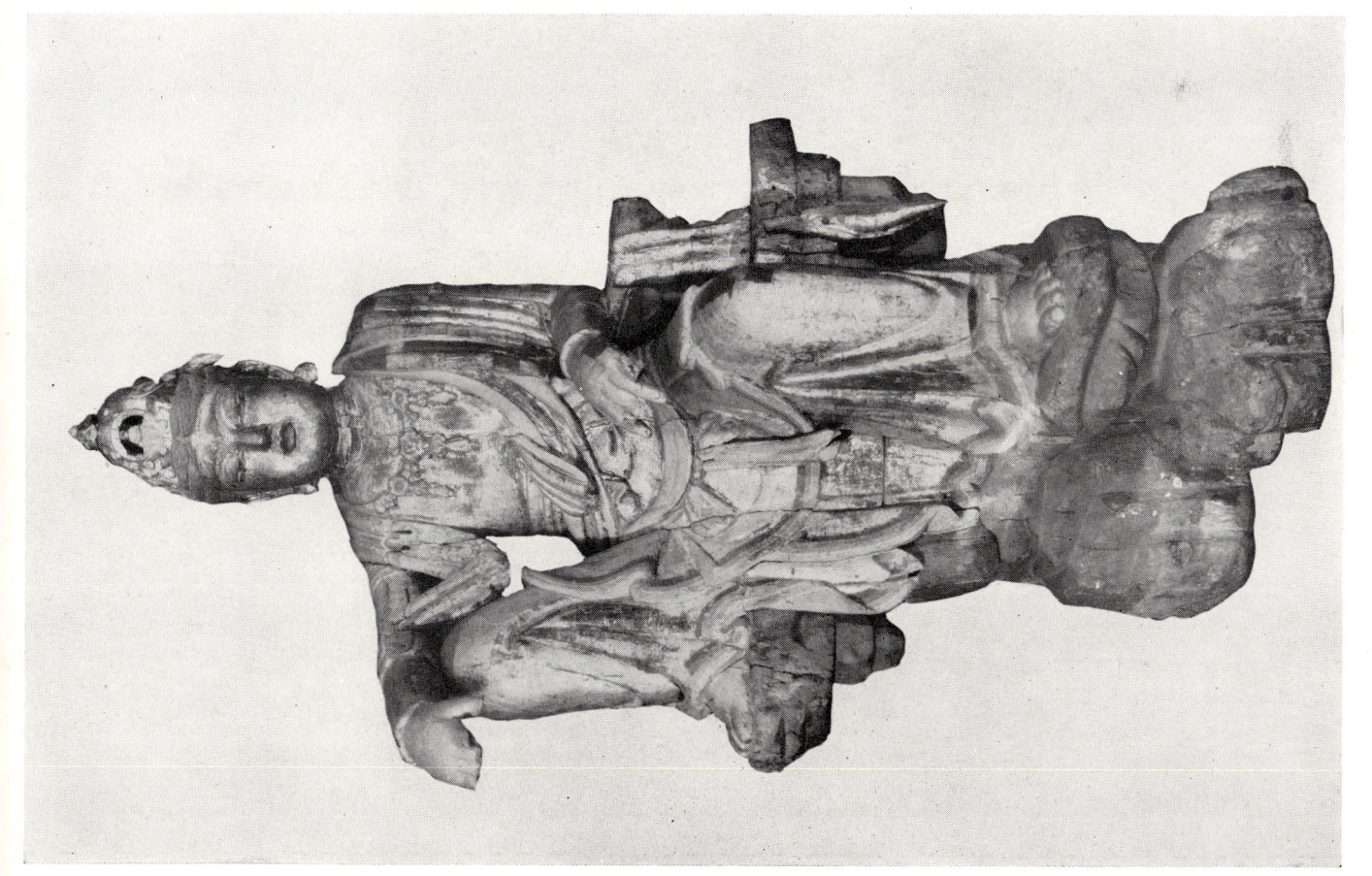

74

76a

76b

77

78

79

80

82

81

83

84

85

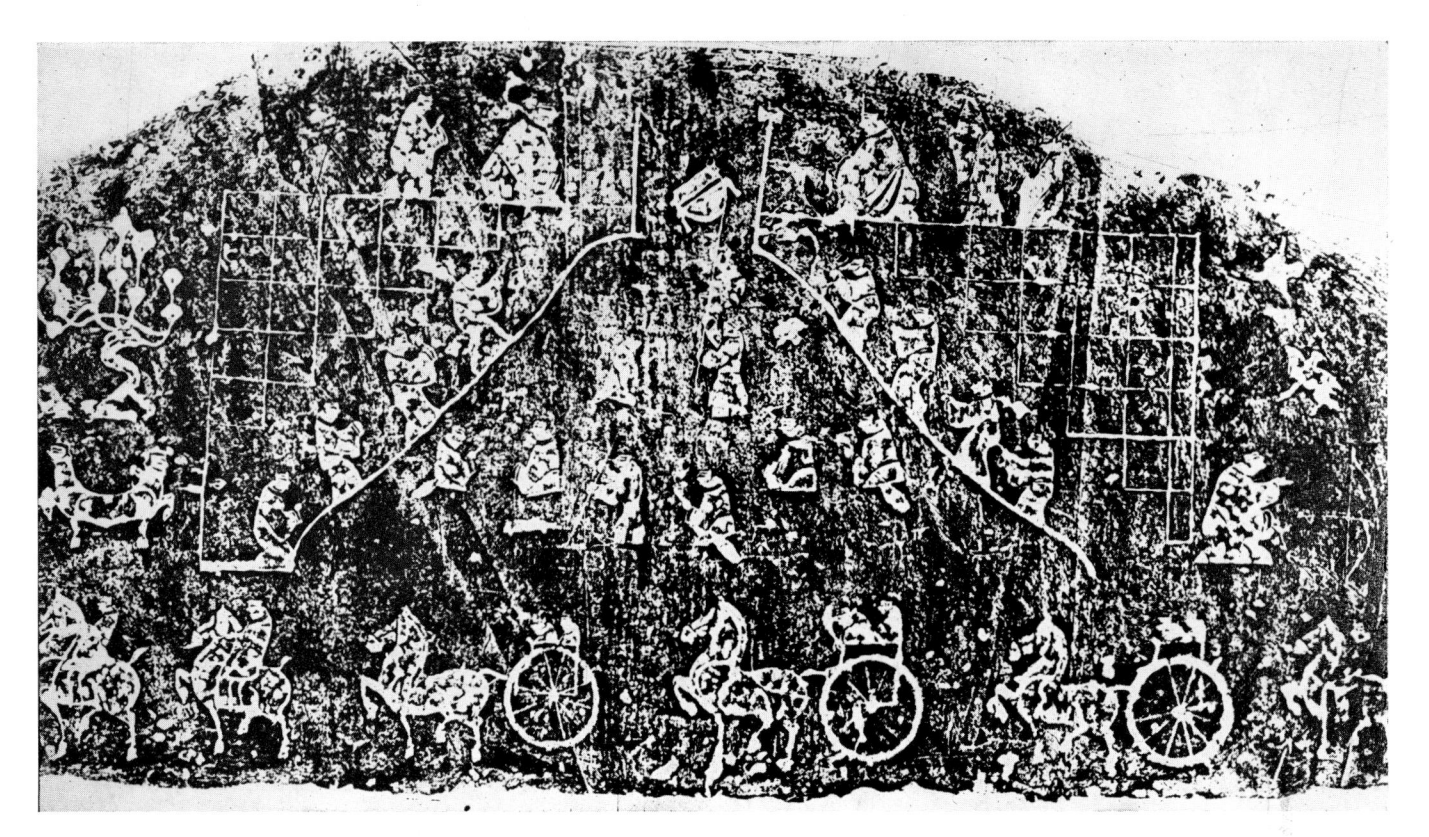

86

87

88

89

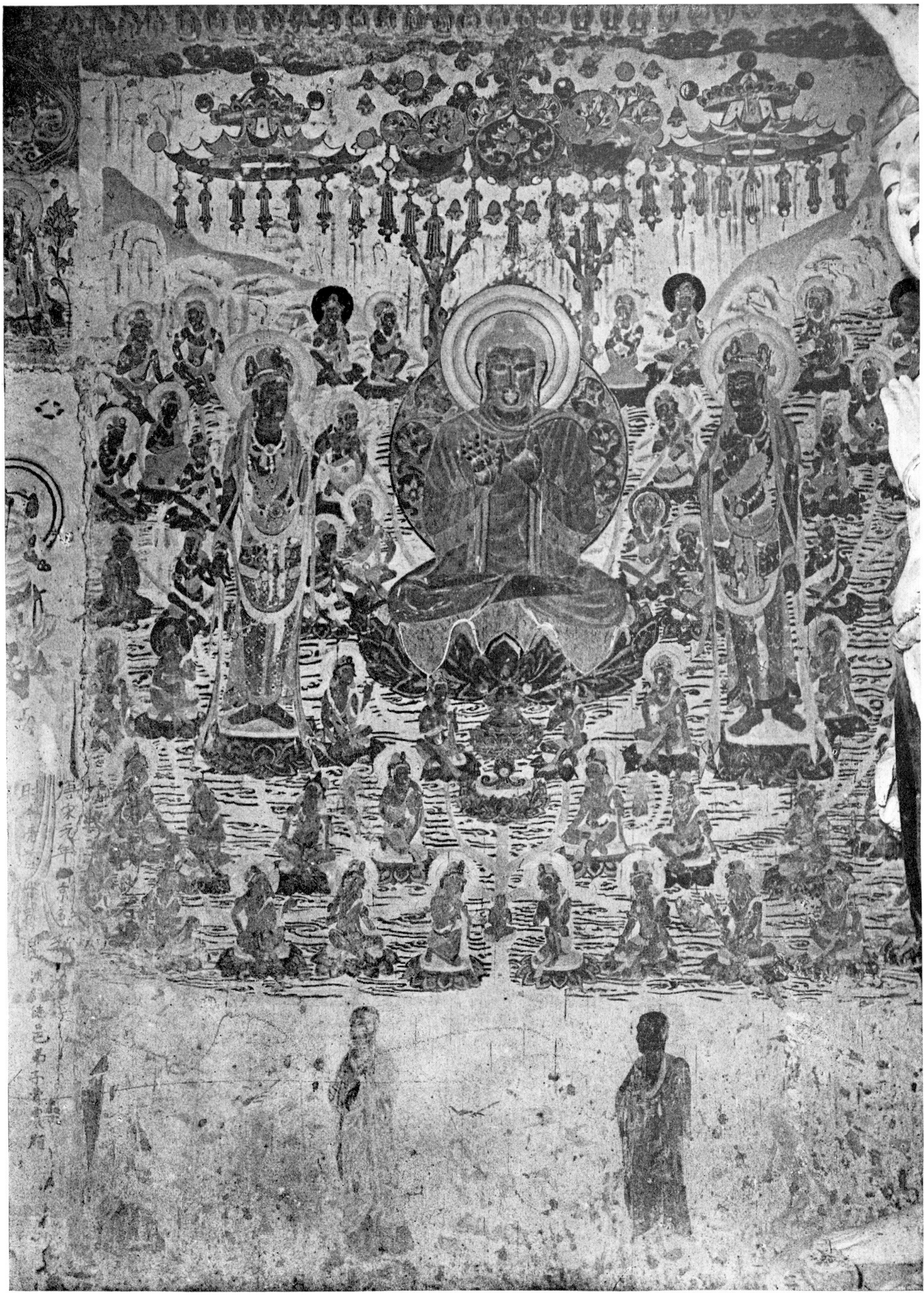

91

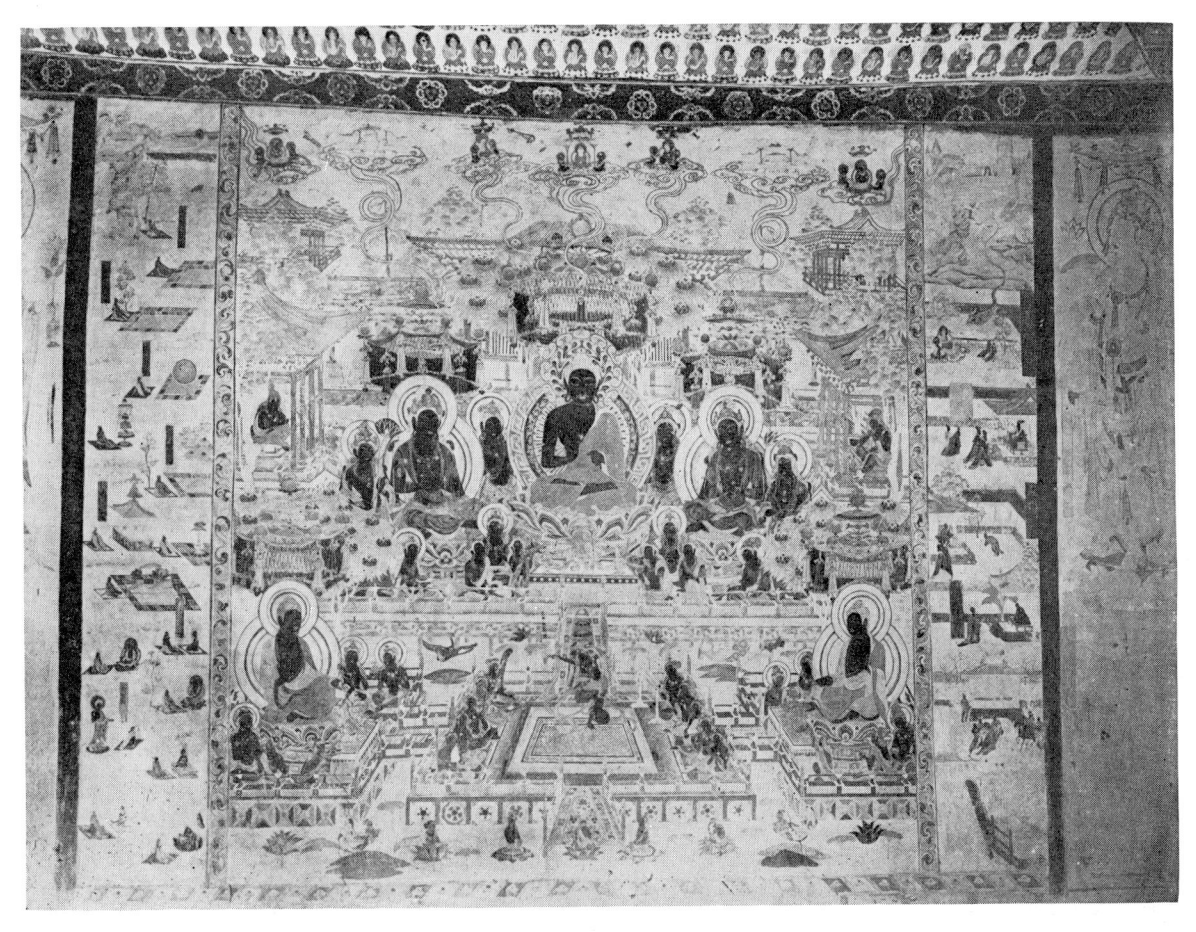

92

93

94

95

96

97

98

99

100

101

102

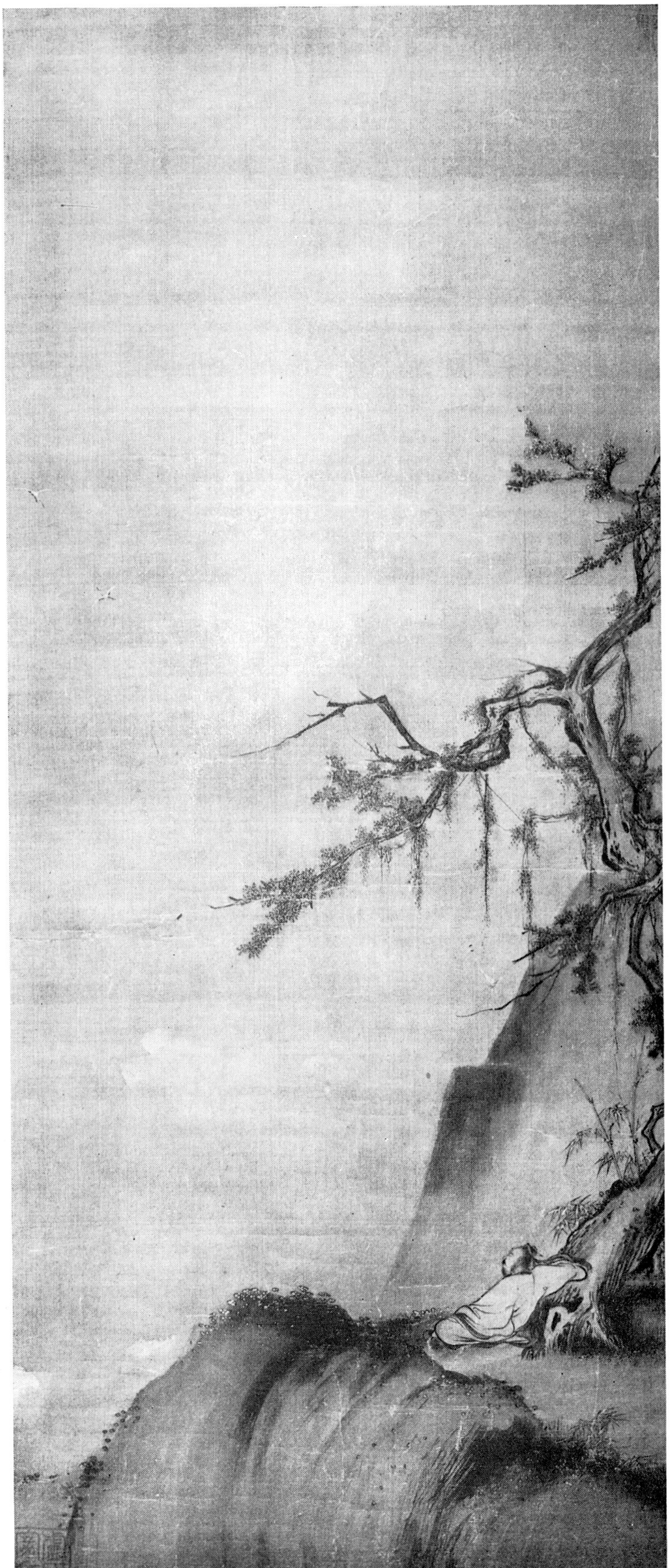

104

105

106

107

108

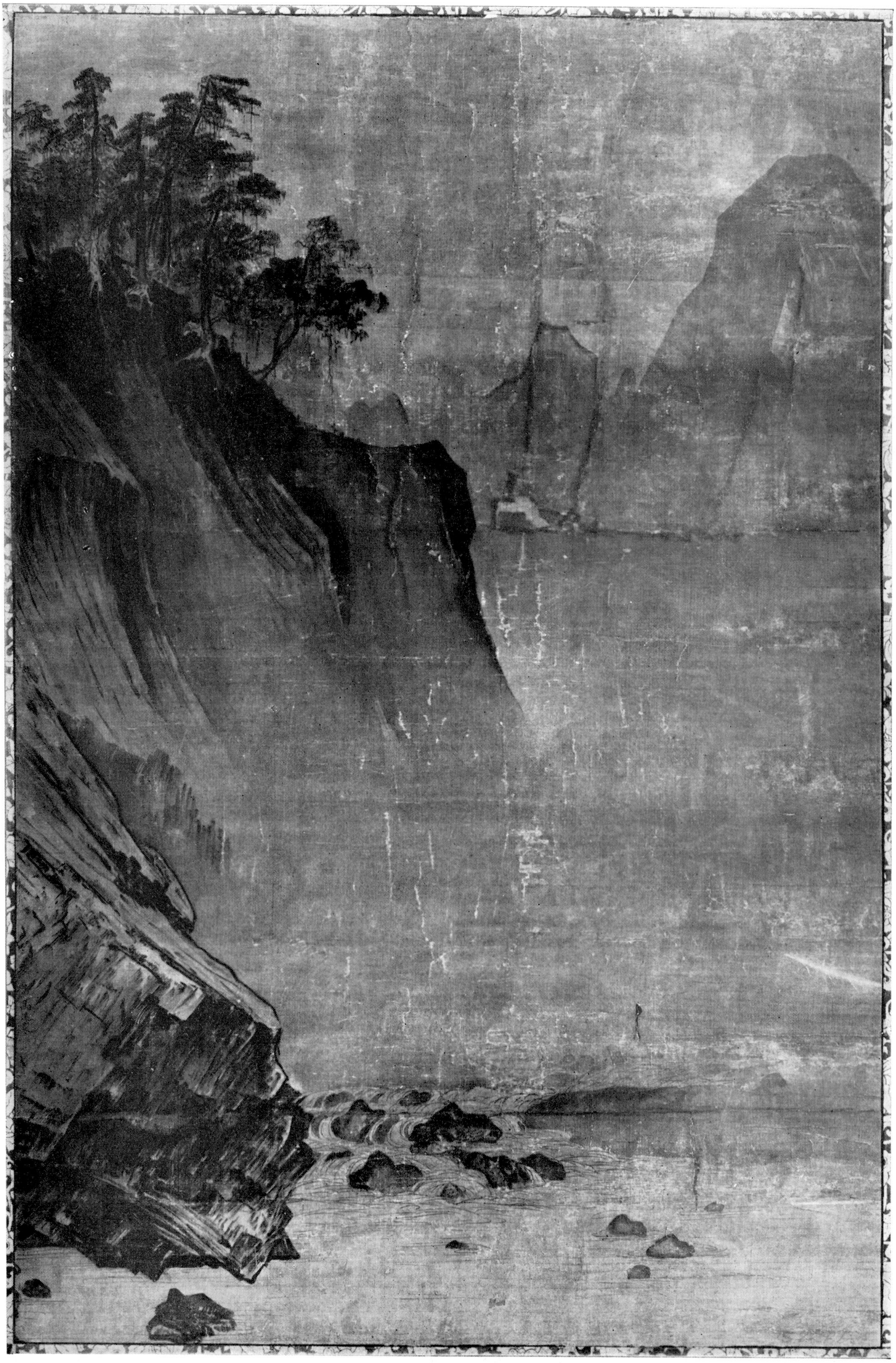

110

111

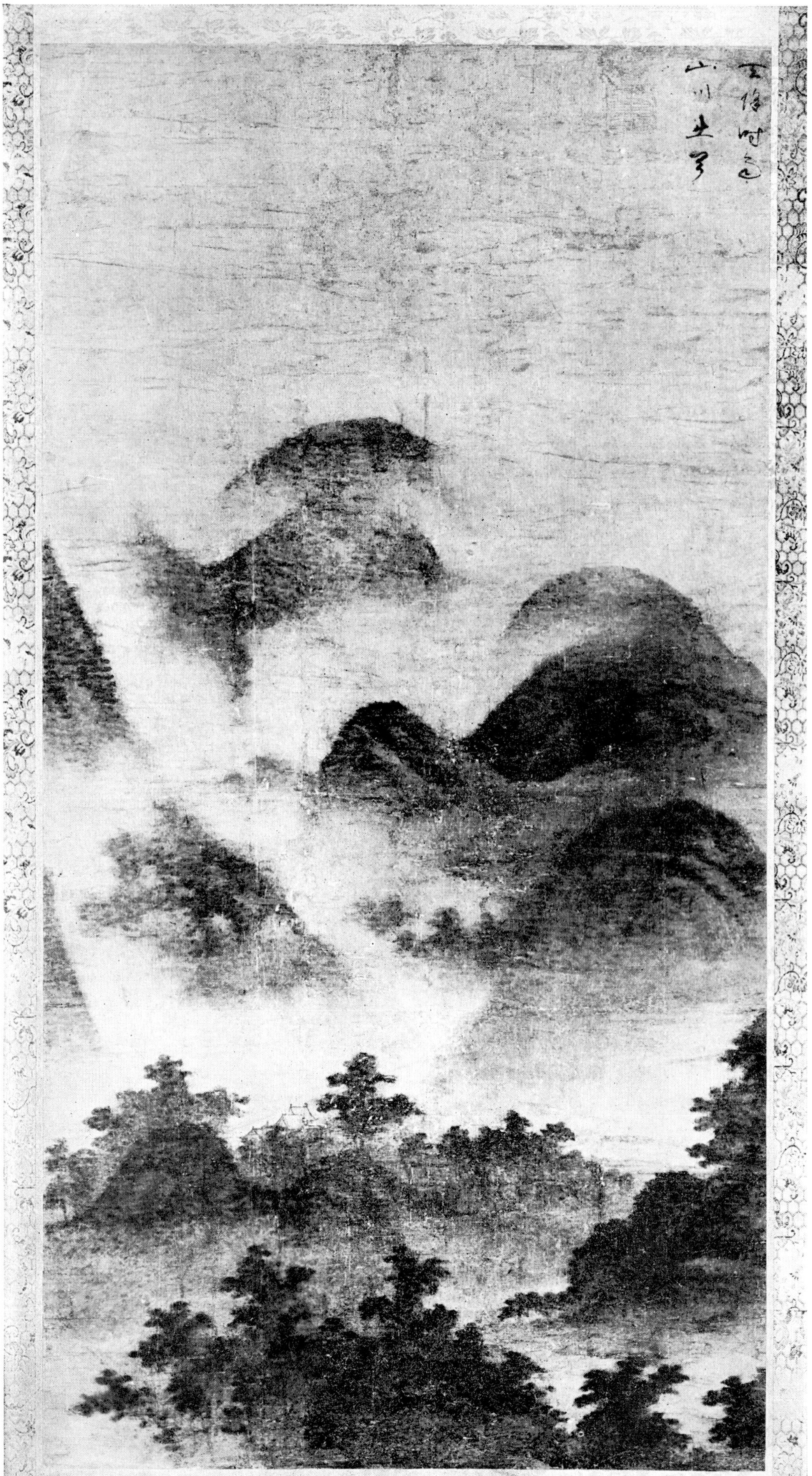

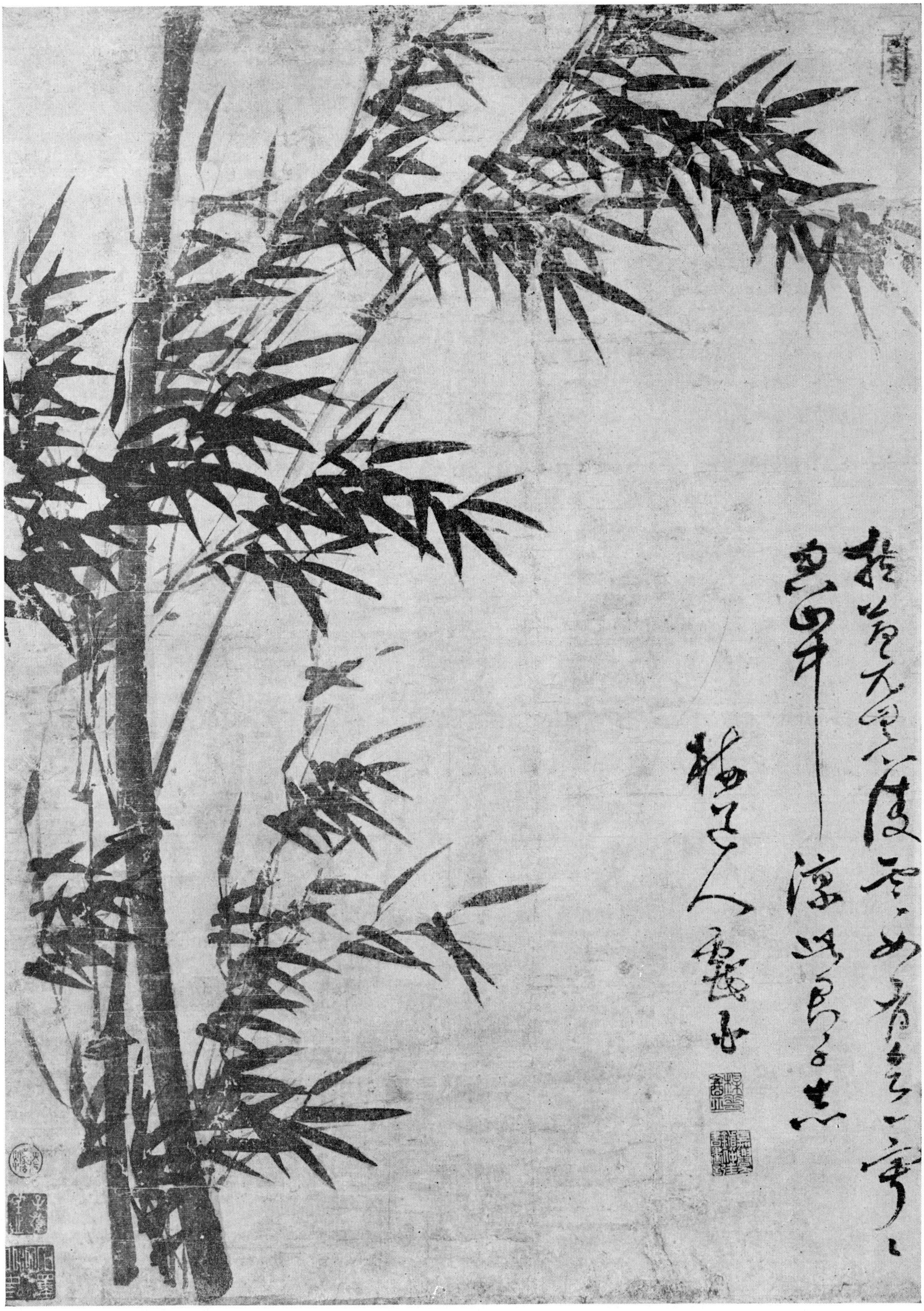

至正十三年五月之望
大癡道人

115

116

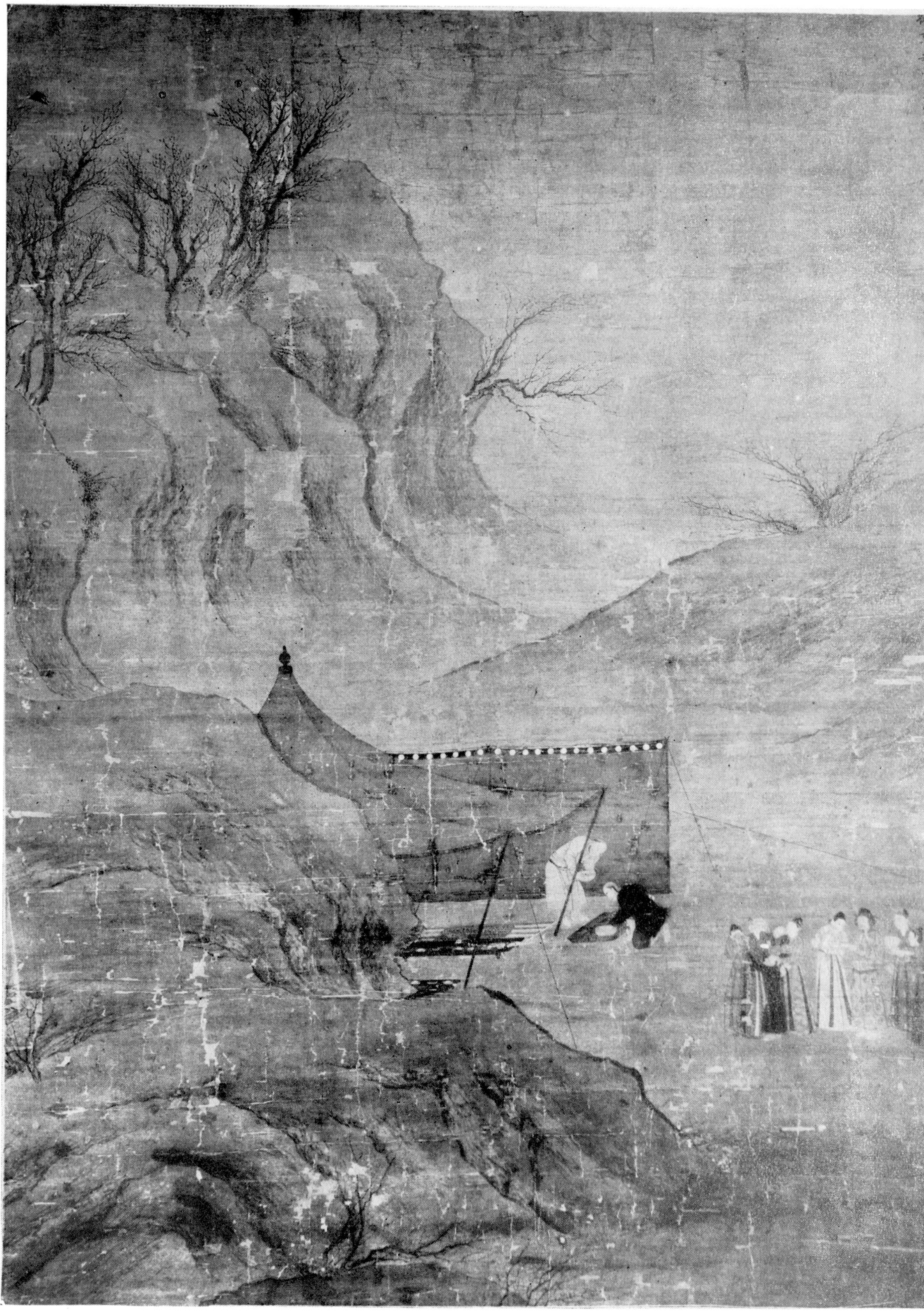

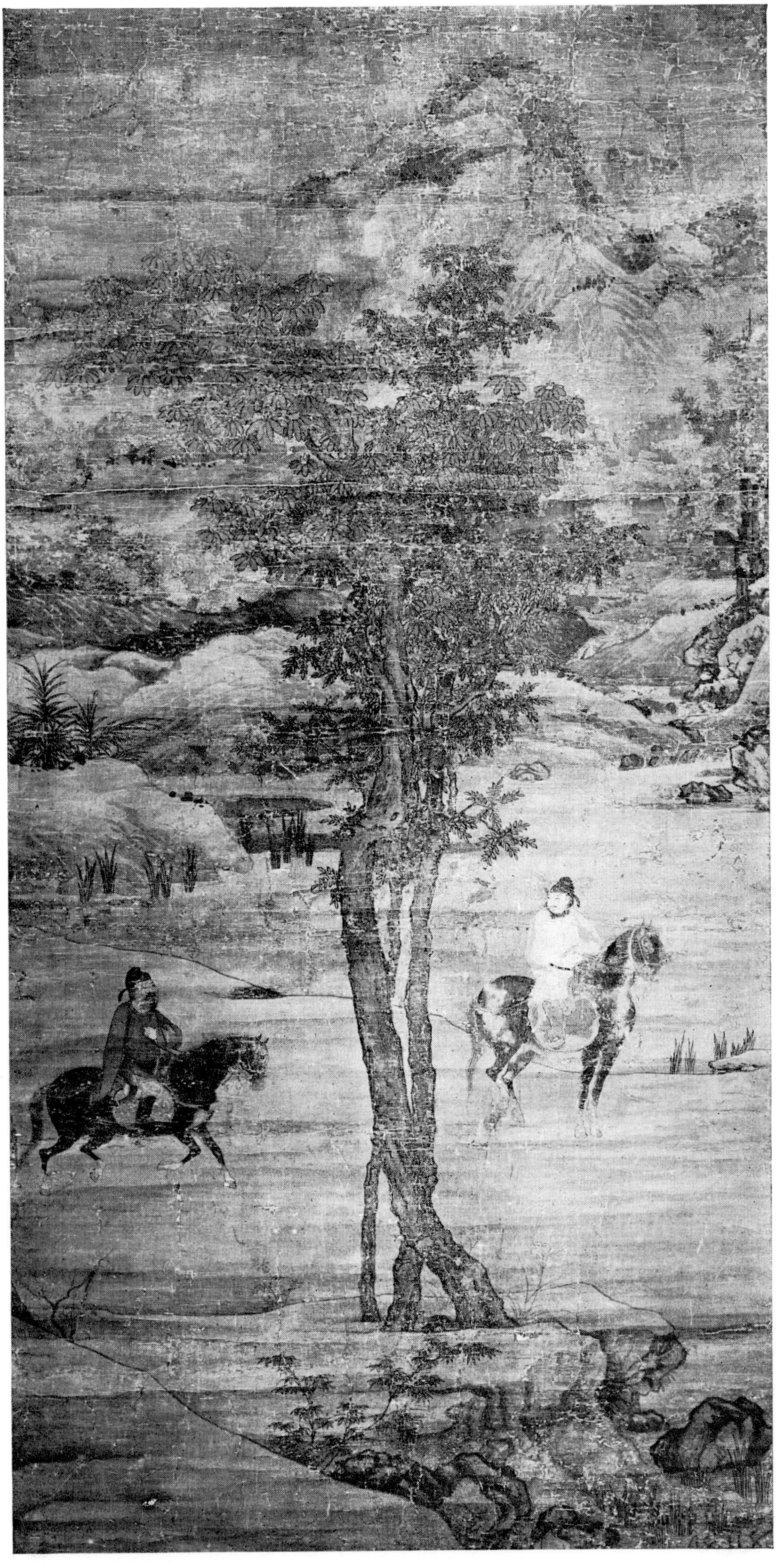

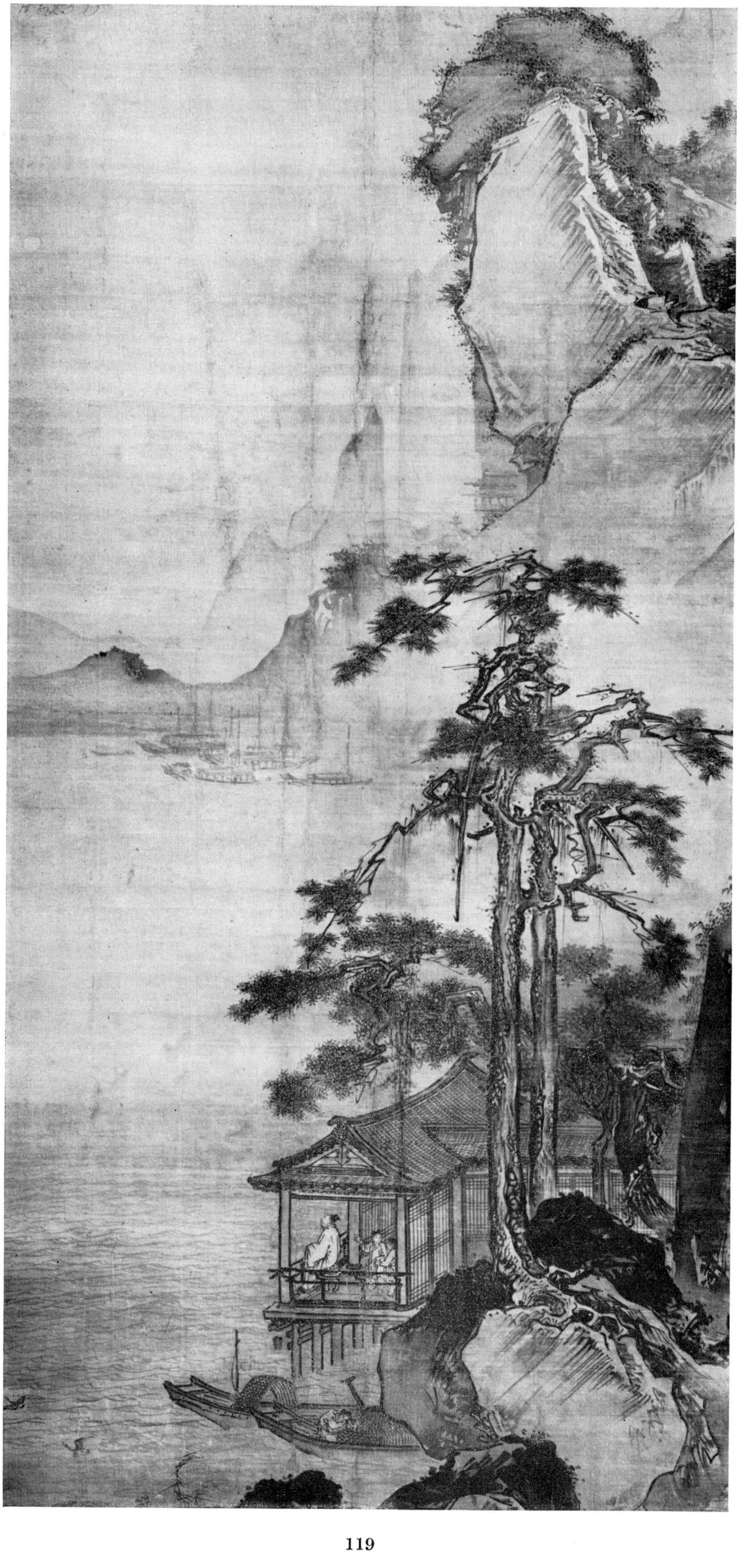

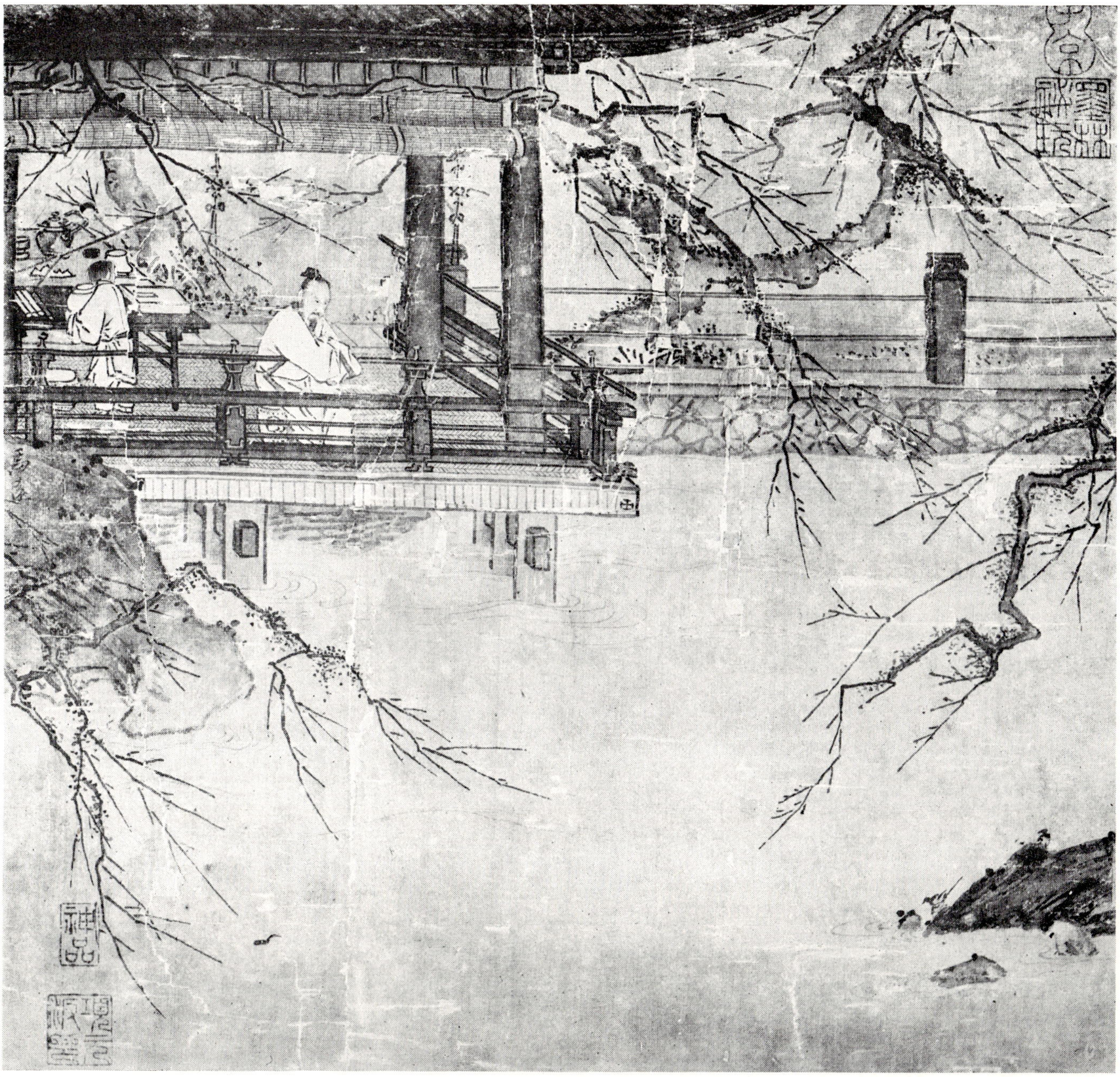

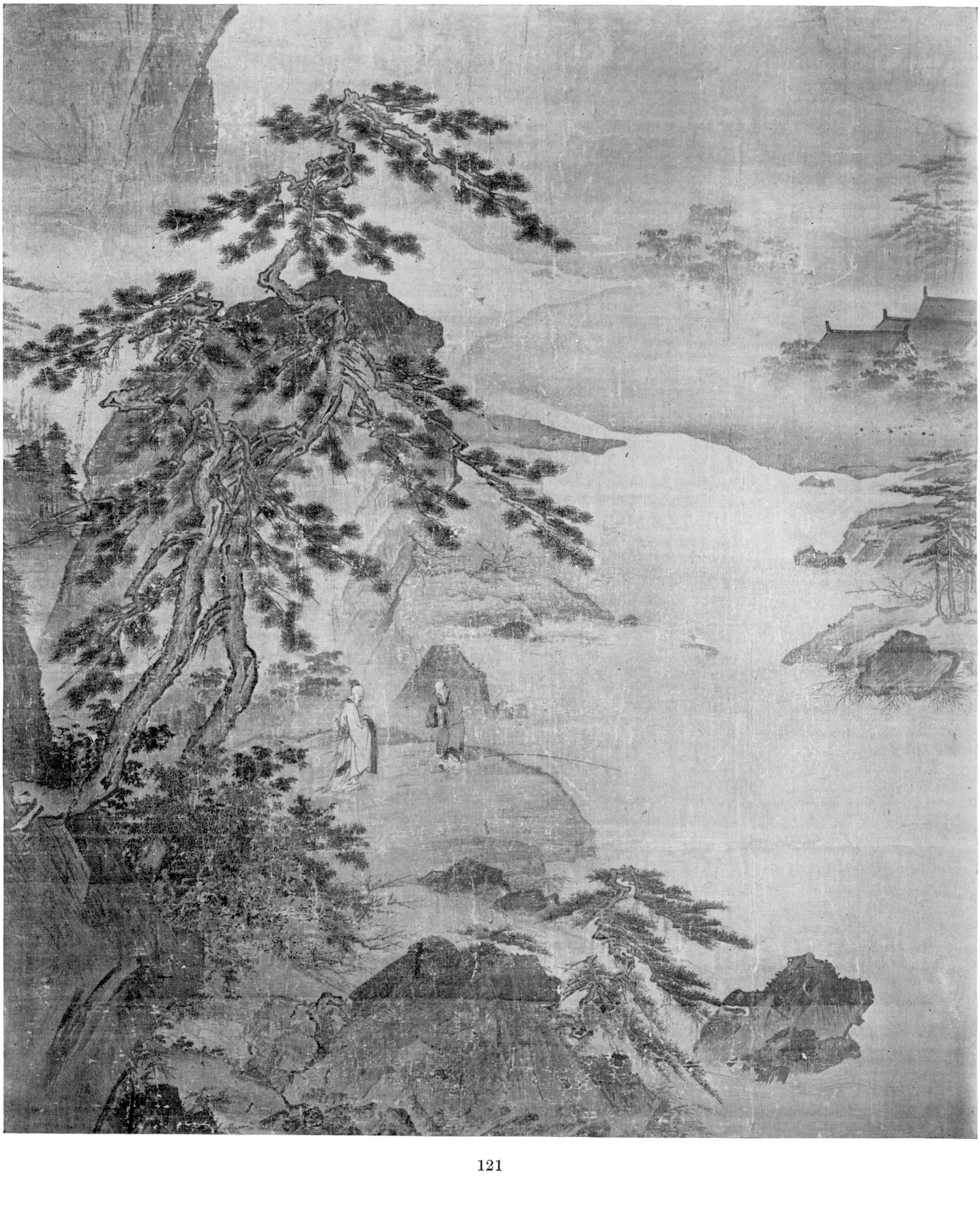

122

123

124

125

126

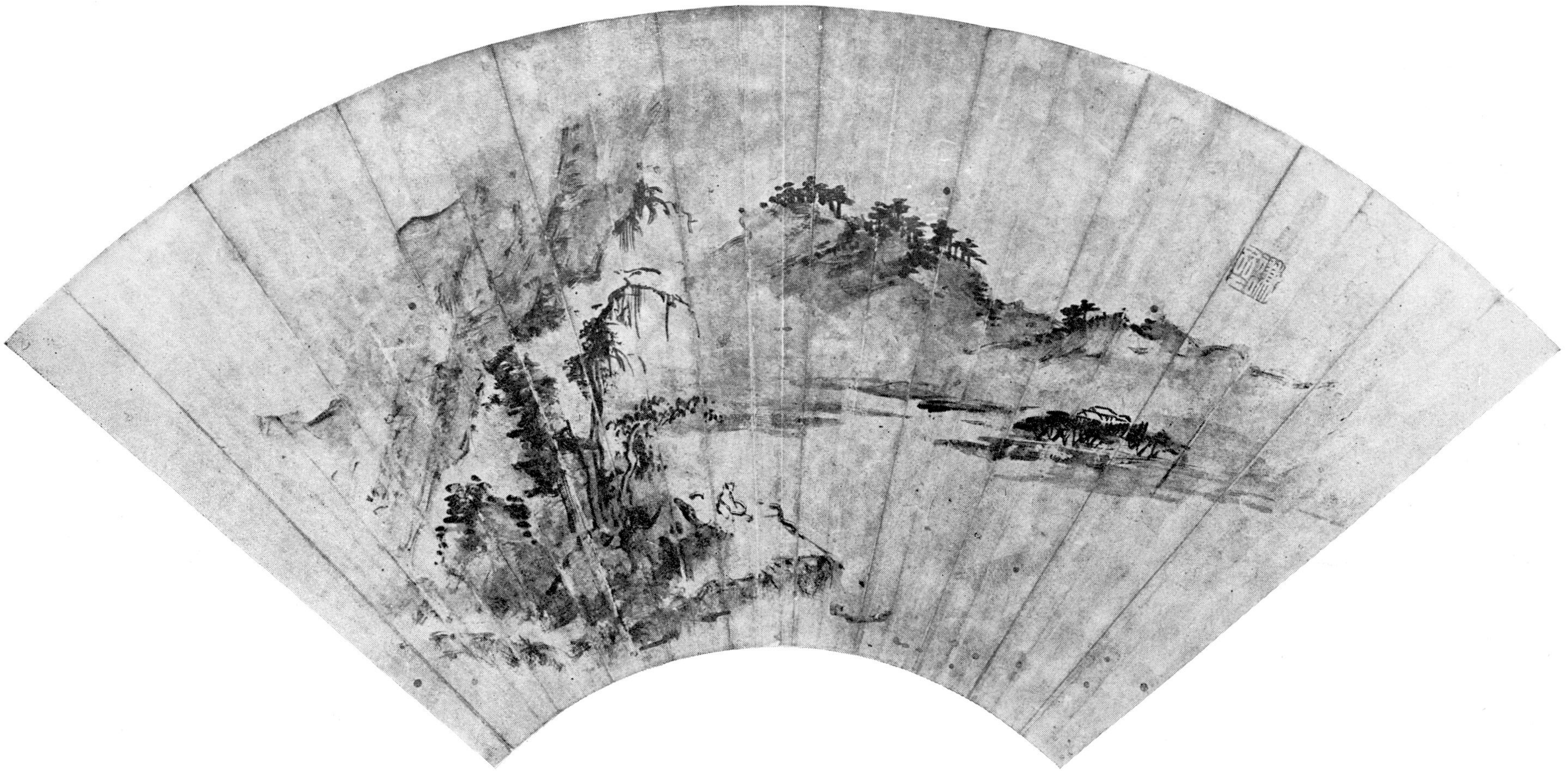

127

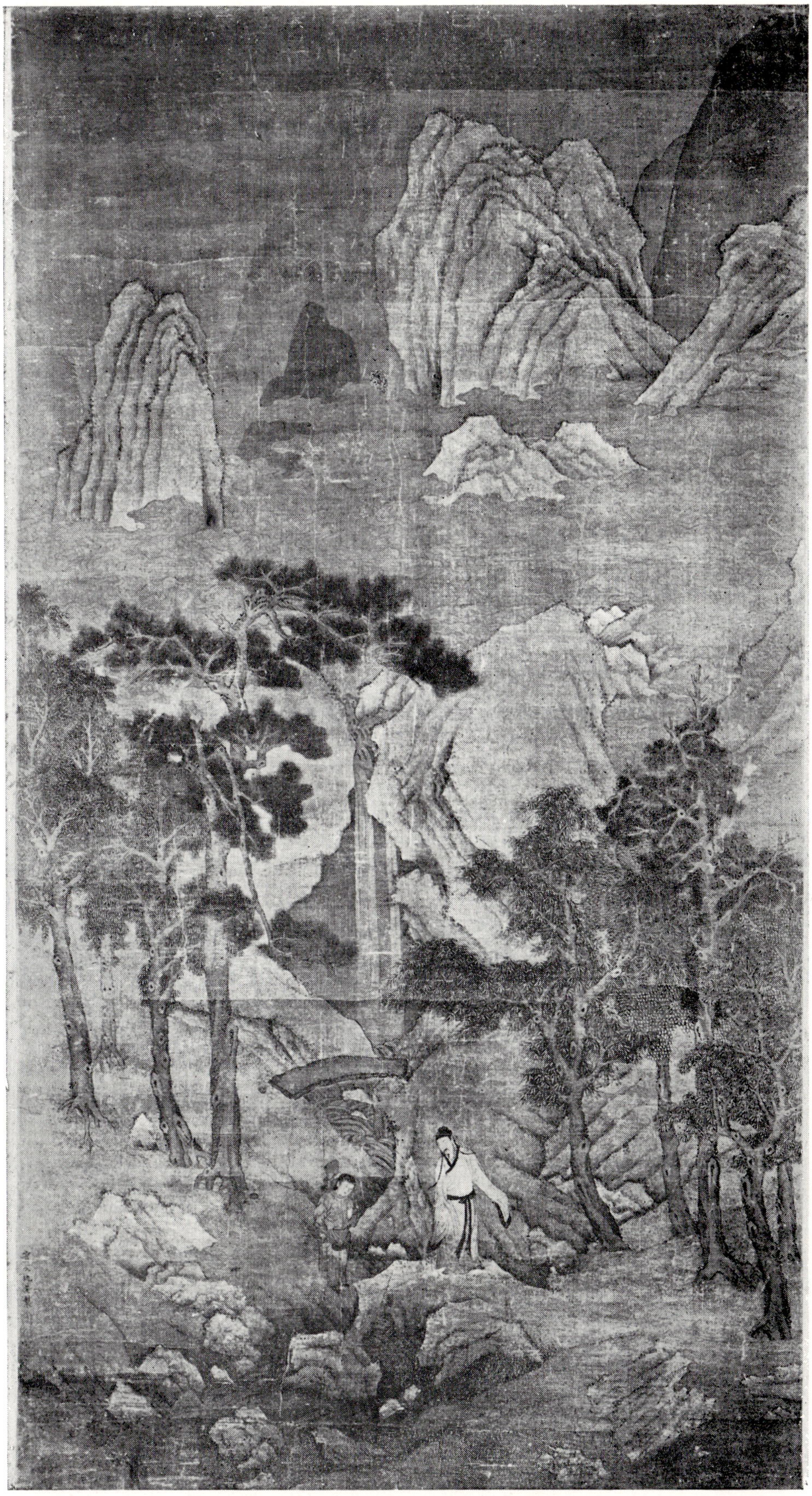

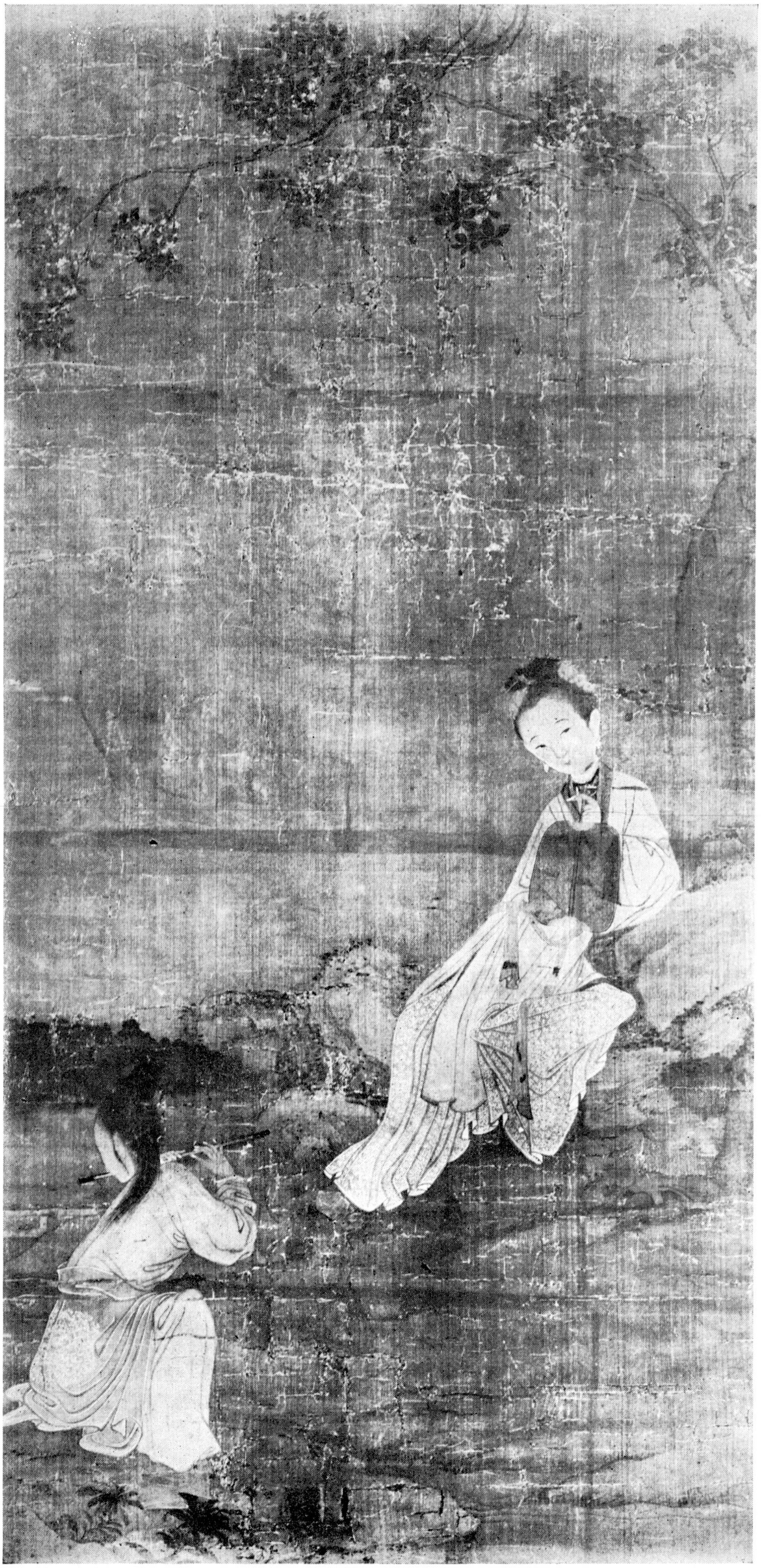